W9-ADF-450

WITHDRAWN

Yale Germanic Studies, 4

RILKE IN TRANSITION

An Exploration of his Earliest Poetry

by James Rolleston

New Haven and London

Yale University Press

1970

Library of Congress catalog card number: 73–99839
Standard book number: 300–01220–9
Designed by John O. C. McCrillis,
set in Garamond type,
and printed in the United States of America by
Connecticut Printers, Inc., Hartford, Conn.

Distributed in Great Britain, Europe, Asia, and
Africa by Yale University Press Ltd., London; in
Canada by McGill-Queen's University Press, Montreal; and
in Mexico by Centro Interamericano de Libros
Académicos, Mexico City.

For Christopher Lancelot

Born August 9, 1967

Contents

Preface

With the publication of the new Insel edition of Rilke's complete works (1955–66), an enormous amount of hitherto inaccessible poetry and prose has been made readily available. Much of this material (three of the six volumes) dates from the decade 1893–1903, a time when the young Rilke wrote and published voluminously. Little attention has been paid to this period, which Frank Wood has called "the early workshop," for the good reason that the bulk of Rilke's earliest writings has little value. But this very fact intrigued me and provoked the question: how could the author of *Leben und Lieder* (1893), a collection wholly dominated by convention, lacking even the contours of poetic individuality, have developed into the craftsmanlike, self-critical, indeed pioneering poet of the early Paris years? There can be few more striking examples of the "self-made poet," and it is evident that the strength and persistence of Rilke's poetic credo in his maturity derive to some extent from the restless experimentation of his youth; there were few literary genres which he did not investigate, few contemporary fads to which he did not succumb. Two of Rilke's early works have become particularly well-known: *Die Weise von Liebe und Tod des Cornets Christoph Rilke* and the first part of *Das Stundenbuch, Das Buch vom mönchischen Leben,* both written in a few weeks in the fall of 1899. By placing the latter in the context of the poet's work both before and after those "inspired" weeks I hope to correct the impression that Rilke sprang ardently into life as a fully fledged mystic, and to argue that the magical fluency of these poems is not necessarily typical of Rilke's work at the time. Nor is it necessarily a sign of superiority. If one is not receptive, the ecstatic tone of *Das Buch vom mönchischen Leben* can seem facile, even monotonous. My study will suggest that the young Rilke was writing poems that stand

up better to critical scrutiny, that his own total rejection of his
early period has too long hindered the search for the precious and
semiprecious gems that lie waiting to be uncovered.

I have been fortunate throughout my studies in having had constant and fruitful contact with professors possessing a special interest in Rilke. At Cambridge I studied with the late Humphry
Trevelyan (Kings) and Ronald Gray (Emmanuel); and at the
University of Minnesota, with Frank Wood, for whom I wrote a
master's thesis, "Rilke's Requiems" (1962). At Yale I have
attended a seminar given by the noted Rilke authority, Jacob
Steiner (Münster). I would like here to express my gratitude
to all these mentors, and especially to my advisor on the doctoral
dissertation, Peter Demetz, whose insistence on clarity and coherence enabled me to understand and remedy some at least of my
deficiencies. I am also deeply indebted to Heinrich Henel, without
whose interest in, and close reading of, the dissertation the present
revised and slightly expanded version could hardly have come into
being. And I am most grateful to Frau Ruth Fritzsche-Rilke for
her personal concern and for her permission to quote extensively
from her father's writings.

Finally I want to thank my wife, Priscilla, the only person both
able and willing to translate my handwriting into a flatteringly
neat typography.

J. L. R.

New Haven, Connecticut
September 1969

1 Introduction

In the late nineteenth century the impetus given to the German language by the early Romantics was becoming exhausted; it was no longer possible to charge a conventional emotional phrase with unmediated significance. At the same time the lingering atmosphere of Biedermeier was being dissolved by movements like naturalism and impressionism, which hoped to renew art by reducing its absolute status. Rilke's early work is thoroughly imbued with the influence of such movements, but the very range of his literary activities during the years 1895–99 reflects his feeling that he was an artist in the classic-romantic mold, filling his *Lehrjahre* with experiments in all three genres, lyric, epic, and dramatic. If, however, he was to return to an art of large statements, he had first to confront the problem of the cliché, of exhausted poetic language. Rilke's solution, on which his whole artistic development was built, was to restrict the range of his vocabulary and, within that range, to adopt certain keywords which, used repeatedly in a variety of contexts, became increasingly his own, emancipated from all associations save those of his personal world.

Many critics have approached Rilke through his key words,[1] but the tendency has been to concentrate on the metaphysically weighted terms (e.g. "Engel," "Puppe," "Spiegel") which so dominate the later poetry and to divorce them from their poetic contexts in order to construct what is assumed to be Rilke's *Weltbild*. In selecting for discussion three highly concrete monosyllables "das Kind," "die Hand," and "das Ding," I want to analyze the role played by these motifs in the poet's early work, while

---

1. Cf. Jacob Steiner, "Das Motiv der Puppe bei Rilke," in *Kleists Aufsatz über das Marionettentheater* (Berlin, 1967), pp. 132–33.

at the same time concentrating on specific poems as entities in
themselves. I shall adopt a historical approach, and by studying
the selected poems in the order of their composition, I hope to be
able to point to a relationship between Rilke's increasingly personal use of the motifs "Kind," "Hand," and "Ding" and the aesthetic quality of his poetry. In thus attempting to combine the
study of poems in isolation with both a developmental approach
and *Motivgeschichte,* my methods will necessarily be somewhat
eclectic. Perhaps I can best define them negatively, by means of a
contrast with the only previous full-length studies of Rilke's early
poetry.

Kurt Berger writes in the portentous style so common in Rilke
studies of the 1930s.[2] His chapters, indeed his subsections, all
have imposing metaphysical titles; he is given to apparently "sci-
entific" discussion of individual poems by means of elaborate
diagrams in which a word is urgently transported by an arrow
up the side of a triangle toward another word. In fact interest
in specific poems is indicated by their relevance to his metaphysical superstructure. As the chapter titles strain ever more desperately toward Nirvana, so Rilke's modest early poems are ruthlessly
inflated into testimonials to his psychic progress toward Oneness.

If Berger depersonalizes Rilke as a creative writer and transforms him into a sage, Mary B. Corcoran goes to the opposite
extreme, treating the poetry as the basis of a portrait of Rilke the
Man. Superficially her approach has much in common with mine,
for she too studies the poet through the medium of emotive words
which he made his own. But her statement of intent suggests the
problematical premises of her work:

> Alles, was Rilke um die gleiche Zeit geschrieben hat und
> was Licht auf ein gewisses Wort werfen könnte, wird unter-
> sucht und in die Besprechung eingeschlossen, wenn es die
> Interpretation des Wortes fördert. Es geht uns darum, aufzu-

2. Kurt Berger, *Rainer Maria Rilkes Frühe Lyrik* (Marburg, 1931).

zeigen, welche Gedanken und Gefühle mit diesen hier unter-
suchten Wörtern verbunden sind und durch welche anderen
Wörter dieselben gefühlsmässigen und gedanklichen Bezie-
hungen ausgedrückt werden.[3]

It seems to me very dangerous to treat everything a poet writes
as of equal psychological, let alone aesthetic, significance. All
forms of writing have their own limitations as sources of self-
expression: a letter is directed to a specific person, and may be
carelessly written; a theoretical essay is a deliberate attempt to be
impersonal; and a poem, quite apart from the formal process
which inevitably distances its content from the psychological
realm, is a distillation of a poet's dreams and fears as well as his
actual experience. It is quite true that a poet, especially a poet like
Rilke, does not use words accidentally. But I strongly question the
assumption that we can deduce from his verbal habits anything
about his personal feelings. Mrs. Corcoran discusses, in varying degree of detail, ten key words, all well chosen, but she subordinates them to the following general chapter headings: "Lebensangst," "Todesangst," and "Lösung von Problemen." Apart from
the un-Rilkean dualism between "Leben" and "Tod," her approach leads, by a curious methodological inversion, to a view of
Rilke not really so different from Berger's. He uses the poems as
pegs on which to hang his insistent generalities, while she uses
them to construct the picture of a poet manfully overcoming his
youthful fears. In other words, both present Rilke as the prob-
lem-solver par excellence.

Of Mrs. Corcoran's primary key words, two are somewhat abstract, "der Rand" and "der Abgrund." Here is her definition of
"der Rand":

> Es ist der Ort, wo der Mensch sich selber fremd wird, da sein
> Ursprung schon hinter ihm liegt, doch ist es auch der Ort, wo

3. Mary B. Corcoran, "Zur Bedeutung wichtiger Wörter in den frühen
Schriften von Rilke," (Ph.D. diss., Bryn Mawr College, 1958), p. iv.

die Zukunft sich ihm noch nicht mit voller Klarheit zeigt, sodass er den Weg dorthin und das Endziel seiner Reise nur dunkel ahnen kann.[4]

Straightforward psychological images are combined with the wholly un-Rilkean notion of "das Endziel." Mrs. Corcoran's language betrays her own bias, which is to interpret Rilke's words in the most "ordinary" way possible. For ordinary problems she then discovers ordinary solutions. This is perhaps the inevitable result of trying to translate words into feelings—it is the critic's feelings, not the poet's, that are described. With her more concrete key word, "die Mauer," Mrs. Corcoran is guilty of distortion. Determined to find the conventional emotion of claustrophobia in Rilke's use of this word, she writes of a letter by him: "Die zwei Erlebnisse von der Einsamkeit und der Angst vor Enge vereinen sich deutlich in einem überaus bedeutsamen Brief vom Januar 1902 . . ."[5] But if we look up the specified passage we find the following references to "die Mauer" in Rilke's letter:

> Als uns um Weihnachten noch eine kleine Tochter Ruth gegeben wurde, da schien der Mauerkreis um die kleine Welt vollendet, und es hätte der Alltag beginnen können, der Arbeitstag, nach welchem wir beide wie nach Brot verlangten. Aber gerade da musste ich, statt in den letzten Mauerkreis gesammelten Sinnes mich zurückzuziehen, selbst anfangen, die Tore zu öffnen und hinauszuspähen auf die Wege der Welt. . . .[6]

It is hard to detect a longing to burst out of "die Enge" in these lines; and few of Mrs. Corcoran's references to "die Mauer" say what she wants them to say. If Rilke's works are to be used as

4. Ibid., p. 32.
5. Ibid., p. 35.
6. An Pol de Mont, January 10, 1902, *Briefe und Tagebücher aus der Frühzeit, 1899–1902* (Leipzig, 1931), p. 148.

quasi-biographical material, then I prefer the approach of Erich Simenauer, whose bias is open and declared.[7] Words belong to the public as well as the private realm, and a poem is an intersection between the two worlds, a summation in public terms of feelings that are in origin private. We can never know the feelings themselves, only their public expression. Nevertheless a poet does not write only *one* poem, and a juxtaposition of several poems by the same author will reveal certain preoccupations with which some or all of the poems are directly or indirectly concerned. Such underlying preoccupations are, in Rilke's work, conveyed by particular words which gather into themselves the resonances of past poems, becoming code words for a whole area of meaning. A reader approaching a late Rilke poem without any knowledge of the earlier work will be both intrigued and baffled by this method. For the late Rilke creates his own world in a few syllables, and draws the reader into it. The language itself, however, is enigmatic, demanding the reader's assent while hinting at dimensions only half-perceived. I shall analyze the genesis of this way of writing, by taking as subjects three words which, in their concrete simplicity, are important in the earliest as in the later periods of Rilke's poetry. The choice of poems to be studied will necessarily be determined partly by their relation to the central motif under discussion, but each poem will be evaluated both as a work of art and as a link in the chain of Rilke's development.

7. Erich Simenauer, *Rainer Maria Rilke, Legende und Mythos* (Frankfurt, 1953).

2 Das Kind

Rilke always considered his own childhood unfulfilled; excessive coddling by his mother followed by an excessively "masculine" period at the military academy left him with the sense of a past that had never truly been his own. The image of the child thus unites his personal with his cultural situation. Just as he had undoubtedly been a child yet felt tantalizingly removed from that state, so he undoubtedly inherited a strong romantic tradition yet somehow could not use it without resorting to cliché. His longing for both a cultural tradition and personal wholeness led him to adopt the romantic image of spontaneous childhood as an article of faith:

> Trotz der Zweideutigkeit der eigenen Kindheit hat Rilke diese später in dem gleichen Sinne wie die Romantiker als eine holde und dichte Daseinsgeschlossenheit begriffen, als Ursprünglichkeit und Welteinverständnis. Tat er dies auch aus dem Kontrast des am Bewusstsein leidenden und des aus der eigenen Verstörtheit die verlorene Einheit wieder suchenden modernen Menschen heraus, so muss er diese Seite des kindlichen Daseins doch auch wirklich und beglückt erlebt haben, wenn er sie so in der Erinnerung zum Symbol ausgestalten konnte.[1]

Kohlschmidt seems to me to make a wrong deduction from accurately stated facts. Although one cannot of course know for certain, the evidence in *Malte* and elsewhere suggests that Rilke's childhood really was dominated by lonely fears. In an early letter he writes:

> Liebster, vielverehrter Meister, wenn man eine sehr dunkle Kindheit hinter sich hat, bei der der Alltag dem Gehen in

1. Werner Kohlschmidt, *Rainer Maria Rilke* (Lübeck, 1948), p. 20.

> dumpfkalten Gassen gleicht und der Feiertag wie ein Rasten
> im grauen, engen Lichthof ist, wird man bescheiden.[2]

His idealization of childhood reflected his conviction that, never having had a real childhood to lose, he could still experience it, and that it was his "Aufgabe" to do so. It was precisely this theme of romanticism that was not a cliché to him. When he spoke of his childhood as "zu leisten," he meant it literally: the way forward was also the way back. Lacking both roots and a usable language, he hoped, in the quest for his own childhood, to discover both the child's natural sense of identity and his ability to see the world simply and coherently. But his idealization was not naïve: it was his goal, not his premise. The premise remained his actual anguish-ridden childhood, and the resultant tension between actuality and symbolic ideal made childhood a central theme from his poetic beginnings to the elegy fragment of 1920, "Lass dir, dass Kindheit war."[3]

In the early poems the child motif predominates over all others, because Rilke's childhood or lack of it is almost his only authentic experience; but it is not so much a theme as a pervasive atmosphere. Before turning to the development of the child image from a mere word into a mature poetic symbol, I should like to examine briefly the figure into which Rilke pours so much of his feeling in these years: the adolescent girl. This figure, which remained an important symbol for him until the *Sonette an Orpheus,* was central to him in the 1890s for more subjective reasons. With a past rapidly losing its meaning and a future longed for yet feared, the girl symbolizes that "Unentschlossenheit" which characterizes Rilke's poetry in these years. Like him, all she can do is state the paradoxes of her position and ask questions of the future.

2. An Ludwig Ganghofer, April 16, 1897, *Briefe aus den Jahren 1892–1904* (Leipzig, 1939), p. 37.

3. Rilke, *Sämtliche Werke,* ed. Ernst Zinn (Wiesbaden, 1955–66), 2, 130.

Gebete der Mädchen zur Maria (1898; *Werke 3,* 243–51) are *Rollengedichte* which project sexuality and devotion, the twin poles of human aspiration, in anguished conjunction. These poems display Rilke's early talent for converting the romantic tradition into something personal. The device of the *Rollengedicht* enables him to heighten clichés of feeling while distancing the reader from them: since it is, after all, a young girl speaking, one expects a breathless and exaggerated tone; as a girl's nature is by definition paradoxical, the reader does not seek a resolution of emotional conflicts, merely an intense articulation of human polarities. Above the struggle hovers the figure of the Virgin, a symbol of perfect and unsullied transition from childhood to full adulthood, a model by definition inimitable:

> Schau, unsre Tage sind so eng
> und bang das Nachtgemach;
> wir langen alle ungelenk
> den roten Rosen nach.
>
> Du musst uns milde sein, Marie,   5
> wir blühn aus deinem Blut,
> und du allein kannst wissen, wie
> so weh die Sehnsucht tut;
>
> du hast ja dieses Mädchenweh
> der Seele selbst erkannt: 10
> Sie fühlt sich an wie Weihnachtsschnee,
> und steht doch ganz in Brand. . . .
>
> (No. 2; May 5, 1898)

The introductory "Schau" makes one think forward to the angel of the *Elegies,* another symbol of perfection before whom the human condition is displayed. But whereas the angel is approached in a spirit of rivalry, even of defiance, twenty-four years earlier the poet is pleading for a little perfection to clarify his, or rather his protagonist's, inner uncertainties. Although inimitable, the Virgin is not unattainable: she is the ideal image of the child, the human source which is also human fulfillment, the mother who has not lost her innocence.

Linguistically this poem stands in the middle of the developmental cycle about to be examined. The first two lines have an effective combination of innocence, rhythmic variation induced by the springy "Schau," and images rendered interesting by the association of "eng" with "Tage" and "bang" with "Nachtgemach." But the next two lines fail completely. The image, though intended to evoke the disproportion between adolescent aspirations and adolescent abilities, lacks any distinctive profile: Rilke has sacrificed concreteness to mellifluous sound, and the resultant alliterations have no impact. The superfluity of "roten Rosen" underlines the fact that the cliché has been neither reshaped nor heightened.

The second stanza illustrates the method of juxtaposition. If the girls have been portrayed in the first stanza as confined and clumsy in their longing, here they are blooming. The nature of the subject precludes contradiction: childhood both thrusts the girl into the future and makes her fearful and inept; it furnishes her with a past yet drives her out of it by suddenly ceasing to fulfill her desires. The analogy with Rilke's poetic situation is fairly clear. Though deeply attached to the romantic tradition, to things gentle and innocent, he feels compelled to go beyond it, to reshape it, however clumsily, to some end as yet unknown. The first couplet of this stanza illustrates three devices employed in this reshaping: the use of the young girl as "speaker" enables him to employ a consciously naïve style, much as the original romantics used the folksong to renovate language. Within this framework he uses his technical gifts to impose a highly sophisticated unity on these two lines, through the alliteration of *m* and *bl* and the overall dominance of the *u* sound. The heavy reliance on technique is made palatable by the naïveté, its obtrusiveness veiled. Then there is the striking image, "wir blühn aus deinem

Blut." Although unconnected with the rest of the poem and not very clear in a concrete sense, it evokes, in its compression and paradox, the authentic Rilkean voice.

This concision exemplifies what Belmore calls "heavy language," in which meaning is inseparable from the terms of its expression. He stresses the problems inherent in such a style: "Since the dense texture of heavy language relies on such a delicate balance of values, represented mainly by words, the principal danger for the poet handling it must consist in lapses from the standard he has himself established."[4] As in the first stanza, the second couplet of the second stanza is a lapse from the level of the first. It is as if Rilke momentarily swerved from his naturally "heavy" style to seek a "light" effect, according to Belmore's definition of lightness as "words being but the bare means for conveying a thought or sensation which, however, is not poetically condensed in them." Instead of being intensified, the cliché is left limply intact as if it could still evoke the resonances it had when first used; the lines are built rhetorically towards the familiar abstraction "Sehnsucht" as if the word would reverberate in the reader. The alliterating of *w* to highlight "weh" is similarly overdone. The emptiness of the rhetoric is underlined by the use of "allein": why, one wonders, should the Virgin be the *only* person to know the pain of longing?

That "allein" has no significance other than a rhetorical one is confirmed by the third stanza, where the use of "selbst" makes the more rational point that, despite her pure transition from childhood to motherhood, the Virgin *also* experienced the pains of adolescence. This stanza attempts to reconcile the conflicting viewpoints of the first two, the clumsiness and the blooming, not through fusing them but by re-presenting them as a single paradox. Appropriately, the stanza is also the only one effective as a whole. The paradox of snow and fire overwhelms the context, but

4. H. W. Belmore, *Rilke's Craftsmanship* (Oxford, 1954), pp. 122–23.

Rilke has amplified his style to match it. The compound words, "Mädchenweh" and "Weihnachtsschnee," intensify clichés to the point where they work anew. Belmore contrasts Rilke's early "ornate" style unfavorably with his later preference for emotional precision.[5] But one of Rilke's talents is for building expressive "ornate" words out of a combination of simple ones: "Weihnachtsschnee" actually evokes a synthesis of two purities. Rilke has embedded his paradox in the naïve style of the young girls, so that it seems a spontaneous representation of their thoughts. It can be argued that this process is forced, that no "real" girls are evoked by these lines; and it is true that the word "Seele," with its abstract vagueness, seriously damages the stanza. Initially it is inconspicuous, inserted between "Mädchenweh" and "selbst" with virtually no accent on it. But "Sie" recalls our attention to it, and its conjunction with the concrete "fühlt sich an" seems confused and unrealized. If, however, one does not press the imagery too hard and accepts the stanza as an attempt to unite opposites in both style (the sophisticated and the naïve) and subject matter (purity and intensity), it reads like a fruitful experiment. Especially well organized is the symmetrical vowelling dominated by the long *e:* the first and third lines begin with a group of short vowels and lead through *ie* to a final accented *e,* while the second and fourth lines open on this *e* and bring it to rest on *a.*

If this examination has appeared excessive for so slight and youthful a poem, I pursued it in order to illustrate the earliest stages of Rilke's emergence from the chrysalis of convention. Moreover when Rilke revised *Mir zur Feier* in 1909 he left this poem intact; he must therefore have considered it a fair expression of his style at this stage. Its final paradox, indeed, of the soul as cool, self-contained snow and as dissolvent fire, expresses what Kohlschmidt views as the central development of the year 1898: the tentative emergence of what was to be the poet's lifelong at-

5. Ibid., pp. 124–27.

titude to life, a "Monismus" based on a dialectical tension between "Einsamkeit" and "Offenheit."[6] The image of "das Mädchen" epitomizes this tension, but is incapable of development. As a subjective viewpoint it can only lead away from itself (its development into an Orphic symbol is another question).

For Rilke the way forward was the way back—to childhood. If his *Weltoffenheit* was strengthened by the Italian journey in the spring of 1898, then the countervailing goal of "Einsamkeit" rooted in individuality was given its primary impetus by his encounter in 1897 with the works of Jens Peter Jacobsen, especially *Niels Lyhne*. This novel was a vital model for the young Rilke. Like the naturalists, Jacobsen rejects romantic dreaminess, but unlike them he accepts the romantic thesis of subjectivity as the primary reality. In the resultant objective analysis of subjective mood Rilke saw a stylistic way forward from the impasse of romantic and naturalist clichés. Thematically, Jacobsen presents childhood as the central experience of the individual, a reality which is not lost but permanently existent, and can therefore be regained: time lived always "is."

> . . . jetzt begann er mit der Leidenschaft eines Entdeckers, sich selbst aus Kindheitserinnerungen, Kindheitseindrücken, aus den lebendigen Augenblicken seines Lebens zusammenzusetzen. . . .[7]

Added to this task of self-construction is the task of constructing others, of seeing them in the submerged reality of their childhood:

> Und er lebte in diesen Erinnerungen, neigte sich zu ihnen mit unruhigem, eifersüchtigem Schmachten, einem vagen Verlangen, zu greifen, zu teilen, eins zu werden mit diesen

6. Kohlschmidt, p. 34.

7. Jens Peter Jacobsen, *Niels Lyhne,* trans. M.v. Borch (Leipzig, n.d.), p. 132 (the authorized translation from the Danish actually read by Rilke).

feinen, zartgefärbten Schatten eines Lebens, das zu reicherem
und reiferem Farbenton erglüht war.[8]

An ambiguity here suggests that maturity is somehow ordinary,
unreal, yet also "reich" and "reif."

The same ambiguity occurs in Rilke's *Florenzer Tagebuch* of
1898, in a passage using similar imagery of light and shadow and
layers of unreality that must be removed:

> In erster Kindheit, da die Pracht noch frei liegt, ist es zu
> dunkel darin, um die Bilder zu sehen, und dann, wenn es
> lichter wird in der Halle, kommen die Knabentorheiten und
> die falschen Sehnsüchte, und diese übertünchen Wand um
> Wand.[9]

If one compares the phrase "die falschen Sehnsüchte" with the
more solemn use of "Sehnsucht" in the "Gebet zur Maria," Rilke's
attitude concerning the transition to maturity appears complex.
The two uses of "Sehnsucht" are not really contradictory. All men
experience longings, and devote much energy to pursuing them;
later they seem to have led ineluctably away from the reality of
childhood. Rilke accepts this process: he proposes neither clinging
to childhood nor constructing a nostalgic dream. He merely asks
how we are to live our own personal reality in such a way that the
balance between "Einsamkeit" and "Offenheit" can be maintained.
The individual must belong to the external world but not merge
himself with it, for that is the way of escapism. Earlier in the
Florenzer Tagebuch Rilke gropes toward the meaning of childhood in the development of genuine maturity:

> . . . unfähige Menschen wollen sich von den Eltern erhalten
> und verantworten lassen. Solange dieser Gott lebt, sind wir
> alle Kinder und unmündig. . . . O wenn doch die wölker in

8. Ibid., p. 198.
9. *Tagebücher aus der Frühzeit* (Leipzig, 1942), p. 117.

der ersten Angst ihrer Kindheit schöpferisch gewesen wären:
dann hätten sie wirklich einen Gott gemacht! . . . Jeder
kommt in Trauerkleidern vom Sterbebette seines Kindheits-
gottes; aber bis er zuversichtlich und festlich geht, geschieht
in ihm die Auferstehung Gottes.[10]

The child, for Rilke an image of responsiveness and creativity, becomes, as we shall see, a surrogate for the artist himself. But in
the years before Rilke's reading of Jacobsen it remains sentimentally conventional. I now turn to poems chosen to illustrate the
simultaneous growth of Rilke's personal style and a complex
child image.

Empor

Manchmal ermattet vom Hasten nach Glück
sehn ich mich wieder nach seliger Blindheit,
rufe die Tage der traulichen Kindheit,
rufe die Tage der Unschuld zurück.

Wo ich mit heiterem Hoffen noch trug   5
kindlichen Glauben im dämmernden Herzen,
und wo zu heilen die kleinsten der Schmerzen
mir noch ein Spielzeug, ein schönes, genug.

Wo ich vom Treiben der Welt nichts gewusst,
nichts noch vernommen von Schuld und von Fehle,   10
wo ich die Wahrheit in jeglicher Seele
wähnte, die Treue in jeglicher Brust.

Wo ich im Innern zu hören geglaubt
Lehre des göttlichen Wortes, wo Friede
ein mich gewiegt, wenn des Abends ich müde   15
drückt in die Kissen mein lockiges Haupt.

Und auch die Träume umfingen mich lind,
trugen auf schimmerndem Arm mich von dannen

10. Ibid., pp. 52–53.

weit in die Welten und woben und spannen
goldige Schleier ums glückliche Kind.   20
[Late 1893; *Werke 3*, 91–92]

These lines belong really to the category of versifying, not poetry, as do virtually all the poems in *Leben und Lieder*. I include them only to show the extreme depths from which Rilke rose. The child image stays wholly within the realm of cliché, and technically the young poet employs to excess certain poetic tools which he later mastered. Thus in the first stanza the contrast between *a* and *e* underlines all too heavily the expressed contrast between exhaustion and longing. Our attention is drawn to the climactic words, and attention is what they cannot bear. "Hasten nach Glück" is undigested cliché, and "seliger Blindheit" introduces an irrelevant dimension. The sole link of "Blindheit" to childhood is the rhyme with "Kindheit." Moreover the device of repetition is, as Belmore points out, much used by the mature Rilke: "There is a contrast between the high complexity of some of Rilke's stylistic devices and the simplicity implied in repetition."[11] Without complex structure for contrast repetition is just repetition, and here it merely emphasizes the rigidity of the rhythm and the superfluousness of the fourth line.

The second stanza illustrates further misused techniques. The "poetically" rearranged word order produces a "unified" stanza, but to no end: the totally regular rhythm nullifies the inverted word order, making it resemble a religious incantation. The exception in the fourth line is what Belmore views as an early mannerism, "the transposition of the adjective behind its noun and at the end of the line so as to catch the rhyme"[12]—here the rhythm. Even this rhythmic effect dilutes the meaning. "Spielzeug" is to become a keyword for Rilke, but its significance lies precisely in its non-aesthetic qualities, its ordinariness. Another technique com-

11. Belmore, p. 111.
12. Ibid, p. 116.

bines the abstract and the concrete ("trug . . . Glauben"), but the biblical phraseology deprives it of interest. Indeed it is primarily the absolute dominance of the Bible, which must have constituted the only "culture" of Rilke's earliest years, that prevents words from acquiring independent meaning. What is the child hoping for ("mit heiterem Hoffen")? What kind of truth is found in the soul? How does one "hear" a doctrine within? Such questions are only answered if one takes the poem in conjunction with, say, the psalms: but then it evaporates, for the psalms say everything better. In the last stanza Rilke attempts an image of his own, but the inspiration is so conventional that the result is grotesque. The variety of activities attributed to "die Träume" forbids closer investigation.

An even more basic weakness than the poem's faded religiosity, so characteristic of Rilke's mother, is the imprisoning rhyme scheme. If Rilke was, as Belmore claims, a "born rhymester,"[13] one can only say that the process of birth was not complete by 1893. The rigid, deadening alternation of masculine and feminine rhymes and the utter predictability of the words chosen ("Blindheit"/"Kindheit," "Herzen/"Schmerzen," "lind"/"Kind"), which Rilke seems able to vary only by the impurity of "Friede"/"müde" or the stiltedness of "Fehle,"[14] muffle each line to prevent any hint of a personal voice.

Träume

Es kommt die Nacht, reich mit Geschmeiden
geschmückt des blauen Kleides Saum;
sie reicht mir mild mit ihren beiden
Madonnenhänden einen Traum.

Dann geht sie, ihre Pflicht zu üben,   5

13. Ibid., p. 17.
14. To illustrate this word Grimm gives a couplet from Schiller of which Rilke's lines are an undistinguished paraphrase: "Wohl dem, der frei von Schuld und Fehle / bewahrt die kindlich reine Seele!"

hinfort die Stadt mit leisem Schritt
und nimmt, als Sold des Traumes, drüben
des kranken Kindes Seele mit.

[Late 1895; *Werke 1,* 29]

The language of this poem seems faded until comparison with
"Empor" shows what enormous technical strides Rilke has made
in the two years intervening. The theme of the dying child, too,
seems at first all too familiar in its folk-romantic pathos. But then
we notice that the child is only mentioned at the end, that "Nacht"
and "Traum" are the dominant motifs. Pathos is thus diminished
to a minimum, and the child's death seen as part of a larger order.
But although Rilke shifts conventional categories to express his
own perspectives, his themes do not yet have a personal force. In
this collection, *Larenopfer* (1895), poetry is mostly "affirmative."
Rilke sees the contradictions, but phrases them so that they harmonize in a traditionally poetic manner. The child's death may be
"Sold des Traumes" but it is also "Pflicht": death is necessary to
generate dreams, and necessity must be affirmed. The child here is
already an essential element in the "real" world, but not a value
in itself. The dream is the primary value because it is "beautiful,"
expressive of all the exquisite sensations Rilke was pursuing or
felt he ought to be pursuing. One thinks of "ein Spielzeug, ein
schönes" in the earlier poem: implicitly Rilke echoes contemporary theories (Huysmans, Wilde) of the primacy of art over
life. At this stage Rilke was indeed, in Angelloz' phrase, "poète du
rêve."

The first couplet illustrates Rilke's ornate style. He first displays
his virtuosity by placing a heavy weight on the word "reich." The
emphatic rhythm coupled with the long *ei* creates a consciously
sumptuous contrast with the simple opening words. The curious
word order, enabling the anthropomorphism of "des blauen
Kleides Saum" to emerge in slow majesty, produces a complete
stasis. We are forced to stop and contemplate this elaborately

ceremonious night. "The diphthong *ei* is ideally suited to vowel music; its tone is rich and long and can . . . be made to sound soft or harsh, according to the way it is used and combined with other sounds."[15] It is certainly soft here, embedded in the consonantal finery of *ch* and *sch*. It is also an essential link between the two halves of the stanza, especially through such parallels as "reich" and "reicht" which foreshadow the more polished *Stundenbuch* lines quoted by Belmore ("mit meinem Reifen / reift / dein Reich"). Indeed when we add the *m* alliteration and the culmination in "Traum" of the sound pattern initiated in the second line, the second couplet exists through technique alone. The whole phrase "mit ihren beiden Madonnenhänden" is inessential; indeed the very compound "Madonnenhände" seems inappropriate here, converting Rilke's night from an Empress into a Virgin. The effort appears misplaced, since the effect of the resounding opening lines is not balanced but dissolved. Rilke's "affirmative" outlook reveals its weakness at this stage: if all phenomena merge into an amorphous whole, then the distinctiveness and coherence of individual realities are dissolved.

The image of the night as Madonna dominates the second stanza, a good example of what Rilke failed to achieve in the fourth stanza of the 1893 poem. The syntax is slightly dislocated to permit the four lines to scan, but the construction is basically simple, as are most of the words used, in contrast to those of the first stanza. The verbs establish a strict symmetry with the first stanza: the sequence "kommt . . . reicht . . . geht . . . nimmt" enacts a single gesture, a gesture that unites within the image of the night such conflicting realities as Rilke can encompass. The meaning of the gesture is summarized in the biblical phrase "Sold des Traumes" (cf. Romans 6 : 23: "Denn der Tod ist der Sünden Sold"). Together with the notion of "Pflicht" it emphasizes the ritualistic nature of the night's gesture. Night is not

15. Belmore, p. 68.

eager for her "reward," but is merely fulfilling an ancient process, a rhythmic circle. Thus the explicit meaning of the poem—that a child must die for the poet to have a dream—is softened to the point of transformation. Neither the dream nor the child's death is in itself important; they are simply aspects of the night's gesture, as inevitable as the cyclic movement of nature. What is important is that the dream can become a work of art, indeed does become one in the shape of the poem "Träume," and that the original source of the dream is a child's soul, transmuted by the macrocosm of the night. The poem's terminology is that of 1895; the subject is not art but dreams; and the child's death is potentially sentimental. Rilke combats the limitations of his subject matter by removing emotion and making the night the overriding reality. The night's gesture becomes, in retrospect, an almost instinctive metaphor for the link between childhood and the creative process.

> Was reisst ihr aus meinen blassen, blauen
> Stunden mich in der wirbelnden Kreise
> wirres Geflimmer?
> Ich mag nicht mehr euren Wahnsinn schauen.
> Ich will wie ein Kind im Krankenzimmer   5
> einsam, mit heimlichem Lächeln, leise,
> leise—Tage und Träume bauen.
>
> [September 13, 1896; *Werke 1, 130*]

No close inspection is needed to perceive the advances that separate this poem from the one written a year previously. The unusual stanza structure and rhyme scheme (*a b c a c b a*) suggest a new confidence in using words, an urge to move beyond the "undecided" stage toward wholly personal verbal units; and the last phrase is one that only Rilke could have written, a construction that leads directly to the world of the monk in *Das Buch vom mönchischen Leben*. This new subjectivity, in the best sense of the word, is paralleled by the speaker's identification with the sick child, a figure with which he was linked only by the night in "Es kommt die Nacht." Indeed the collection *Advent,* in which this is one of the earliest poems (*Advent* spans the period September 1896 to July 1897), is filled to a startling extent with the pronouns "Ich" and "Du." The young poet seems determined to emancipate himself from his poetic models by passionate self-assertion and by invoking the "Du" of his dreams; he seems almost to be preparing himself for the meeting with Lou Salomé in May 1897—the seasonal implications of the collection's title could not be more appropriate. At this stage of his struggle with the cliché, with second hand language, a new avenue seems to open: total empathy, identification with the images used. The sick child embodies Rilke's self-awareness at this stage unusually well. The familiar romantic contrast is invoked to express the child's isolated purity: busy world against private dreams. The world outside is discordant, confused, the child's world pale, refined; the child's apartness in the sickroom suggests the artist's apartness from humanity. If the "decadent" aesthetic of the 1890s (with which Rilke must have become familiar in 1896 in the Prague literary world) did not yet identify being an artist with being sick, it did insist on the "unnaturalness" of the artist's activity summarized here in the phrase "Tage und Träume bauen," a phrase which looks two ways. Coupled with "Tage" the verb "bauen" points to *Das Stundenbuch* and beyond, to Rilke's theory of "Arbeit" as the only viable relationship between the artist and nature; coupled with "Träume" it looks backward, to a small-scale, willfully subjective view of art. Both images imply the separateness of the artist from "normal" living. At the same time the contrast between the two spheres is not absolute. The simplicity of the verb "bauen" suggests that the difference between poet and artisan is little more than a difference of material, while the word "Kreise," as an evocation of the outside world, belies the disorderly imagery attached to it. It is a distant anticipation of the cosmic images Rilke was to use in evoking the figure of

Rodin in 1902. The artist is somehow at the centre of these "Kreise" as they revolve around his sickroom. The mingling of temporal and spatial terminology strengthens this impression: what the poet rejects is not the world as such but the suggestion that he abandon his central place in it. At the heart of the maelstrom time has meaning and shape, and the world's activities are like "Kreise." In the outside world such patterns are invisible, and time becomes merely a dimension of spatial "Geflimmer."

The bipartite structure observed in previous poems is very much in evidence here. As the rhyme scheme (*a b c a c b a*) suggests, the fourth line is the pivot of the first three lines and the last three. The two halves are strongly contrasted rhythmically, but Rilke cannot yet control language sufficiently to convey such emotional contrasts. In the first three lines the word "mich" signals the change from long vowels suggesting tranquillity to an increasingly insistent *i* vowel; its positioning for rhythmic purposes, to create dactyls in the first two lines, is less convincing: the clash with normal word order is so pronounced that we notice the rhythmic effect and feel it as a trick. The profusion of visual images suggests the child's feverish imagination, but the adjectives add little to the nouns they qualify, and the whole terminology is too imprecise to convey the intended contrast between "Stunden" and "Kreise." The effect is further reduced by the inappropriately moralistic word "Wahnsinn" in the fourth line. This line is altogether weak: the prosaic effect, presumably intended to separate the two mood pictures, is overdone. The alliterative monosyllables at the beginning sound cluttered, and the awkward coupling of "schauen" with "Wahnsinn," while conveying the idea that to the child everything is visual, heightens one's discomfort.

Rilke succeeds better in the last three lines. Very simple words ("Kind," "Tage") are effectively merged with more elevated terms ("einsam," "leise," "Träume"). Still the penultimate line reveals the poem's limitations: "einsam," "heimlich," and "leise," with a cumulative affectation, perversely emphasize the cliché elements of the image. The sick child, once gentle and self-contained, becomes fragile and self-consciously posed. This is because the child is still idealized; the word "Kind" is not yet permeated with either the reality of observed children or the subjectivity of remembered childhood.

> Das ist dort, wo die letzten Hütten sind
> und hohe Häuser, die mit engen Brüsten
> sich drängen aus den grauen Baugerüsten
> und schauen wollen, wo das Feld beginnt.

> Dort bleibt der Frühling immer bang und blass,   5
> der Sommer fiebert hinter diesen Planken:
> die Kirschenbäume und die Kinder kranken,
> und nur der Herbst hat dorten keinen Hass.

> Und seine Abende sind manchesmal
> windschwingenstill und schön in ihrem Schmelze: 10
> Die Schafe schimmern und der Hirt im Pelze
> lehnt lauschend an dem letzten Lampenpfahl.
>   [November 19, 1897; *Werke 3, 226*]

This poem has been chosen less as a contribution to the development of the "Kind" motif than as evidence of the very great poetic strides Rilke made in the year since the preceding poem. Indeed, in the collection *Mir zur Feier* (1898) it stands out as something of an exception—Belmore thinks the first stanza suggests *Neue Gedichte*.[16] The image of the suburb as the boundary between the real and the unreal looks even further ahead to the Tenth Elegy, which twice echoes the phrase "hinter diesen Planken": "Oh aber gleich darüber hinaus, / hinter der letzten Planke, beklebt mit Plakaten des 'Todlos' . . . gleich im Rücken

16. Ibid., p. 176.

der Planke, gleich dahinter, ists *wirklich.*" The atmosphere of the
poem has some affinities with Georg Trakl, as in the first stanza
of his *Im Dorf:*

> Aus braunen Mauern tritt ein Dorf, ein Feld.
> Ein Hirt verwest auf einem alten Stein.
> Der Saum des Walds schliesst blaue Tiere ein,
> Das sanfte Laub, das in die Stille fällt.[17]

The differences are as instructive as the parallels. Both poets present landscapes simply by listing associatively the features that
strike them; both convey their sense of decay by personifying
structures, natural objects, seasons. In doing so Rilke looks beyond his normal range. A verbal comparison with Trakl's stanza
suggests, moreover, that Rilke's style really points in a different
direction. The simplicity and economy of Trakl's mature style enable him to present "unnatural" visions as part of the natural
world: the visible decay of the shepherd is noticed, but not com-
mented on—it is simply registered, as if through an X-ray lens.
The coherence of the vision is assumed; the word "und" occurs
nowhere in the poem's nine stanzas. By contrast, it occurs eight
times in Rilke's three stanzas. This additive method suggests his
intention, which is to accumulate emotional impressions in order
to contrast them with their opposites. The last line of the second
stanza is the turning point: if for Trakl autumn, a season of decay,
symbolizes man's permanent state, for Rilke it offers the peace
of evening, a relief from sick striving. The shallowness of the
third stanza compared with the first two reveals the limitations of
Rilke's poem in his insistence on a harmonious vision. Moreover
the "dynamism" of the verbs in the first two stanzas undermines
the initial pessimism of the images and dilutes the subsequent contrast: "sich drängen" conveys the claustrophobic narrowness of the
lots on which the houses stand, but insists on life and longings

17. Georg Trakl, *Die Dichtungen* (Salzburg, 1938), p. 79.

within; "fiebert" and "kranken" express a cyclical malaise, anticipating the relief of autumn; such verbs writhe between death and life, far from the finality of Trakl's "verwest," "schliesst," "fällt" in successive lines.

The colloquial yet enigmatic opening removes this poem at once from the descriptive style of *Larenopfer,* recalling rather the imagery of a mature poem like "Ausgesetzt auf den Bergen des Herzens" (1914). Clearly this landscape is as much interior as it is exterior. The image of the suburb reflects the poet's interest at this time in the sensation implied in the term "Rand," to which Mrs. Corcoran devotes much of her study. As the suburb feels itself on the edge of the fuller life of "das Feld," so the adolescent girl, as in "Schau, unsre Tage sind so eng" (written six months after the present poem), hesitates on the edge of maturity. It is not necessary to equate the "hohe Häuser" of the first stanza with the awkward, self-conscious girls of Rilke's many "Mädchenlieder," but the resonance is clearly there. It gives the living houses a special vividness, without diluting the social aspect of the poem. As *Malte* was to demonstrate, social and private issues were never separate for Rilke; he invariably employed a subjective correlative to convey public suffering. The first three lines are both desolate and feverish, like an expressionist painting: "die letzten Hütten" are the outskirts of the suburb, yet the way they are introduced thrusts the temporal meaning of "letzten" into conjunction with the spatial. The very informality of the sentence suggests the anguish of something about to be lost, of childhood, of human life itself. Upon this informality is built the complexity of the middle lines: the internal rhyme of "engen" and "drängen," followed by a dominant diphthong *au* and a dominant consonant *g,* draws the image together. The accumulation of emotion is well managed until it founders on the word "schauen." As in the previous poem discussed, Rilke seems to want to invest this word with a dignity it cannot sustain; it is certainly an anti-climax after "sich drängen." It also stresses the subjectivity of the stanza: the poet, himself in the position of the "hohe Häuser," cannot fulfill his own imagery. The collapse of the stanza embodies the awkwardness and anguish of the "Rand" situation. Rilke seems to have become aware of this, for in his 1909 revision he altered three words in this stanza: "hohe" to "neue," "grauen" to "bangen," and "schauen" to "wissen," changing the pace of the lines completely (*Werke I*, 166). The word "neue" introduces a more specifically naturalistic element, reducing the sense of the houses as adolescents; "bang" does not seem an improvement on "grau" in itself, but it does heighten the alliterative unity of the line while removing the sense of climax through the *au* diphthong. The disappearance of "schauen" reduces the parallel between the houses and Rilke's "Mädchen," and the alliterating "wissen" gives the last line a quality more like the others, to echo the social implications of "neue." Adolescent involvement has been subtly dislodged by mature detachment—what the stanza gains in harmoniousness it loses in immediacy.

The second stanza, which Rilke left more or less intact in his revision, resembles Trakl's in that separate but related impressions are simply listed; yet it lacks Trakl's mesmeric quality because the poet works too hard to impose unity on the stanza with the framework of the successive seasons and the unnecessary emphasis on place ("Dort . . . hinter diesen Planken . . . dorten"). Where Trakl simply presents a dying world, Rilke attempts to exorcize the horror of it by pushing to extremes his images of the natural world in dislocation. Spring is the time of gentle beginning, but here it never really starts. Summer is the time of warmth, but here there is only feverish heat. The cherry trees, symbols of spring, and the children, symbols of the future, seem unable to bloom. This brief appearance of the child motif suggests a new stage in its meaning for the poet: the child, still "krank," is no longer identified with "Träume"; instead he is objectified in a context both social and natural. Instead of standing for the poet's alienation, the sick child represents the alienation of the half-

world the poet is evoking. Rilke feels able to approach larger
issues without self-assertion. Spring, image of childhood, is pale
and remote; summer, image of maturity, is constricted and over-
ripe. Rilke conveys vividly a trapped, self-perpetuating despair,
but the very delineation of this claustrophobic world impels him
to a positive assertion, to the juxtaposition of his anguish with the
negative refuge of autumn, image of old age. This is the kind of
poetic movement Rilke would later, in his own terms, have condemned as "unehrlich." It seems, rather, "unentschlossen."[18] The
young poet, seeking unity of experience, tried to combat the
dominant images of disharmony with a traditional harmonious
construct.

As the power of Rilke's imagery grows so does his difficulty in
fusing opposites within a single poem. The central fourth line of
the second stanza recalls the equivalent line in the poem previously discussed, "Ich mag nicht mehr euren Wahnsinn schauen."
It is prosaic in contrast to the highly colored lines preceding it,
and it contains an uncomfortable combination of words, "Herbst"
and "Hass." Granted the poet has been personifying both houses
and seasons, yet it is hard to accept suddenly the notion of autumn
having "feelings." This shift from external symptoms to an inappropriately internal word reveals the precariousness of Rilke's
hold on his imagery: he has succumbed to the temptation of stat-
ing a feeling instead of realizing it in words. A comparable in-
security prevails throughout the over-generalized third stanza. In
the first couplet "windschwingenstill" is a delicate inspiration, but
it is surrounded by an excessive use of "und," the diluting word
"manchesmal," and the sheer alliterative padding of "schön in

18. "Mein Können war damals so gering, mein Fühlen unreif und ver-
ängstigt, und es kommt noch dazu, dass ich für alle ersten Veröffentlichungen
immer das Schlechteste und Unpersönlichste zusammenstellte, weil ich mich
nicht entschliessen konnte, das was mir wirklich lieb war preiszugeben" (To
Ellen Key, March 3, 1904, quoted by Zinn, *Werke 3,* 867).

ihrem Schmelze." In the second couplet the sheep are incorporeal, and although the poet tries to finish in the singular rather than the plural with an image a little more concrete, the shepherd is all too romantic in comparison with the concrete atmosphere of the earlier stanzas. Moreover the excessively alliterating last line causes him to dissolve into the background. That Rilke felt these weaknesses is clear from his 1909 revision:

> und nur der Herbst hat dorten irgendwas
>
> Versöhnliches und Fernes; manchesmal
> sind seine Abende von sanftem Schmelze:
> die Schafe schummern, und der Hirt im Pelze
> lehnt dunkel an dem letzten Lampenpfahl.

Most of my specific objections are here rectified: With "Hass" removed the enjambement makes the central line less flat, with the rhythmically light position of "manchesmal" the first couplet now flows easily, and the substitution of "dunkel" for "lauschend" both interrupts the alliteration and objectifies the shepherd in the manner of the *Neue Gedichte*. What cannot be rectified is the general insubstantiality of the imagery in the context of what has gone before. "Versöhnliches und Fernes" represents a good attempt to soften this contrast: autumn is no longer felt so positively, but rather alleviates distress by distancing the reader from it. Although the poem's structure is thereby improved, the deterioration of the poetic vision, the inappropriateness of the pastoral atmosphere, cannot be hidden.

It is this final version which Berger describes when he writes:

> Durch das Gedicht geht eine eindeutige Entwicklung; die seelische Stimmung wird anfangs aus den tatsächlich gege- benen Umrissen des Motivs Vorstadt (Häuser, Hütten) entwickelt, dann wird sie vertieft und erweitert über Jahres- zeiten und Mensch, die Schlusstrophe bringt die Lösung in

der allerengsten Verbindung von Zeit, Wesen und Ding.
(Herbst, Abend—Schafe schummern—Hirt lehnt dunkel—
letzter Lampenpfahl.) Während Stefan George im "Jahr der
Seele" die Natur und die Zeit vermenschlicht, sucht Rilke
über Mensch und Natur hinaus die Einheit, in der alles ruht
und aus der heraus alles letzte Wirklichkeit und Dasein emp-
fängt.[19]

The perversity of such writing is what my study seeks to combat.
The intentional fallacy is carried to the point where the poem itself disappears, despite apparent references to the text. It is useless
to assume that what Rilke "seeks" he therefore achieves. One can
agree that Rilke is indeed seeking "Einheit," but one must deny
that he conveys such a unity in this poem, and, further, that such
a metaphysical aim offers any criteria of merit. There are many
who preach unity of experience, but there are very few to whom
one listens. Although Rilke became one of those few, naturally he
did not start with a complete and absorbing vision. Berger's approach offers no way of distinguishing between *Mir zur Feier* and
the *Duineser Elegien;* moreover the constant quest for metaphysical progression leads to failure to recognise whatever actual merit
the poem has. If Rilke's first stanza is "about" a suburb and his
third is a dreamy vision of autumn, the third must therefore be a
Vertiefung of the first. I have tried to show, however, that the
opposite is true. The earlier stanzas, in which the author's insights
are implicit in a social vision rather than explicitly stated, are the
more successful.

> Du musst das Leben nicht verstehen,
> dann wird es werden wie ein Fest.
> Und lass dir jeden Tag geschehen
> so wie ein Kind im Weitergehen
> von jedem Wehen   5
> sich viele Blüten schenken lässt.

19. Berger, pp. 80–1.

Sie aufzusammeln und zu sparen
das kommt dem Kind nicht in den Sinn.
Er löst sie leise aus den Haaren,
drin sie so gern gefangen waren,   10
und hält den lieben jungen Jahren
nach neuen seine Hände hin.

[January 8, 1898; *Werke 3*, 211]

Written only two months after the preceding poem (November
1897), these stanzas offer a kind of counterpoint to it. Where
the earlier poem accumulates images from disparate sources, the
present one develops a single theme through all its twelve lines;
if the former gives the impression of tortuousness and concentration, here we see an apparently expansive elegance. The simplicity
is of course deceptive, as Kohlschmidt, writing of the first two
lines, points out:

Aus dem für die Allgemeinheit einen Mangel aussagenden
ersten Vers macht der zweite Vers eine Tugend, einen Ge-
nuss. Der Sinn ergibt sich erst, wenn man unter "verstehen"
einen willkürlich ausgewählten Teilsinn des Wortes begreift,
nämlich die blosse Aufnahme durch die ratio. So ergibt sich
aus dem Paradox, das die beiden Verse bilden, eine ganz neue
Reizschwingung und Verdichtung des Gefühls der Lebens-
festlichkeit. So ist auch der Ton, den die Reime jetzt an-
schlagen, der eines leisen schwingenden Getragenseins, das
auf eine betonte Klausel zuströmt und in ihr ausklingt, ohne
dass nun noch ein Pathos vonnöten wäre.[20]

Undoubtedly the poet displays here a new security of tone, sup-
ported by two major elements. There is the cumulative rhyming
scheme which, as Belmore puts it, is "with its repetitions so expressive of his urgency to exhaust an idea or an image to the
last."[21] Through it Rilke achieves what Kohlschmidt terms a

20. Kohlschmidt, p. 37.
21. Belmore, p. 8.

"Getragensein," an ability to construct a stanza around two terminal points without turning these points into portentous climaxes: the stanza floats on the feminine rhymes in the third, fourth, and fifth lines, and barely touches ground with the unobtrusive word "lässt." The continuity and plasticity of imagery seem to reflect Rilke's instinctive personal identification with the theme now moving to the center of his poetry, the theme of "das Kind," which is on the threshold of expressing the creative act. What is stressed is not the child's innocence, not the pathos of its sickliness, nor even its capacity for dreams, but its spontaneous acceptance of the world. The implication, for the adult, is that childhood must be seen not as nostalgic ideal but as "Aufgabe." This was the meaning to Rilke of Jacobsen, whom he had just read for the first time (1897):

> Jacobsen hat keine Erfahrung gehabt, keine Liebe, kein Erlebnis und keine Weisheit, nur eine Kindheit. Eine grosse, ungeheuer farbige Kindheit, in der er alles fand, was seine Seele brauchte, um sich phantastisch zu verkleiden.[22]

The impact of Jacobsen can be felt behind the imperious didacticism of the present poem. Once a young poet groping for his own identity, Rilke has suddenly become an educator, a bearer of a message, a role he was to play until the end of his life. In each stanza the opening couplet expresses the thesis and the other four lines illustrate it. In each the vowel in the dominant feminine rhyme (*e* in the first, *a* in the second) dominates the stanza as a whole; in each the danger of monotony in the fourth line is averted by a playful dactyl-like beginning ("so wie ein . . . ," "drin sie so . . ."); and in each the last two lines artfully reflect the poem's meaning. The short fifth line in the first stanza gives a special prominence to the word "Blüten" in the final line: the blossoms seem to overflow into the second stanza. The penulti-

---

22. *Briefe und Tagebücher aus der Frühzeit,* p. 357.

mate line of the second stanza, by contrast, seems longer than it really is, as its decorative adjectives turn our attention away from the child to the world he is welcoming. In the short-sounding final line he slips away from us, pointing to the reality we must embrace. The child's gesture fulfills the "Fest" promulgated at the beginning.

The poem is technically a gem. Not surprisingly, Rilke left it intact in his 1909 revision. Yet close comparison with the flawed poem to which I have called it a counterpoint seems to diminish its superiority. Although the child image is perfectly realized, the result is somehow contrived. The poem's impetus derives from the image of childlike freshness, yet in the second stanza the child's behavior is studied, statuesque, even pretentious, like a *Jugendstil* picture. What exactly do these flowers mean to him? One can accept the ideas of spontaneity and non-possession, but how are they illustrated by a refusal even to notice the natural world embodied in the flowers? The phrase "nach neuen" suggests something has occurred, yet one feels an emptiness at the core of this particular gesture. The only purpose of submitting so delightful a poem to such questions is to suggest that Rilke is not yet capable of projecting a single image that will sustain an entire poem. The convictions generating his child image are still literary rather than experienced, and this is why the poem "Das ist dort, wo die letzten Hütten sind," with all its imperfections, looks further into the future.

> Und der Abend wird schwer:
> Alle gleichen verwaisten
> Kindern jetzt, und die meisten
> kennen einander nicht mehr.
> Gehn wie in fremdem Land
> langsam am Häuserrand,
> lauschen in jeden Garten,—
> wissen kaum, dass sie warten,

5

bis das Eine geschieht:
　　heimliche Hände heben   10
　　tief aus dem Leben
　　ein Lied . . .
　　　　　　　[April 25, 1898; *Werke 3*, 255–56]

This poem is again rooted in a juxtaposition of harmony and disharmony, but Rilke's growing technical skill has enabled him to weld the disparate elements with more success than hitherto. One can see two interlocking structures. First, the tripartite shape suggested by the rhyme scheme (*a b b a, c c d d, e f f e*), in which the first four lines and the last four lines differ from the middle four lines. Within this framework the first section presents the lost people, the middle section shows them longing and waiting, and the last represents the "Umschlag," the positive revelation. A closer look reveals a definite break in the center of the poem after the sixth line. In this line the previously dactylic rhythm slows almost to a standstill with the words "langsam am"; the world of *Malte* is evoked in the loneliness of the imagery. Then, almost imperceptibly, the word "lauschen," though deriving in both sound and context from "langsam," starts a new rhythm, the metaphorical motion of "in jeden Garten" expresses a tension, a possibility of change, absent from the static "in fremdem Land . . . am Häuserrand." The language prepares the "lost" people for the revelation at the end. In this way the poem is rendered seamless, and the transition from despair to hope appears inevitable.

Ten days after the present poem Rilke wrote another very similar in shape which he later omitted from his *Frühe Gedichte,* a decision worth analyzing:

　　　　Immer wenn die Nacht beginnt,
　　　　treiben in den alten Gassen—
　　　　willig einem jeden Wind—
　　　　Lieder, die leise müde sind.

> Und ein jedes ist wie ein Kind
> ganz in Angst allein—
> wollen sich alle von mädchenblassen
> Händen heimlich heben lassen
> in weisse Träume hinein . . .
>
> [May 4, 1898; *Werke 3*, 255]

Much of the same imagery is employed as in "Und der Abend wird schwer," with a different focus: instead of people, the songs ("Lieder," not "ein Lied") are anguished, and for them redemption consists of being lifted "in weisse Träume hinein." The imagery takes us back to the poems of 1895 and 1896, and indeed these dream-seeking "Lieder" resemble children "ganz in Angst allein." The difference between the two poems lies essentially in the different resonances of the word "Kind." In the poem Rilke discarded the word stands alone, an unadorned image on which the poem stands or falls; and it falls because the image points only to "Träume," to self-indulgent dissolution. In the poem under discussion here, in contrast, the word coupled with "verwaist" meshes into the texture of an image larger than itself. In this integrated state "das Kind" gains new possibilities of expressivity. The concreteness of the word "verwaist," despite its sentimentality, ties the child into a genuine social context. It suggests simultaneously man's loneliness, his anguish at the loss of all protective covering, and the positive aspects of this situation. The word "schwer" in the first line foreshadows Rilke's many statements about "das Schwere" in his later correspondence: the image of St. Christopher was clearly important to him, and its social relevance is suggested here. As the individual must expose himself totally and seek out "das Schwere" to achieve understanding, so these lost people, by becoming "verwaiste Kinder," bare their souls sufficiently to make a revelation possible. They are not poets, they "hardly know that they are waiting," but they embody a new validity for the child image. Spontaneity cannot simply be willed, but perhaps it can be attained through acknowledgement of, and absorption in, one's own orphanhood.

There remains the question of the revelation itself. As it stands, the poem dissolves in alliterations and solemnity: the word "heben" recalls "schwer" and the association with St. Christopher, but it is embedded in a background intended to evoke pure sound. The "Lied" cannot be sung, merely suggested. Later Rilke clearly felt this to be too vague, too much like the "Träume" he was striving to put behind him. His 1909 revision runs:

> bis das Eine geschieht:
> Unsichtbare Hände heben
> aus einem fremden Leben
> leise das eigene Lied.
>
> [*Werke I*, 194]

Of this revision Hagen writes:

> In der Urfassung wird das Numinose durch die Wahl von drei Worten auszulösen versucht, die im Stabreimverhältnis zueinander stehen. In der Umarbeitung dagegen wird nun dieses Numinose dadurch vorbereitet, dass ein stetiger, starrer Rhythmus von vier Trochäen zwischen die daktylischen Verse geschoben wird, die vorangehen und folgen.[23]

I would go further, and say that "das Numinose" is more closely defined and above all more relevant to the social atmosphere of the poem than in the original version. The change from "heimlich" to "unsichtbar" is important: whereas the former placed an aesthetic barrier between the people and the "Lied," the latter's scope is deliberately restricted. The hands are invisible, but not mysterious; they are the hand of the "absolute" (a term I shall discuss shortly), the force which enables man to fulfil his own

---

23. H.–W. Hagen, *Rilkes Umarbeitungen,* Form und Geist 24 (Leipzig, 1931), p. 48.

nature. Certainly they offer a model for construction, not self-dissolution. For the song is within the singer. If the strangeness of life is fully experienced, the answer to questioning will arise within the individual, as if hands had plucked it from the enigma without and placed it inside the orphaned psyche. But in 1898 Rilke was not yet able to formulate such a conclusion. An alliterative, fluent phrase seemed a natural ending to a poet for whom self-fulfillment and absorption in the external world still seemed synonymous. The harmony of the world was an unexamined premise, an anchor in his quest for images of disharmony. "Das Kind" here embodies man's orphaned state, and we know, from the previous poem, "Du musst das Leben nicht verstehen," that it has also retained its value as a positive image. Rilke's problem is to reconcile the instinctive aesthetic values associated with the child with his own growing sense of concreteness and social reality.

> So bin ich nur als Kind erwacht,
> so sicher im Vertraun,
> nach jeder Angst und jeder Nacht
> Dich wieder anzuschaun.
> Ich weiss, sooft mein Denken misst: 5
> wie tief, wie lang, wie weit,—
> Du aber bist und bist und bist,
> umzittert von der Zeit.
>
> Mir ist, als wär ich jetzt zugleich
> Kind Knab und Mann und mehr,   10
> ich fühle: nur der Ring ist reich
> durch seine Wiederkehr.
>
> Ich danke Dir, Du tiefe Kraft,
> die immer leiser mit mir schaft
> wie hinter vielen Wänden;   15
> jetzt ward mir erst der Werktag schlicht

und wie ein heiliges Gesicht
zu meinen dunklen Händen.
[October 5, 1899; *Werke 3*, 368]

Das Buch vom mönchischen Leben (1899) occupies a problematical position in Rilke's oeuvre. If, as do most readers, one
first approaches it as the poet's starting point, one is enthralled
by its confident use of language and its paradoxical imagery. The
style seems both simple and personal. Yet in relation to what has
gone before, and especially in the context of Rilke's need to syn-
thesize the traditionally aesthetic with the concrete and the social,
the cycle appears less satisfactory. Russia, of course, is the great
experience behind it, but one must question whether the renewal
of his mother's religiosity combined with the illusion of infinite
space within himself were the experiences Rilke needed most at
this time. E. M. Butler has pointed out at length the flaws in
Rilke's presentation of Russia, and while this does not affect the
poetic result of the experience, it does suggest that, when a
sharpening of his sense of the particular (already stimulated by
the Italian journey) was his most pressing need, the generalized
pantheism, the "Träume" of his youth, received a new lease on
life:

> But he sensed the inner piety of the people, saw that this
> was not the loathed externalized religion of his own youth,
> and his soul, thirsting not only for freedom but also for
> harmony, surrendered to a surface aesthetic feeling without
> penetrating the kernel of this religion which was rooted in
> life.[24]

It is of course futile to criticize a great poet's development, to
speculate about alternative paths open to him. Had Rilke not
become so absorbed in the ideals of art and community during

24. F. W. van Heerikhuizen, *Rainer Maria Rilke* (New York, 1952), p.
99.

the years 1899–1901, the shock of the Paris experience might not have been so severe or so fruitful; and but for the experience of Russian religion, renewing Rilke's sense of absolute perfection, the aspirations that impel the *Elegies* might never have developed. One can only observe generally that the inspirational flow of *Das Buch vom mönchischen Leben* seems less interesting than the more experimental workshop poems of the years immediately following; and particularly that the present poem seems more prolix, less well knit than "Und der Abend wird schwer" (1898).

The Russian experience does seem to have led Rilke to place his identity problems in perspective. Using the "Rolle" of a Russian monk, he subordinates the stages of a man's life to the centrality of religion. The first stanza portrays the child's combination of awe and intimacy, the short middle stanza expresses the simultaneity of human experience if oriented toward God, and the third stanza shows us the adult being molded by his God, the synthesis between faith and life complete. The unifying statement ("der Ring") no longer needs to be placed last, because man's progression is consummated in his daily life. But the replacement of the anguish of isolation by wholehearted devotion exacts a heavy poetic price, for the poem is no longer wholly independent. It assumes the acceptance of a point of reference (God) outside itself, and without such an acceptance on the part of the reader the fervor becomes empty posturing. Many readers, of course, have found no difficulty here: *Das Buch vom mönchischen Leben* is the starting point for the innumerable studies of "Rilke the Mystic." But in terms of poetic texture the present poem contains some disturbing elements.

Most striking is the regression from what could be called *Wortkunst*. In "Und der Abend wird schwer," we observed the subtleties of structure and the suggestive use of the word "Kind." Here it entirely lacks resonance—it stands for a stage of life dominated by minor hopes and fears. In this respect it represents the poem's style as a whole. Rilke has temporarily exchanged a symbolist style for a rhetorical one: just as the whole poem is merely a part of a wider sequence, so too the words are not significant in themselves, but only as the tools of an emotional statement. The word "jeder" implicitly devalues "Angst" and "Nacht." We are to look beyond these particulars to the general, which alone is of value. The word toward which the first two stanzas build, "der Ring," is a metaphysical image of unity, the summation of the preceding invocations. Such a poetry of statement, which subordinates individual images to a forward impetus, is appropriate to an epic writer, to a Milton or a Klopstock. Since Rilke's God has no real independence, no existence outside the poet's images, his style is an uneasy compromise between an assumed religious grandeur and an absorption in his own actions and reactions. The first two stanzas contain excessive references to the speaker, as if repetition could convince: "Ich weiss," "Mir ist," "ich fühle." Lines like "so sicher im Vertraun" and "wie tief, wie lang, wie weit" represent a devalued language, in which emphasis seeks to mask the banality of the religious imagery. The phrase "umzittert von der Zeit," the kind for which these poems are famous, renders the abstract concrete. Although expressive, it cannot bear the weight imposed on it as the fulfillment of "Du aber bist und bist und bist," a line epitomizing the failure of Rilke's rhetorical style.

The third stanza, however, set apart from the others by its integrated rhyme scheme, displays both the worst and the best of this stage in Rilke's development. Initially the first two lines seem empty: the pomposity of the "Ich," the superfluity of "tiefe," the apparent irrelevance of "leiser," the vagueness of "schafft"— such language shows Rilke at his weakest. But the third line, touching on the concrete for almost the first time in the poem, casts new light on the first two. Suddenly we have an image, the image of a monk in his cell listening to a voice very far away, which he no longer needs close by him. "Leiser" is appropriate after all, and although the first two lines are not redeemed, it does at last appear possible that Rilke will be able to incorporate rhetorical elements into his style without dissolving it. The last three lines strengthen this impression; the emphasis on "schlicht" seems emblematic of the new atmosphere. There is still something imprecise about the simile of "der Werktag" as "ein Gesicht," but it is exciting, only Rilke could have coined it. The relationship of face and hands, to be discussed at greater length in my second chapter, successfully resolves the inherent tension between man's creative drives ("Hände") and his need for a consistent personal identity ("Gesicht"). If Rilke's monk were always so concrete, the new abstract tendencies would not be disturbing, for the words themselves would embody his fervor.

> Ein einziges Gedicht das mir gelingt,
> und meine Grenzen fallen wie im Winde;
> es gibt kein Ding, darin ich mich nicht finde:
> nicht *meine* Stimme singt *allein:*—es klingt.
> Die Dinge werden heller und metallen,   5
> und wie sie atmend sich im Raum berühren,
> sind sie wie Glocken, die mit seidnen Schnüren
> spielenden Kindern in die Finger fallen:
>
> die Kinder ziehn zugleich an allen Strängen,
> die sie erstaunt in ihren Händen spüren,   10
> so dass die Töne vor des Himmels Türen,
> die viel zu langsam aufgehn,—schon sich drängen.
>
> [January 12, 1900; *Werke 3,* 674]

I described two earlier poems as counterpointed with each other, and in a sense the present poem and the twelve-line stanza to be studied next stand in a similar relationship. As Rilke's technical mastery grows, his awareness of the world's problems grows also. Moods of exhilaration and pessimism alternate. The present rhapsodic outburst reads like a conscious escape from the monk's cowl donned three months earlier: the poet exults in his own creativity without paying tribute to any higher force. As in the poem "Du musst das Leben nicht verstehen," a wholly positive utterance is built on the image of "das Kind." The children are confined to a single spontaneous action ("ziehn zugleich an allen Strängen"). Convincing in its naïveté it establishes a bond between the child image and the creative act.

We have already seen how reading Jacobsen convinced Rilke that childhood was the poet's basic source material. By now he goes further, viewing the child's actions as the model for artistic creation. These ideas are lucidly formulated in an important letter of April 7, 1899:

> Um so nah an die Dinge zu kommen, gibt es nächst dem Vertrauen zu ihnen ein Mittel, unsere Eindrücke und Erinnerungen nicht zu verlassen und auf ihren einsamsten Wegen ihnen gern und gläubig nachzugehen und nachzusehen, bis sie klein in dem Tal der Heimat angekommen sind und brüderlich neben Blumen und Bäumen, Bergen und Burgen stehen. Denn dort in unserer Kindheit sind sie gerecht und rein. Dort ist Kraft und Kern unseres Könnens. Dort ist der Beginn. Dort ist die weisse Eins, mit der wir immer wieder beginnen können zu zählen. Dorthin müssen wir uns auf weitem Weg zurückfinden, um uns zu vollenden . . . Wahrlich: Die Kindheit ist das Bild der Kunst. Sie ist der Schein jener Schönheit, von der wir träumen, dass sie einst sein werde . . . Dann ist keine Gefahr darin, sich alles geschehen zu lassen und abzuwarten, zu welchem Werke der Mut mündig werden will: zum tiefen Gedicht oder zum breiten Leben.[25]

Rilke insists here that an artist's work is in a sense already done, that the lived experience of childhood is a complete manifestation of everything the adult will achieve, and that art is only one way

25. An Charlotte Scholtz, April 7, 1899, in *Die Erzählung 1* (1947), no. 3, pp. 12–13.

of re-enacting one's childhood, of achieving that identification with the whole of life which to a child is self-evident. Indeed childhood itself depends on the larger flow of life that has preceded it and surrounds it. The concept of "der junge Tote," first developed at length in the "Requiem" for Gretel Kottmeyer (1900; *Werke 1*, 469), embodies this mature view of childhood. "Dein Tod war schon alt, / als dein Leben begann," and "von dem, was du sehntest, bist du erlöst / zu etwas, was du hast" are key lines in that poem illustrating Rilke's view of personality as an almost accidental intersection of spatial and temporal factors. The child is a symbol of wholeness because the voices of the past speak freely through him while he is wholly involved with the "Dinge" of the present. The adult has the impossible task of using his consciousness to regain an unconscious state. All the tensions of a man's life arise from this task: the need to develop forward against the need to discard the trappings of adulthood, the urgency of speaking with one's own voice against the certainty that an individuality is merely the product of a past collectivity, the rightness of merging oneself with the stream of life against the human task of creating something apart from life.

That art can resolve such contradictions is the theme of "Ein einziges Gedicht." The poem mentioned in the first line is not in itself of value to the poet; it is no solemn work of art to be contemplated. Rather it is like a key that unlocks the world of nature as the child sees it. It is akin to Proust's madeleine except that it is a product of the poet's striving, not of chance. If Proust seeks his childhood to transmute it into art, Rilke does the opposite, creating in order to gain access to his childhood. The *Grenzen* imposed by adulthood are dissolved, and the poet is able to sing the song greater than the one he has written, to merge his voice with all the voices of nature the adult cannot hear. Actually there is a complexity of levels here: the present poem *is* an attempt to capture in words that intoxicated feeling of synthesis between successful assertion and joyful dissolution of the self. It may be reasonable to relate this poem to Rilke's experiences of the previous year. The Russian trip had revealed to him the possibility of a childlike response to the world. In *Das Buch vom mönchischen Leben* he had written a cycle of poems he knew were successful. Perhaps only after the expression there of his exalted feelings and aims did he feel released into a newly vibrant world of the concrete. Only now could he begin the task of integrating adult visions and a sense of adult identity with the minutiae, the simplicity of a child's perception.

The fifth to eighth lines seem to adumbrate this very process. "Die Dinge" had been subordinated to the somber atmosphere of the monk's cell; now they are becoming brighter, beginning to breathe. They are still encompassed by the "Raum" of the religious vision, and the image of the bell expresses their effect on the poet. "Die Glocke" was much used by Rilke in these years of grappling with his new perceptions,[26] for it is a powerful synthesis of the abstract and the concrete. Situated proudly at the top of a church tower, the bell unites man's aspirations with the religious certainties of the ages; a landmark in the visual world, its true realm is that of sound; majestic and self-contained, it depends on man to achieve fullest life, indeed a tug on the rope is accessible to the smallest child. This bond between the highest visions and the child at play generates the present imagery. These four lines bind together a wide variety of sounds through the poet's growing ability to alliterate with discrimination: the consonants *r*, *l*, *s*, *g*, *k*, and *f* play upon each other to suggest both the range of the bells and the spontaneous harmony of the playing children.

The last four lines maintain this linguistic level, with tactful alliterations enhancing the meaning: the sudden motion of *z* in the first line is contrasted with the metallic thinness of *t* in the third.

26. The bell motif is strikingly developed in a poem of March 1901 (*Werke* 3, 741).

The last line is perhaps slightly awkward—Rilke is not yet a master of grammatical displacement—but his purpose is clear: to slow the verse down, signifying the resistance of the absolute, and then to end as it were on a jerk, on the unceasing force of human inspiration when merged with the world around it. For the first time in the poems discussed in this chapter, Rilke has developed a single image to a wholly personal conclusion without sagging into the conventional. That the children should tug at all the ropes is both naïve and expressive of their total commitment to experience. Their surprise echoes the poet's delighted surprise at his entry into their world, and their absence from the final couplet in favor of "die Töne" suggests the final merging of the spontaneous and the creative. These "Töne" are neither wholly the poet's nor wholly the children's nor even a product of the two together; they are independent. They assault the heavens, and yet they could not come into being without the children's symbolic gesture. The poet occupies a kind of middle ground between the children and these revelations of nature. Rilke often said that nature needed man's voice to fulfill her; this poem suggests that childhood similarly needs the adult to crystallize its meaning. The poet thus has a mission to develop his vision to the point where it annihilates itself, dissolving in the absolute reality that exists all the time unseen, that "Schönheit, von der wir träumen, dass sie einst sein werde."

> Ich bin nur einer deiner Ganzgeringen,
> der in das Leben aus der Zelle sieht
> und der, den Menschen ferner als den Dingen,
> nicht wagt zu wägen, was geschieht.
> Doch willst du mich vor deinem Angesicht,   5
> aus dem sich dunkel deine Augen heben,
> dann halte es für meine Hoffahrt nicht.
> wenn ich dir sage: Keiner lebt sein Leben.
> Zufälle sind die Menschen, Stimmen, Stücke,

Alltage, Ängste, viele kleine Glücke,   10
verkleidet schon als Kinder, eingemummt,
als Masken mündig, als Gesicht—verstummt.

[September 19, 1901; *Werke 1*, 316]

Although not a complete poem, this stanza is reasonably self-contained, and it stands in direct contrast to the exultant rhapsody we have just studied. I pointed out earlier that Rilke's renewal of the romantic ideal of childhood was based on poetic conviction not on anything experienced. His own childhood, indeed, provided the negative evidence against which to measure the ideal. A pessimistic stanza like the present one does not invalidate the vision of the preceding poem; it is its necessary antithesis, the bitter experience which alone can ensure the genuineness of the vision. One of the sources of Rilke's greatness is that all levels of reality are included in his poetry. Those who see him as a glorifier of "art" have missed the point. If he exulted in moments of inspiration, he also grappled with the greyness of daily life. If he stressed the need to turn inwards and seek one's own childhood, he did not therefore ignore man's social vicissitudes. Indeed the root of his dialectic is that man's most intimate being, his childhood, merges with the collective past of humanity. We find Rilke in these years pondering the problem of his military school and his proposed novel about it, for it embodied the human paradox in its most acute form, the transformation of individual children into a frightening collectivity:

Denn der einzelne ist ja eben,—auch der verdorbenste— Kind, was aber aus der Gemeinsamkeit dieser Kinder sich ergibt,—das wäre der herrschende Eindruck,— eine schreckliche Gesamtheit, die wie ein fürchterliches Wesen wirkt, welches bald diesen und bald jenen Arm verlangend ausstreckt.

[November 5, 1899][27]

27. *Briefe und Tagebücher aus der Frühzeit*, pp. 206–07.

Statements like this enable us to place the Paris experience in perspective. The distress he felt in August 1902 was so intense only because Rilke's inner senses were ready for it: the *Malte* experience, so evident in a word like "eingemummt" in the present poem, was latent within him. E. M. Butler has pointed out how Rilke seemed to divert his morbid feelings into the short stories of the early years, while his poems themselves remained almost sickly sweet. However a poem like "Das ist dort, wo die letzten Hütten sind," although isolated in 1897, is a forerunner of Rilke's attempt, from 1899 onwards, to integrate his fears with his visions.

This attempt, psychologically so demanding, suggests a reason for the religious framework of *Das Stundenbuch*. We have seen the damage done to Rilke's language by his invocation of the absolute in "So bin ich nur als Kind erwacht" (1899), but we have also seen the brilliant results of his symbolic assault on the absolute in "Ein einziges Gedicht," written only three months later. In the present poem, where Rilke returns to the "Lyrik der Zelle," the underlying framework of the absolute generates a deep pessimism about the possibility of achieving an identity. A condition of his maturation was his sense of himself as an intermediary: by the time of the *Neue Gedichte* he thought he could fuse his personality with his poetry. The poems themselves would no longer need to invoke the absolute, but implicit in their self-contained perfection is the assumption that God would read them, or at least accept them. The personality of the young Rilke had been so divided between vision and anguish that the mature poet could never discard the thought that some higher force was holding him together and warding off chaos. Always with him is the question he asks in a poem written on the same day as the stanza under discussion: "Wer lebt es denn? Lebst du es, Gott,—das Leben?" (*Werke 1*, 317).

In the present poem the poet insists on his relationship with the absolute as a guarantee of personal identity. As in "So bin ich nur als Kind erwacht," it is only at the end that the verse attains a high level. The first eight lines, although less cliché than before, exaggerate the personal nature of the confrontation and the monk's pose of humility. Rilke has used the monk as a vehicle for mystic exultation that would be improper in a layman; now he attempts to convey a comparable degree of self-abasement. But the relative clause structure of the first four lines prevents the verse from flowing. Attempts to ameliorate this by assonance ("einer"/"deiner") and alliteration ("wagt"/"wagen") seem obtrusive. Although a phrase like "den Menschen ferner als den Dingen" has the Rilkean ring, the conventional sentiments Rilke is trying to express just will not come naturally to him. The middle four lines seem even more strained: the attempt to make the absolute concrete is most awkward—the alliterating *d* reads like an effort to counteract this by returning the verse to an incantation. Yet through this stilted style we can feel the poet nurturing the general statement that really matters to him. Suddenly it is there. Nothing could be simpler or more Rilkean than "Keiner lebt sein Leben," and the final lines marvelously unite the disjointed rhythm of adult life with the soft blanket of illusory answers that smothers the budding perceptions of children. The staccato of *t* and *k* is succeeded by a ubiquitous neutralizing *m*. Alliterations are far more numerous than in the earlier lines, yet they do not obtrude, for the meaning is built on them. After all that has been said in this chapter, the terrifying importance of the phrase "verkleidet schon als Kinder" must be evident. Rilke can accept that adult life involves role playing—what else is his assumption of a monk's attitudes? But to have been deprived of the directness and spontaneity of childhood will turn one's roles into masks with only emptiness behind them. The theme of the Fifth Elegy is adumbrated here: premature adulthood is inner death, the finality of being "verstummt" despite all outward signs of vigor. The word "verkleidet" conveys not only Rilke's personal deprivation, but also the symbolic custom of dressing children as little adults. From this we can understand Rilke's passionate addiction to "Einsamkeit." "Verkleidet" as a small child, then caught up in the collective distortion of the military school, he must have known he was irredeemably a part of the role-playing world. Yet if there was no bridge between the reality of his childhood and his ideal image, he could at least try to reassemble the scattered and submerged fragments of a childlike perception that must once have existed. The only way to free his energies from role-playing to devote them to such a task was to withdraw from human contact. Simenauer mocks Rilke's efforts in this direction, but he misses the point, for there was nothing arrogant or affected about such an aim. When Rilke says "Keiner lebt sein Leben," he makes no exception for himself. And in the last lines he is no Zarathustra berating humanity: these experiences are his own, and it is his life's struggle to stave off the threat of the final word, "verstummt."

> Das ist nicht wie wenn Kinder irrgehn im Wald;
> nein, sag das nicht.
> Ich bin alt.
> Und mein Wald ist: von Stein die Gestalt,
> und aus Lärm ist sein Angesicht.   5
> Das ist wie wenn einer sterben will,
> und die Kinder im Hofe schrein;
> und er wartet lang in den Tag hinein,
> aber die Kinder im Hofe schrein.
> Und da weiss er: so wird mein Sterben sein: 10
>   nichteinmal *still.*
>   [September 17, 1902; *Werke 3*, 760]

If Rilke's experience of Paris did not so much change him as bring out what was latent in him, it did have a fundamental effect on his technique. Where formerly his "Ängste" were associated with childhood and contrasted with the aesthetic actuality of Worpswede, suddenly he sees them manifest on all sides, incarnate in the outsiders of Paris. Thus the relationship between the poet and his absolute is radically transformed; no longer does he sit in a symbolic cell mediating between positive aesthetic experiences and the fears of childhood long past. All at once the elements of life have coalesced. Rilke, thrust back into his "Ängste" is aware that aesthetic experiences, if any, will have to be forged from what has hitherto seemed to be their negation. The absolute is not eliminated from the equation. Indeed the urgency with which Rilke invokes the "Herr" in *Das Buch von der Armut und vom Tode* (1903) far surpasses the slightly self-satisfied relationship with God in the earlier parts of *Das Stundenbuch.* But the excess rhetoric has been swept away. The new thematic source is a tension between the need to penetrate the meaning of man's urban life and the need to keep one's head above water, to cling to the belief in the absolute which alone can give aesthetic shape to the new experiences. Thus neither the poet himself nor his absolute appears frequently in the poems of this period: both are implicit in the external reality which the poems try to encompass. This does not mean that the dialectic is resolved. Rilke was not to know a synthesis of all his faculties until February 1922, and a mere subordination of the self to an external reality would have meant a return to the wooden objectivity of the French Parnasse or its obverse, naturalism. Rather, in his Paris period Rilke sought symbols into which he could pour his simultaneous sense of *Offenheit* and *Einsamkeit,* symbols both expressive of the world around them and inwardly withdrawn from it. Famous among these are the panther and the various outsider figures in *Malte.* The child, with its established affinities with the artist and also its raucous ubiquitousness in the visible world, is clearly eligible for a new symbolic dimension. One of the greatest of the Paris poems is entitled "Kindheit" (1905–06), and the present stanzas point towards it in a number of ways.

The most striking innovation here is the dissolution of poetic viewpoint. "Ich" slides into "einer" and both are combined with lines in an apparently neutral tone ("und die Kinder im Hofe schrein"). There is also an implied interlocutor ("nein, sag das nicht"). To ambiguity of perspective Rilke adds ambiguity of subject: it is never stated what "Das ist . . ." specifically describes; rather we are offered similes, variations in search of a theme. The whole is remarkably prophetic of the *Telegrammstil* developed by the expressionists, and suggests Rilke's unique position. Alone among his contemporaries he could surmount the dissolution of the impressionist sensibility as described in Hofmannsthal's "Chandos Letter" and create new verbal forms without withdrawing into a private world. In this his apparently anachronistic devotion to the ideal of the child played a crucial role. For the child the world simply "is," and does not have to be filtered through a categorizing subjectivity. If the poet refuses to categorize his perceptions, he will be able to perceive again the significance of purely spatial relationships, which are the essential element in the child's world. A wholly new meaning is thus given to Rilke's youthful method of juxtaposition: if in his early poems he combined contradictory realities in order to veil his uncertainty, now he does so with the aesthetic aim of recreating a contradictory world, a world unified only by the perceiver's intellect. One can see in this another link between the groping youth and the mature *Nuancenmensch,* and the opening line of the poem seems to proclaim this link by rejecting the past. The "Kinder" here are the romanticized wraiths of the poet's youth; in attempting to describe his disorientation in Paris, Rilke peremptorily rejects the old categories. To be lost in a forest implies the positives of natural harmony and of a way out. In Paris there is no nature and no way out. Nor is the poet a child—the ideal must not be confused with reality. "Ich bin alt," with brutal simplicity, goes beyond sentimental yearnings. The value of children, or even of forests, is not thereby negated, but these things are lost for Rilke and he must acknowledge their loss before they can be regained.

Another habit that in an earlier poem seemed a weakness is a strength here: the repetition of "und." From the second line onward the verse has had a heavy staccato tread. "Und" maintains this monosyllabic emphasis. Discrete experiences are forcibly conjoined: the reader contrasts the wispy lightness of "irrgehn im Wald" with the stark rhyming phrase in the fourth line, "Stein die Gestalt." Both "mein" and "Wald" receive a stress, but the heavier is on "mein" because the new "objectivity" Rilke is adopting is in fact intensely subjective; and the word "Wald" looks in two directions. The dreamlike connotations of the first line, still echoing, are absorbed in the resonance of the word as "wilderness," formless natural chaos. By adopting the chaos as "mein," Rilke sees a chance of symbolically reunifying the two meanings of "Wald." He knows there is no other choice. These lines embody the possible solution, the rendering concrete of what is abstract or unmanageably vast. If we compare the closing lines of "So bin ich nur als Kind erwacht" (1899) with the present couplet, we see the progress Rilke has made. There the metaphor involving "Gesicht" is intangible, investing the monk's reality with a mystery that excludes the reader; here it is immediate, drawing the reader into the poem's world. Noise is indeed the city's face, thrust unwelcomely close to our own.

In the first stanza Rilke speaks to us directly, involving himself in the city and relating it to his past. In the second stanza he evokes a city dweller, a poetic persona who is also trying to involve himself in the city in his quest for the moment of reconciliation which is the "eigener Tod." That both stanzas deal with the same theme is implied by the opening "Das ist wie wenn." The dying man's quest for harmony is essentially the poet's own. The enemy in this stanza is the intractability of reality, symbolized by the potential horror contained in the child image, a horror greater for its perversion of fundamental innocence. If the children in the first stanza evoked the dreamy aestheticism of Rilke's past, here they suggest the "schreckliche Gesamtheit" of the military school. No better illustration of the poet's mental tension could be found than this dual use of the same paradoxical image.

Again Rilke creates the weapons to wage the struggle he evokes. For this "Sterben" is in no way portentous, it has nothing in common with the "eigener Tod" of the 1900 "Requiem." In context it is simple and inevitable. There is no breach of style between the lines evoking the dying man and the interspersed cries of the children outside. Indeed the rhyming of "hinein" and "schrein" suggests the merging of the two levels, the abandonment of the dying man's struggle described in the last two lines. The brief final line with its colloquial directness suggests the bitter realism of the man's death. After the accumulating "ein" rhymes evoking conflict, "still" closes the circle by rhyming ironically with "will." Death does indeed come, but it is not the dignified death that was sought.

The poem is, on a literal level, wholly pessimistic, but the consistency and concreteness of its language embody new hope through new clarity. The quest for harmony and its constant frustration are juxtaposed and intertwined, their contradiction unresolved within the poem; indeed the negation seems dominant. But "nichteinmal still" does not sound final. As the dying man ends his complaint with an almost humorous cynicism about death rather than with death itself, so Rilke prevents himself from being overwhelmed by the city through the simple particularity of his vision. Questions of hope or happiness have in a sense become irrelevant. The poem need no longer express positive values, for it has in itself become the poet's best hope, the temporary resolution of the conflict it expresses.

The tension between the romantic idealization of childhood, which Rilke made his own, and the actual memory of a lonely and frightening period in his life gives the child motif its ambivalent force in these poems. The ten poems discussed can be divided into three groups representing the broad stages through which the motif passes in Rilke's early years. The first four poems (1893–97) are dominated by dreams: the child is a central figure whose separateness is constantly emphasized, surrounded by a protective shield of dreams. In the next three poems (1898–99) the child, more consciously used by the poet, exchanges its early independence for a symbolic role in a larger context of artistic and social themes. In the last three poems (1900–02) the child regains a central position, this time as something close to a real child.

In "Manchmal ermattet vom Hasten nach Glück" (1893) the general harmoniousness is rounded out in the last two stanzas by the total enclosure of the child in dreams. The separateness of public and private realms is implicit in every line. In "Es kommt die Nacht" (1895) this separateness, no longer assumed, is underscored by a special factor: the child is sick. The surface of the poem remains unruffled by discordant elements, but the implications threaten the child's world. The child's death is part of an overall harmony, but it is brought swiftly and arbitrarily by the night from which the child cannot be protected. The dream for which his death pays is not his. This poem has something in common with the first poem to be considered in my next chapter, "Ich weiss, als Kind" (1896), in which the "second hand" disrupts the child's world. In both works Rilke seems to be saying more than he intends, namely that the self-contained world of the child must be destroyed before art can be created. It is the poet's desperate attempt to resist a truth he has himself perceived which makes a reading of "Was reisst ihr" (1896) an uneasy experience. The poet strives to identify himself with the protected sick child. The rejected outside world seems to revolve around the self-contained sickroom. Such an atmosphere cannot be maintained, and the outside world is impressively re-entered in "Das ist dort, wo die letzten Hütten sind" (1897). Here the child's sickness is projected into the half-world of the outermost suburbs, which become charged with the atmosphere of adolescence. The claustrophobic imagery expresses the growing child's urge to pass over "der Rand" into "das Offene." But the poem's resolution still occurs in terms of the dream. The third stanza reaffirms the intimate and desirable connection between sickness and dream.

"Du musst das Leben nicht verstehen" (1898) is built around the image of a wholly spontaneous child, but the very emphasis on his spontaneity injects an element of self-consciousness. For the child is not really visualized as an individual; he is introduced as a metaphor, "so wie ein Kind," a model for the lesson in living of the opening couplet. In "Und der Abend wird schwer" (1898) the child motif is again used metaphorically: "Alle gleichen verwaisten / Kindern." Here Rilke is more successful in integrating the motif into a world of adult preoccupations. The image of orphans is well adapted to the poem's social context. It also conveys the child's fundamental isolation and, through the vision earned at the end by these exposed people, the child's instinctive openness to life, an openness that will always ultimately be rewarded. The metaphorical use of the motif is less impressive in "So bin ich nur als Kind erwacht" (1899)—the very words "nur als Kind" are uncharacteristically restrictive. Where the poet had, in "Was reisst ihr" (1896), attempted to enter the child's world, here he draws the child into his own world, as a device of contrast. The motif is subordinated to a schematically imposed meaning.

We are closer to the mature poet in "Ein einziges Gedicht" (1900). Rilke achieves here what he failed to achieve in "Du musst das Leben nicht verstehen": a presentation of spontaneous children whose spontaneity expresses a wider truth. Here they embody the proof of his dictum in a letter of April 1899 (quoted above): "Die Kindheit ist das Bild der Kunst." The children are presented as a metaphor in the first stanza, a metaphor which arises from the artist's creative achievement. So compelling is the image that, in the second stanza, the children's reality is complete, their gesture a decisive act. A drastic contrast to this emblematic fulfillment is provided by "Ich bin nur einer deiner Ganzgeringen" (1901), which conveys the subjective reality of a distorted childhood.

In "Das ist nicht wie wenn Kinder" (1902) two contrasting pictures of children are presented, both of metaphorical significance as the introductory "wie wenn" stresses. The first line

rejects the dream child of the early years; the second stanza
presents the horror of children as a collectivity. Neither image
encompasses the meaning of childhood, but together they express a grasp on reality which reflects Rilke's achievement of a
child's vision, an ability to connect outwardly unrelated phenomena (the dying man and the children at play) and to face the
dissolution beneath life's surface. In the second stanza of "Kindheit" we see how Rilke eventually achieves the perspective of
childhood through an intuitive understanding of a child's priori-
ties:

> Und in das alles fern hinauszuschauen:
> Männer und Frauen; Männer, Männer, Frauen
> und Kinder, welche anders sind und bunt;
> und da ein Haus und dann und wann ein Hund
> und Schrecken lautlos wechselnd mit Vertrauen—   5
> O Trauer ohne Sinn, o Traum, o Grauen,
> o Tiefe ohne Grund.
>
> [Winter 1905–6; *Werke 1*, 384]

Nothing is excluded from this vision. The word "Traum" no
longer has exclusive connotations, it is a reality of childhood like
any other, alternating with the equally childlike sensations of
"Trauer" and "Grauen." The concrete and the emotional loom
equally large, and the ability to see all phenomena intensely but
separately is a prime defense against being overwhelmed by them.
The artist cannot actually be a child, cannot live in terms of gestures and uncoordinated reactions, but through his art he can
attempt the paradox of "conscious spontaneity," of seeing the
world as a child and organizing it as a poet.

3   Die Hand

Of the ten poems chosen for their relevance to the child motif, five contain references to the human hand endowing it with qualities beyond the expected:

> sie reicht mir mild mit ihren beiden
> Madonnenhänden einen Traum.

[Autumn 1895]

> und hält den lieben jungen Jahren
> nach neuen seine Hände hin.

[January 8, 1898]

> heimliche Hände heben
> tief aus dem Leben
> ein Lied . . .

[April 25, 1898]

> Jezt ward mir erst der Werktag schlicht
> und wie ein heiliges Gesicht
> zu meinen dunklen Händen.

[October 5, 1899]

> die Kinder ziehn zugleich an allen Strängen,
> die sie erstaunt in ihren Händen spüren,

[January 12, 1900]

The last of these comes closest to a conventionally instrumental view of hands, yet here too a separation is implied between the cognitive faculties and the purely sensory reaction expressed by "spüren." The children's hands pull the ropes instinctively, astonished at their own situation. In the first three examples one can see the hands being associated with increasingly metaphorical gestures. Although the imagery in the 1895 poem is conventional,

the emphasis on the night's "Madonnenhände" underlines the act
of giving rather than the dream given: a sacred act is being per-
formed. In the second example (1898), the feeling of a symbolic
action is even stronger. The child, by merely stretching out his
hands, affirms his bond with the infinite present; or rather, the
hands do this for him, connecting what is wholly spontaneous in
the child with the creative self-renewal his actions symbolize for
the poet. In the third example (1898), the hands are detached
from any kind of body, and their autonomous function as a bridge
between life and art can be seen clearly. A song is intangible,
though shaped by human creativity, and the absolute is responding
to something in man when it lifts a song from the depths of life,
inducing harmony where before there was only alienation and
change. The child's gestures turn constantly toward life, and his
hands are themselves the song. The adult, having lost this unity
of perception, must wait for "heimliche Hände" to restore the
song to him. The difference between "hinhalten" in the second
illustration and "heben" in the third is the difference between
the child's immediacy and the adult's self-consciousness.

Sacredness, independence and creativity: these qualities are all
suggested in the lines quoted from *Das Buch vom mönchischen
Leben.* The contrast between "heiliges Gesicht" and "dunkle
Hände," yoked together in a single image, illustrates the tension
between the creative power of the hands and their independence
from conscious control: "Rilke employed the hand-image not
only to embody artistic creativity, but also to give expression to
the opposite, namely to his own poetically unproductive periods".[1]
The adult cannot control the movements of his hands, he can only
seek a way of life in which they will sustain rather than destroy.
Incapable of the child's gesture, he cannot spontaneously evoke
the sacred. Instead he must strive for a "Werktag" in which his
hands find fulfillment. The synthesis of the conscious "Werktag"

1. Frederick C. Tubach, "The Image of the Hand in Rilke's Poetry,"
PMLA 77 (1961), 242.

and the unconscious drives of the "Hände" will then appear as a "heiliges Gesicht," a genuine personal identity. The intangible quality of the sacred can reappear in the adult's life but only as the result of a sustained tension, when the activity of the hands runs in the channels of creation. For this activity can veer away from the conscious mind at any time, and then the owner of the hands is at a loss, cut off from his own powers, from his "dunkle Hände."

> Ich weiss, als Kind: Mein Spielzeug fiel.
> Ich bückte mich. Da kalt und knöchern
> kam eine Hand die Wand durchlöchern
> und griff danach. Ich blieb ihr Ziel.
> Wie oft greift jetzt dem müden Ringer
> mit ihrem dürren Knochenfinger
> die Totenhand ins Saitenspiel.
> [November 20, 1896; *Werke 3,* 548]

A corollary to the hand's independence is the suggestion that it derives its power from an external force. The present poem shows the "second hand" to be a very early image in Rilke's writing, and it becomes a central element in the complex of motifs to be discussed. Rilke conceived the absolute as a perfection to be invoked, but essentially remote from man. The one human attribute constantly associated with the absolute is hands, however, as the semi-humorous opening story of *Geschichten vom lieben Gott* (1899) demonstrates: man escapes from God's hands before they can finish him, and God is so angry with his hands that they too are in a kind of limbo: "sie können nur *beginnen,* was sie auch tun. Ohne Gott giebt es keine Vollendung" (*Werke 4,* 293). The extent to which Rilke develops this image justifies a slight schematization. If the absolute, perfect consciousness is by definition self-contained and man's mind, a consciousness condemned to imperfection, longs for the perfection it can never reach, then the hands of both, symbols of blind creativity and undirected power, grope towards each other in the gulf between the finite and the infinite. To be constructive, man's hand must seek to grasp the hand of the absolute, since it offers the only way forward from imperfection to perfection; yet such contact is terrifying as well as life-giving, and its results unpredictable. In 1898 Rilke adumbrated an image with biblical overtones, suggesting the ambiguity of the situation, of man's need to seek his strength outside himself:

> Wenn zwei oder drei Menschen zusammenkommen, sind sie deshalb noch nicht beisammen. Sie sind wie Marionetten deren Drähte in verschiedenen Händen liegen. Erst wenn eine Hand alle lenkt, kommt eine Gemeinsamkeit über sie, welche sie zum Verneigen zwingt oder zum Dreinhauen. Und auch die Kräfte des Menschen sind dort, wo seine Drähte enden in einer haltenden herrschenden Hand.[2]

The comparison of man with a marionette, not in a negative sense but rather with the favorable connotations of Kleist's essay, brings the ambivalence of the "Hand" theme into proximity with that of the "Puppe" which, as Steiner and others have demonstrated, was already developed by Rilke in the 1899 story "Frau Blahas Magd."[3] The child pours his feeling into the doll until the moment when he suddenly feels dried out and sees the doll as a grotesque corpse inflated by his subjectivity. Similarly the apparently life-bringing hand of the absolute can suddenly turn away from its marionette. At any time the "herrschende Hand" is at liberty to withdraw man's "Kräfte" from him and leave him groping in the void, his hands more like monsters than instruments.

"Ich weiss, als Kind" hints at the horror of such a relationship. The fourth line especially suggests the frightening connection between hand, toy, and child. The hand reaches for the toy, but the child is its real goal. The toy, laden with the child's emotions,

2. "Zur Melodie der Dinge" (1898; *Werke* 5, 416).
3. Jacob Steiner, "Das Motiv der Puppe bei Rilke," pp. 132–70.

is a mere agent through which the hand can reach the child—
the verb "blieb" emphasizes that this process has gone on before
this moment of awareness and is likely to continue after it. The
hand is the ambivalent power on which the adult depends, and the
experience suggested is the child's first loss of spontaneity, the first
awareness that he is "schutzlos." These elements, although they
can be seen in the poem in retrospect, lie below the surface of
the lines written in 1896. The exceptional terseness and vividness
of the first four lines suggest rather the direct transcription of an
experience, while the relative banality of the last three lines reads
like a youthful poet's attempt to interpret the given experience.
One feels the undecided character of the early poetry. Rilke is
writing of something very personal, but since it is an enigma to
him the lines remain in the *Nachlass*. Poems on less intimate
themes were finished and sent to the publisher.

The first line and a half act like chords in a recitative, provid-
ing in three sober statements the factual base for what follows.
The first phrase, "Ich weiss, als Kind," deliberately compressed,
concerns the truthfulness of the experience—the fantastic elements are to be rooted in the prosaic. The little word "da" initiates a line and a half of visual horror which remains, however,
within the compressed style of the opening. There is no loss of the
child's perspective, yet the anguish is vividly suggested by the alliterating *k,* the internal rhyme "Hand"/"Wand" and the extremely rich "Knöchern"/"löchern." So tightly knit are the
phrases that the extraordinary is at once believable. The dactyl
preceding "Hand" thrusts the word forward just enough for the
reader to visualize the hand's eerie power. In the fourth line the
image loses its impetus, as if the child had become confused by
the hand's proximity. "Danach" seems consciously vague; it must
refer to the toy, yet the first line of the poem seems far away
now. Basically the hand thrusts toward the child himself, as he
acknowledges both explicitly and implicitly by juxtaposing "nach"
and "Ich."

The last three lines appear cut off by more than just a caesura. It is as if the poet has wrenched his attention away from the specific horror of his actual perception to the less demanding, more platitudinous level of his 1896 preoccupations. The word "jetzt," underlining the change of tense, turns our attention to the theme of death as the adult sees it. If Rilke were seeking to dramatize the difference between the child's and the adult's viewpoint, these lines would stand up well as the exposition of the adult *Rolle.* The gesture described is no longer concrete but generalized, infused with a mediocre consciousness: the hand's "dürre Knochenfinger" seems a cliché in contrast to the immediacy of "knöchern" in the second line, and the identity of the "müde Ringer" is vague in contrast with the precision of the opening lines. The very last word, however, takes the poem beyond the *Rollengedicht* and makes it clear that Rilke is seeking a metaphorical equivalent for his youthful experience. As the "second hand" violates the child's world, so unexpected death plays a violent discord on the fragile instrument of the adult's "Saitenspiel." The word lends a certain unity to the stanza as it stands: the rhyme "fiel"-"Ziel"-"Saitenspiel" establishes the successive stages, from initial loss of innocence to constant confrontation with death, as having a kind of logic. But the gap between the sharpness of the child's experience and the adult's struggle for an adequate imagery remains too great. The poem was left in a suggestive but undeveloped state.

The scene is re-enacted in *Malte Laurids Brigge,* except that it is a pencil, not a toy, that falls, and the terse "Ich bückte mich" expands into a lengthy description of the child's sense of his own awkwardness:

> . . . ich erkannte vor allem meine eigene, ausgespreizte Hand, die sich ganz allein, ein bisschen wie ein Wassertier, da unten bewegte und den Grund untersuchte. . . . Aber wie hätte ich darauf gefasst sein sollen, dass ihr mit einem Male aus der Wand eine andere Hand entgegenkam, eine grössere,

ungewöhnlich magere Hand, wie ich noch nie eine gesehen
hatte. Sie suchte in ähnlicher Weise von der anderen Seite
her, und die beiden gespreizten Hände bewegten sich blind
aufeinander zu. Meine Neugierde war noch nicht aufge-
braucht, aber plötzlich war sie zu Ende, und es war nur
Grauen da. Ich fühlte, dass die eine von den Händen mir
gehörte und dass sie sich da in etwas einliess, was nicht
wieder gutzumachen war. Mit allem Recht, das ich auf
sie hatte, hielt ich sie an und zog sie flach und langsam
zurück, indem ich die andere nicht aus den Augen liess, die
weitersuchte. Ich begriff, dass sie es nicht aufgeben würde,
ich kann nicht sagen, wie ich wieder hinaufkam.

[1908–09; *Werke 6,* 795]

The idea of the second hand's persistence is retained from the
early poem; but any suggestion that the hand is interested in
the dropped article rather than the child is eliminated. There is
now a lengthy description of the child's own hand, its apparent
independence from him before the second hand appears, and his
desperate reassertion of authority over it after its eager approach
to the second hand. This scene has been variously interpreted.
Idris Parry tends to discount the frightening aspects and concentrate on the general meaning of hands, in other writers as well
as Rilke, as a creative force:

> Although he is at first unprepared, is one of little faith, and
> withdraws from the hand of God which comes to him from
> the wall, he finds that to fulfil his artistic mission he must
> seek and clasp that hand, which will guide him in the pure
> gesture of art.[4]

Simenauer, in contrast, seizing on the combination of horror and
curiosity, the fatefulness implicit in the child's reactions, regards

---

4. Idris Parry, "Malte's Hand," *GLL 11* (1957), 12.

the passage as descriptive of a loss of independence, as the child's
surrender to auto-erotic enslavement:

> Die libidinöse Beziehung zu seinen Händen ist, wie zu er-
> warten, nicht jedesmal leicht einzusehen; sie ist dem Schrei-
> benden weitgehend unbewusst, und ihre Verknüpfung in der
> manifesten Aussage mit bewusstseinsgemässen willentlichen,
> auf ein reales Ziel gerichteten Tendenzen geeignet, den
> ursprünglichen Sinnzusammenhang zu verdecken.[5]

If one looks at the *Malte* scene alone, Simenauer seems closer
to the truth than Parry. It is hard to transmute the horrifying
hand seeking out the child into the "hand of God," but if the
act of creation is viewed a little less idealistically than Parry's
conclusion implies, both interpretative tendencies can, I think, be
accommodated. For the artist, in Rilke's view, is not himself
capable of "pure gesture"; only the child or the young girl
achieves such gestures. What the artist can do is to utilize his
conscious awareness of the world to re-enact such gestures, to reproduce the dance of a girl like Wera Knoop in words. There
is nothing spontaneous about such a task. One could almost call it
an enslavement to the world of appearances, a lifelong submission of one's own powers to the absolute in an attempt to recreate
a pure gesture.

This passage about the hand could be seen as the child's first
awareness of his all-demanding vocation, the first dislocation
from the world of "pure gesture." Such an event naturally seems
like total loss, loss of self and loss of world. As his hand moves
away from him, he knows it can never be wholly "his" again;
and the anguished cry in a later letter, "Au lieu de me pénétrer,
les impressions me percent,"[6] is the inevitable outcome of this
moment. Having clasped the second hand Rilke has nowhere

5. Erich Simenauer, *Rainer Maria Rilke*, p. 476.
6. An Lou Andreas-Salomé, December 19, 1912, *Ausgewählte Briefe* (Wiesbaden, 1950), *1*, 421.

else to turn if it thrusts chaos instead of harmony at him. All he
can do is strive to maintain contact between his consciousness and
the enigmatic agent of creation, his hand.

> Zwei weisse Nonnenhände mühen
> nie sich um einen lichten Preis,
> zwei weisse Nonnenhände blühen,
> ohne dass es der Frühling weiss.
>
> Zwei weisse Nonnenhände halten   5
> nichtmehr das Leben, das sie unspinnt;
> müssen sich fest zusammenfalten
> weil sie beide so einsam sind.
>
> [June 27, 1897; *Werke 3*, 177]

In discussing the first poem I concentrated on the theme of
hands in relation to their "owner" because that brief stanza was so
intensely subjective in its concerns. The present poem, from the
collection *Dir zur Feier* written for Lou Salomé, shows hands as
symbolic of everyone's connection to the world outside, not just
the artist's. Folded hands, indeed, are almost a *Wunschbild* for
Rilke, the image of an enclosed life in which the approach of
the second hand can simply be ignored. Here the attitudes of
Phia Rilke, his mother, can be sensed. In a story also written in
1897, entitled "Einig," the sick youth Gerhard talks to his mother
in a way that manages to combine irony with longing:

> Was ist Frömmigkeit? Freude an dunkeln Kirchen und
> lichten Christbäumen, Dankbarkeit für den stillen, von
> keinem Sturme gestörten Alltag, Liebe, die den Weg ver-
> loren hat und sucht und tastet im Uferlosen. Und eine Sehn-
> sucht, welche die Hände faltet, statt die Flügel auszu-
> spannen.
>
> [*Werke 4*, 91]

The last phrase reveals the tension within the poet which produces the ambivalence of the hand image. With one part of him

he yearns to immobilize his life, as it were, at the moment of
withdrawing his hand in the *Malte* scene. Why not know the
power and the horror, yet reject it? Why not simply protect
what is valuable instead of leaving it for the unknown? This
instinct is powerfully embodied in the religious motion of folding
hands. The clasping of the second hand propels one into the unknown, whereas the pure gesture of folding hands seems to align
the ideal of self-containment with the sanctity of tradition:

> Die Mädchen lieben dieses duftende Dunkel mit seinen
> schönen unerschöpften Möglichkeiten. Sie wohnen darin.
> . . . Und sie erschrecken leise, dass es Stube und Garten und
> Abend giebt. Und sie heben die Furcht vor diesen vielen
> Dingen in das seidene Dunkel ihres Lebens hinein und fal-
> ten die Hände davor. So sind ihre Gebete.
>
> ["Intérieurs," 1898; *Werke* 5, 412]

The previous poem combined the immediacy of a personal
experience with an immature attempt to provide a framework
of ideas for it. Here Rilke tries to eliminate this inconsistency by
centralizing his poem on a single symbol, invoked in an incantatory manner. He intends the hands to become vivid through the
variety of images built around them, to link themselves by association to the reader's own ideas. But Rilke cannot yet make
symbolist techniques work effectively for him. The first stanza
is static—the hands do not come to life through the enumeration
of what they are not; and the second stanza tends toward the
abstract in a way that ultimately restricts the image instead of
enlarging it—the last line tells the reader what to think. This abstractness, of course, characterizes Rilke's mature style; whereas
the young poet tends to dissolve an image in a high-sounding
phrase, the later Rilke seeks an idea and a form of words strictly
appropriate to the image being evoked. In this poem we can feel
the struggle to pass from the one stage to the other. The first two
lines establish a rather labored relationship between the hands

and the vaguely worldly image of a "Preis." The unavoidable stress on "nie" in particular arouses expectations of clarity that are not fulfilled. The second two lines are better matched: the image of hands as chaste flowers blooming according to their own laws is delicately contrasted with the luxuriant, unchaste blossoming of springtime flowers. Rhythmically the two images are bound into each other. The first and third lines smoothly evoke the hands as objects, and the second and fourth, with their greater rhythmic movement, suggest a contrasting restlessness, a movement from within. Paradoxically, though, these are the negative lines, denying movement. A tension thus grows between the drives felt by the hands and the stasis they have chosen, a tension that generates their autonomous "blooming."

In the second stanza the same effect is achieved in a more sophisticated way. A single image—the hands holding each other instead of life outside—develops through the four lines, and all but the first have a gently propelling stress on the opening syllable. The fourth line, however, is much closer to the first in tone than to the second and third. The stress on "weil" is very slight; the repeated *ei* vowel strongly recalls the incantatory "Zwei weisse," and the retarding effect of these open vowels contrasts with the forward movement of the middle two lines. This last line reads like a synthesis of the poem's rhythms, which is appropriate to the explicitness of its meaning. Whether that meaning—the motivation of the hands by loneliness—is appropriate to the image as it has been developed is more dubious. The first two lines of the stanza seem to embody more intensely the implication of the first stanza that their self-enclosed blooming is a purposive choice by the hands. The juxtaposition "halten/nichtmehr" adds the dimension of the past: the hands have held on to life, but now they have relinquished it, although the verb "halten," like the preceding "mühen" and "blühen," is not really cancelled by the negation that follows. The hands fulfill their holding function without actually holding anything specific, just as they bloom without reference to the springtime. The gesture of folding hands has now been prepared most positively as an assertion of self-contained value vis-a-vis the "busyness" of life strikingly embodied in the meaningless intricacy of a spider's web, a web that surrounds them without being able to infringe on them. At this point Rilke turns off his own path. The word "müssen" dissolves the image at a stroke and turns the poem away from the impersonal strength of the hands towards the sentimental "fear" of the nun herself. What had seemed a positive gesture is now an expression of anguished retreat from the world.

This simultaneous assertion and denigration of the folded hands reflects the poet's ambivalence. For the use of hands to protect one's identity is not confined to the young. In old people Rilke could see a lifetime of experience both nurtured and protected by the hands, as in the following description of Clara's grandmother:

> . . . wie sie hinter den seltenen Zärtlichkeiten ihrer Hände diese fast beschämt zu verstecken suchte, wie sie überhaupt immerfort diese Hände wie Zugbrücken einzog, so dass sie in jedem Augenblick wieder einsam sein konnte, neben den Dingen, von keinem her zu erreichen, unzugänglich, ein langes Leben hinter vielen Mauern.[7]

The old lady embodies so much that Rilke thought desirable, yet the walls around her life merely magnify the self-protective wall of adolescence, rendered impenetrable by age. He is fascinated by but cannot wholly endorse a life that has simply accepted and adopted such restrictions. Nevertheless, in conjunction with its religious meaning, the gesture of folding hands can come to symbolize the spontaneity the artist seeks. The nun folding her hands in prayer acknowledges the absolute and consciously, fearfully, retreats from it. When the gesture is repeated many times the

7. October 3, 1900, *Briefe und Tagebücher aus der Frühzeit,* p. 366.

anguish expressed by it fades and only the bond with the absolute remains. The aging nun becomes the antithesis of the child: the child lives the fulfilled life without knowing that it is doing so, the nun "knows" the whole of life without ever having lived it.

The following passage, written much later as part of the original conclusion (1909) to *Malte Laurids Brigge,* develops the image of the nun's hands in the context of the observing artist:

> [Das Porträt] stellte eine Nonne dar, die Äbtissin eines Klosters in ihrer verschlossenen Ordenstracht . . . plötzlich, bei den Händen, war ein Wunder geschehen: es waren deutliche, sehr eigene Hände, unsymmetrisch aneinandergelegt zu der oft gebrauchten Haltung des gewohnten Gebets. Gott weiss wie es geschehen sein mochte: der schlichte leibeigene Maler hatte es aufgegeben, seine sonstigen erlernten Hände zu malen; es war über ihn gekommen, die Hände nachzubilden, die er in Wirklichkeit vor sich sah,—und man musste zugeben, dass es ihm wunderlich gelungen war, sie in ihrer Realität zu erreichen. Er hatte sie wichtig genommen, als gäbe es nichts als diese alternden gefalteten Hände, als hinge eine Menge davon ab, sie nicht zu vergessen. Über dem Bestreben, alle Einzelheiten, die er nach und nach entdeckte, in ihrem Umriss unterzubringen, waren sie ihm viel zu gross geworden, und nun standen sie vorn in dem Bilde, hoch wie ein Kirchturm, ein für alle Mal.
>
> ["Tolstoj," 1909; *Werke 6, 974*]

Rilke's reality includes the weight, the distortions of subjectivity; objects are heavy with the meaning lent them by humans. Folded hands represent a key that can unlock this total reality for him. In the picture described here, they contain the fullness of the nun's subjectivity, her awareness of the absolute, while they occupy the world of objects, "hoch wie ein Kirchturm." If the act of folding hands expresses initially a withdrawal from reality, a loss of childhood's "pure gesture," within time the hands again become capable of a valid gesture through the very purity of their constantly repeated withdrawal. In the poem, the threefold repetition of "Zwei weisse Nonnenhände" points toward this dimension, and the tension between stasis and movement embodies the arc of the gesture, the two hands neutralizing and stabilizing their thrust toward the absolute by clasping each other.

> Wenn ich manchmal in meinem Sinn
> ein Begegnen dem andern vergleiche:
> du bist immer die reichende Reiche
> wenn ich der dürftige Bettler bin.
> Wenn du mir leise entgegenlebst   5
> und, kaum lächelnd, mit einem Male
> deine Hand aus Gewändern hebst,
> deine schöne, schimmernde, schmale . . .
> in *meiner* Hände hingehaltne Schale
> legst du sie leichtgelenk,
> wie ein Geschenk.
>
> [November 25, 1897; *Werke 3*, 191]

The first two poems displayed the metaphysical roots of the hand image, its relationship to the second hand. In the present poem, also from *Dir zur Feier,* the hand becomes a central element in the physical world of objects and gestures which Rilke seeks to penetrate. Later, in his essay on Rodin (1902), Rilke identifies the gesture of contact between human beings with the stable world of objects:

> Eine Hand, die sich auf eines anderen Schulter oder Schenkel legt, gehört nicht mehr ganz zu dem Körper, von dem sie kam: aus ihr und dem Gegenstand, den sie berührt oder packt, entsteht ein neues Ding, ein Ding mehr, das keinen Namen hat und niemandem gehört.
>
> [*Werke 5*, 165]

At this stage, however, Rilke is fascinated by the dimension of time rather than that of space. The gesture in the present poem is comparable to the child's motion in "Du musst das Leben nicht verstehen" (January 1898): "und hält den lieben jungen Jahren / nach neuen seine Hände hin." The emphasis is on the tableau, the crystallization of the dramatic with the purpose of transforming adult emotions into the pure gesture of childhood.

This was a period for Rilke of intense activity as a playwright, and the extensive stage-directions in all his playlets reveal that the rather inadequate dialogue is intended as only a partial element in the total effect. A possible answer to the problem of the cliché presents itself: if language cannot be renewed, it can be reduced to its barest components and ultimately to the silence of the tableau:

> Und auch die Worte und die Gebärden wirkten in diesem Sinne, stark und neu. Das einfache Heben der Hände bedeutete wieder etwas, wie in der Kindheit, und bedeutete viel. Liebkosungen glänzten, und Flüche wuchsen wie Lawinen in der Luft.
>
> ["Maurice Maeterlinck," 1900; *Werke 5*, 481]

This description of Maeterlinck's theater throws into sharper focus the connection of the hand image with the lost perfection of childhood. The peculiar resonance of the image for Rilke derives from its dual role. In the poem on the second hand and in its development in *Malte* the hand is the agent of loss, the sinister independent force that destroys the child's equilibrium. But the hand is also an agent of possible redemption: the repetition of the nun's gesture of withdrawal and the elaborate tableau of giving and receiving hands in the present poem both seem to exemplify the *Aufhebung* of the temporal, the restoration of the timelessness of childhood.

In 1897, the year of the present poem, Rilke read the works of Jacobsen. He develops Jacobsen's notion of the constant immanence of the past in an essay written much later, after he had become involved with Rodin's spatial world. The two dimensions, the temporal and the spatial, are of course complementary rather than contradictory. Both are rooted in the gesture, the instrumentality of the hand:

> Ich glaube, dass alles, was wirklich geschieht, ohne Todesfurcht ist; ich glaube, dass die Willen langvergangener Menschen, dass die Bewegung, mit der sie ihre Hand in einem gewissen bedeutungsvollen Augenblick öffneten, dass das Lächeln, mit welchem sie an irgend einem fernen Fenster standen,—ich glaube, dass alle diese Erlebnisse von Einsamen in fortwährenden Verwandlungen unter uns leben.
>
> ["Fragmente von den Einsamen," 1903; *Werke 5*, 644]

Like the tableau poem from the same period with which I have just compared it, the present poem stands poised at a moment of transition. It is finely wrought; the elaborate rhyme scheme (*a b b a c d c d d e e*) encases a single luxuriant image which develops at one with its formal framework. At the same time the effect is studied, unreal. Rilke has successfully refined the clichés of his earliest years to the point where he has made them wholly his own, yet one still feels the *origin* of many of the expressions, their faded aura cannot be entirely absorbed. When Rilke writes "Gewändern," a certain conscious austerity is perceptible: the word has been deliberately stripped of the ornate adjectives to which it has grown accustomed. There is then a sense of release in the next line, when the alliterating adjectives come tumbling out. Formally they are justified (this climactic line describes the hand poised in the arc of the gesture), yet they are such a well-worn group that the accumulation tends to diminish rather than enhance the image. On the other hand a verbal construct like "entgegenlebst" partakes of the future as well as the past. It matches the mood of the tableau, yet in its compression of the separate dimensions of motion and growth into a single word it points toward the effortless paradoxes of *Das Buch vom mönchischen Leben*.

The syntax is entirely unlike that of the second hand poem

of 1896. Bald, monosyllabic statements barely modified for verse
have given place to the effect of a single sentence, a developing
flow rooted in the rhythm of the verse line. The poem illustrates
both the strengths and the weaknesses of the ornate structure.
Weakness is apparent in the repeated use of "wenn": lacking
genuine complexity, Rilke is forced to induce his single sentence
effect artificially, by repeating the subordinating conjunction.
From the fifth line onward one is not troubled by this technique,
since the image generates its own movement. But the first four
lines limp along. It is a weakness of Rilke's, which persists into
the *Stundenbuch* period, to attempt a rhetorical framework for his
imagery. Here the first two lines are really superfluous: "in
meinem Sinn" is a tautology, and the theme of comparison leads
nowhere, cancelled by "immer" in the third line. Even if the poem
began with the third line, there remains something trite about the
contrast between "Reiche" and "Bettler." The alliterative participle "reichende" attempts to bind the lines into the imagery
that follows, but the social framework limits rather than enlarges
the theme of the gesture. This could be explained biographically;
the purpose of the poem, after all, is to flatter Lou Salomé. More
intrinsic to the poetry itself is the implication that Rilke is not yet
committed to the self-sufficiency of the gesture. The phraseology
is all there: the hands are described like objects, they are lifted
and set down in a motion much closer to religion than to "nature," and at the end they seem transubstantiated into the "Schale"
and "Geschenk" of a holy communion. At the same time there
is a constant reiteration of the "ich" and "du" who own the hands,
down to the italicizing of "meiner." This stress on the personal
pronouns characterizes poems written in this year, in *Dir zur Feier*
as well as in its contemporary collection *Advent.* Rilke seems intent on maintaining his identity, his sovereignty over the creative hands.

The special merit of the poem is its rhythm, which is admi-
rably coordinated with the meaning. The meter is trochaic and

dactylic, but by placing several unimportant words at the beginning of lines Rilke can vary widely the number of actual thematic
stresses in a line. With the first line hardly stressed at all, the
dactyl "manchmal in" initiates the rocking rhythm in a manner
that is barely noticeable. "Begegnen" brings the first felt stress,
and this is appropriate to the word's symbolic status as a kind
of title to what follows. This second line has two dactyls—the
rhythm is becoming more apparent. The third line then surges
from these beginnings, enveloping "Du" with radiance. All four
metrical stresses are emphasized, and three dactyls seem to carry
the line's impetus over to the "wenn" of the next line. The word
"ich" brings all this to a halt. Not really in a stressed position,
it still negates the flowing rhythm and provides a telling contrast to the "du" which inaugurated the flow. The fifth line,
continues the dactylic rhythm and resembles the first in its rhythmic smoothness, with only "entgegen" receiving a gentle emphasis. The sixth line again has a weak first syllable and two felt
stresses, "lächelnd" and "Male." In the seventh one again feels all
four metrical stresses. The rhythm receives a special upsurge towards the words "Gewändern hebst," which express the actual
gesture toward which the lines have been building. Even more
than the third the eighth line underlines each beat of the meter,
with commas adding further emphasis. The second four lines
thus stand in an oblique relationship to the first four. Whereas the
fourth line, with the introduction of "ich," slows the rhythm that
was building up, the eighth line heightens still further a similar
growing movement (I have discussed above the problematic
quality of these adjectives *qua* adjectives).

In the ninth line the rhythm changes completely. The insistently trochaic measures of the first eight lines, reflecting the
growing gesture, are followed by five regular iambic beats, expressing the passive "Schale" waiting to receive the gesture. The
trochaic rhythm returns in the last shortened lines as the hand is
placed in the "Schale," reaching a fusion of the two rhythms in

the finality of "Wie ein Geschenk," a line that can be read both iambically and trochaically. Both rhythms can be felt, even if it is hard to enunciate them. The slight required emphasis on "ein" also suggests the unity of the hands in fusion. Within the scope of the conventional vocabulary at his disposal in 1897, Rilke has achieved here a masterpiece of formal art.

Aus Nächten

Nach dem Tage naht das Namenlose—
    Lass uns beide biegsam sein und weich,
    ich entbreite mich und bin ein Teich
    und du steigst aus mir als erste Rose . . .

Und wir schauen, was um uns begann;—   5
nur noch eine Weile Angst und dann:
    Dämmerungen, die sich glänzend glätten,
    Stunden, welche in die Stille steigen,
    feierlich, als ob sie goldene Geigen,
    kaumverhallte,—in den Händen hätten . . .   10
    [September 20, 1898; *Werke 3*, 628]

It is a short step from the elevation of a concrete gesture into a quasi-sacred metaphor to the transformation of what is essentially metaphorical into something concrete. The present highly uneven poem, not included in any collection, envelops the hand motif in an awkwardly experimental "Monismus" characteristic of the year 1898. Rilke is almost visibly struggling to emancipate himself from the individualistic framework of *Dir zur Feier,* to convey in words the broader gestures of the world to which all lovers belong. Through a stylized use of the hand motif Rilke seeks the capacity to penetrate the particularity of objects and fulfill them by supplying the dimension they lack. In the following passage the poet moves without difficulty from the controlling hand in nature to the hands of the human being. By unfolding one's hands, allowing them their independence and accepting the bond with the second hand, one can achieve one's vision. The strong emphasis on the social aspect suggests that Rilke saw his metaphor as applying not only to artists but to all who will clasp the unseen hand:

> Aber in dem fortwährenden Ergriffenwerden von allem, was mächtig wird über uns und über den Dingen, wächst unser Vertrauen zu den Händen, die uns das antun an jedem Tag und in jeder Nacht, in der wir einsam wachen oder tief träumen . . . Wenn die hart gewordenen Hände eines Verzweifelten, eines Verlassenen oder Hilflosen aus dem krampfhaften Falten, mit dem sie einander aufreizten, voneinander gehen und nebeneinander, als ob keine von der anderen wüsste, zur Arbeit kommen, dann sind sie, die Überzähligen, Vielzuvielen, Verschmähten, einem Dinge notwendig geworden. Die Dinge haben an sie, die von allen vergessen waren, gedacht, und was sie vorbereitet haben, ist wie ein Bad, aus welchem die Hände warm und wie Verklärte steigen werden.
>
> [September 26, 1900][8]

The paradoxical union of work and passivity in these lines is explicable only in terms of "das Ding," to which my next chapter is devoted. This union, however, a rarefied synthesis of the tangible and the spiritual, is frequently embodied at this period in musical imagery. The musician is clearly working to produce something, but it is not tangible; much of the work consists of passively listening to the tone of his instrument, be it violin or lute. In the resulting totality it is impossible to separate musician and instrument:

> Stärker in Beziehung zum persönlichen Erlebnis und Wesen des Dichters gelangt das Geigenmotiv von den *Frühen Ge-*

8. *Briefe und Tagebücher aus der Frühzeit,* pp. 344–45.

dichten an. Da wird ihm der geheimnisvolle Geigenleib, dem soviel Aussage von sonst Unsäglichem entströmen kann, zum Sinnbild der eigenen, ihm selbst unübersehbaren Dichternatur⁹

This statement can be richly documented by poems from the years 1898–99:

> Bis einst das Fürchten von mir fiel
> und ich ein leises Saitenspiel
> in deinen Händen bin . . .
> [May 11, 1898; *Werke 3, 616*]

> Denn wir sind wie silberne Geigen
> in den Händen der Ewigkeit.
> [undated, ca. 1899; *Werke 3, 636*]

The role of the second hand as performer on the poetic instrument is quite explicit, yet here too Rilke is capable of turning the image completely around. Writing of this period later on when he had rejected the ideal of self-immersion in nature and with it the musical images that expressed it, he says:

> War mir die Natur noch ein allgemeiner Anlass, eine Evokation, ein Instrument, in dessen Saiten sich meine Hände wiederfanden, ich sass noch nicht vor ihr . . . sah nicht die Natur, sondern die Gesichte, die sie mir eingab.
> [October 18, 1907]¹⁰

It is perhaps legitimate to read an additional nuance into the verb "sich wiederfanden." Clearly the hands are not clasping each other, for then they could not play an instrument. Rather they are "finding themselves" in the sense of discovering their counterpart hands in nature and absorbing their strength. The two images

9. Clára Mágr, *Rilke und die Musik* (Vienna, 1960), p. 107.
10. An Clara Rilke, October 18, 1907, *Briefe 1906–07* (Leipzig, 1930), p. 377.

of the poet as the instrument of the second hand and nature as
the instrument of the poet's hands are virtually interchangeable,
because both express the essential: an access of creative inspiration.

Neither image appears in the poem under consideration, but
the notion of the poet as nature's instrument is very close to its
surface. As in "Wenn die Uhren so nah," a poem written on the
same day (I will consider it in my next chapter), Rilke seeks to
depict an internal development parallel to the transformation in
nature brought about by the approach of night, the coming of the
"nameless" time, when daytime categories are dissolved. In lines
that somewhat embarrassingly attempt to unify the human and
the natural, the lovers prepare themselves, able through a combination of passivity and mutual involvement simply to become
part of the changing world. Then, after a bridge passage in which
the natural event already occurring merges with the human anticipation, we witness the revelation of spatial and temporal
phenomena united in a musical image. Because music occurs in
time, Rilke has endowed the "Stunden" with hands holding the
violins. One sees how completely metaphorical the hand image
has become for him. The very concept of a "Stunde" is human.
This revelation is clearly inseparable from the observing lovers,
who are thus both the willing tools of the absolute ("biegsam
und weich") and the consciousness without which the hands of
the absolute could not become manifest. As if to emphasize the
necessity of this consciousness, the evening hours seem to be in
some way altering the "Stille," yet their violins are "kaumver-
hallt," not actually heard. The ultimate paradox of music already
past suits the poem's purpose: the evocation of an absolute which
can absorb man's aspirations precisely because it is empty of all
reality, even of the reality of its own music.

Two perspectives are presented in the first stanza, and are
heavily underlined. "Das Namenlose" is expressed through the

alliterating *n,* the dominant *a,* and the line set back towards the margin. The contrasting, subjective "wir" have their three lines set forward and a dominant *ei* diphthong. The exhortation "Lass uns" introduces the poet as an active persona, controlling his beloved by being the origin of her experience, the "Teich" in which the "Rose" has its roots. The human element in the coming revelation is embodied in the word "das Namenlose," a strictly conceptual term which assumes man's centrality. Similarly, the phrase "ich entbreite mich und bin ein Teich" implies the autonomy of the human will at the very moment when the poet is shedding his humanness. This simultaneous flexibility of all categories and centrality of the poetic "Ich" is to become the dominant mode of the *Rollengedichte* in *Das Buch vom mönchischen Leben* (1899).

The brief middle stanza represents the intermediate stage, in which the lovers gradually shed their subjectivity ("Angst") and become witnesses of the "Dämmerungen" which are in part their own creation. The words "um uns" suggest that nature is responding directly to their act of concentration and submission. In the final stanza, poetic technique dominates, somewhat to the detriment of the imagery. The constant alliterations *gl, st, g, h,* and the concentrated fusion of sense dimensions are clearly intended to express the complete suspension of human categories in a higher unity. The result is confusing rather than convincing. There are simply too many images lacking any inner connection. One can appreciate the beauty of a line like "Stunden, welche in die Stille steigen," yet feel that the development of the image in musical terms fails to enhance it, indeed casts the shadow of obscurity on the initial beauty. Rilke's inventiveness goes far beyond the rather studied terminology of "Wenn ich manchmal in meinem Sinn," but although the poem's large aims can be felt, in the quality and development of its imagery it must be accounted a failure.

Wenn ich gewachsen wäre irgendwo,
wo leichtre Tage sind und schlanke Stunden,—
ich hätte Dir ein grosses Fest erfunden,
und meine Hände hielten Dich nicht so,
wie sie Dich manchmal halten, bang und hart.   5
Dort hätte ich gewagt, Dich zu vergeuden
du grenzenlose Gegenwart!
Wie einen Ball
hätt ich Dich in alle wogenden Freuden
hineingeschleudert, dass einer Dich finge,   10
und Deinem Fall
mit hohen Händen entgegenspringe,
Du Ding der Dinge.

Ich hätte Dich wie eine Klinge
blitzen lassen!   15
Vom goldensten Ringe
liess ich Dein Feuer erfassen,
und er müsste mirs halten
über die weisseste Hand.

Gemalt hätt ich Dich: nicht an die Wand   20
an den Himmel selber, von Rand zu Rand,—
und hätt Dich gebildet, wie ein Gigant
Dich bilden würde: als Berg, als Brand
als Samum, wachsend aus Wüstensand—

oder: 25
es kann auch sein: ich fand
Dich einmal . . .
                    Meine Freunde sind weit,
ich höre kaum noch ihr Lachen schallen—
und Du—Du bist aus dem Nest gefallen—   30
bist ein junger Vogel mit gelben Krallen
und grossen Augen und tust mir leid—
(meine Hand ist Dir viel zu breit),
und ich heb mit dem Finger vom Quell einen Tropfen

und lausche, ob Du ihn lechzend langst,—   35
und ich fühle Dein Herz und meines Klopfen—
und beide aus Angst.

[September 24, 1899; *Werke 3*, 321–23]

The years 1898–99 were the years of Rilke's first great "experience," the visits to Italy and Russia, the flowering of the relationship with Lou Salomé. At the same time Rilke became possessed of an idea rooted partly in his own poetic development, partly in the literary atmosphere of the time (especially the theatre of Maeterlinck), partly in his interpretation of what he saw in Russia: the idea of total self-immersion in nature, of poetry as the unmediated expression of nature's laws. This idea, as "Aus Nächten" shows, tended to burst open the forms Rilke had been using; the conjunction of totally disparate images within the confines of a tight stanza is rather bewildering. In *Das Buch vom mönchischen Leben* the technical problem is solved: each image is fully developed within a free form conceived for it alone. The result is a strange combination of great emotional energy and pure intellectuality. For the images have little independent force; they are all vehicles for the overriding idea of unity—unity among nature, man, and the absolute which endows man with his power to create.

I cannot regard the work as religious in any meaningful sense. The very idea of "der zukünftige Gott," which Ruth Mövius rightly emphasizes, surely negates all piety and reverence. Such a notion, as the present poem underlines, is essentially a function of the poet's own creativity. Mövius is also right to stress the technical dependence of the poems on the *Weltanschauung* which drives them. What is religious about them in the loosest sense is their inseparability from the central idea of unity, which the reader must accept wholeheartedly if he is to enjoy them as poems:

Rilke findet im Reim eine göttliche Gesetzmässigkeit. Aus dem Zufälligen seiner "fremden Gedanken" findet er sich

in "willigen Versen" zu Gott zurück. Das heisst: er muss
seine Gefühle zwingen, dass sie sich binden lassen zu einer
Einheit. Wenn er sie aber bezwingt, so beugt er sie unter
Gott, der Rilke nun im Vers entgegenkommt und seine
"zufälligen Gefühle" umwandelt in reine Gesetzmässigkeit.
Dichtend erlebt Rilke eine Läuterung seiner Gefühle, sie
gehen ein in Gottes Gesetze, er "erkennt" lächelnd sein Lied.
Es gilt also nicht, den Reim zu "bauen" (wie vielleicht
andere es für einen Dichter nötig erachten), sondern es
gilt, ihn zu "finden," ihn zu "erkennen."[11]

The emphasis Mövius places on "zwingen" is suspect. Rilke himself encourages this disciplined image in the original prose prelude to the present poem: "Und der Mönch hatte die Hände ge-
faltet. . . . Und so bezwang er seine vielen Gefühle, dass sie doch
Verse wurden, obwohl sie aus Wirrnis und Wildheit in die Worte
sprangen." Given the resonances for Rilke of folded hands, the
implication here is clearly that the monk has had excessive contact
with the second hand and must withdraw consciously in order to
impose form on his emotions. But such "form" is really tautol-
ogous, because nothing dictates it but the emotions themselves.
As Mövius says, God very willingly comes to meet the poet,
transforming feelings into "Gesetzmässigkeit." Since the simple
technique of rhyme has been elevated into a "göttliche Gesetzmässigkeit," the process of shaping the emotions amounts to little
more than rhyming them, cf. the six consecutive *-and* rhymes in
the present poem. Rilke has temporarily succumbed to such
unconstrained methods because of the infinite potentiality of his
idea of unity. There seems literally no limit to the variety of
images which an abandonment of the barriers between man and
nature makes possible. Ideals can be paired with everyday images,
mountains with seeds, God with a tiny bird. Rilke cannot yet see

11. Ruth Mövius, *Rainer Maria Rilkes Stundenbuch* (Leipzig, 1937), p.
129.

that such limitlessness is itself a limitation, that an image lacking any congruity with the reader's experience will not move him.

The poem is divided into five parts. The first introduces the world of the monk and the contrast between his actual experience and his dream of the absolute, the next three project versions of that dream, and the last section suggests that the dream may have been fulfilled after all in a simple incident of daily life. The cunningly rhetorical structure creates an artificial climax, with the only concrete image at the end, when the bird falls from its nest. Contrast with the vague invocations that precede it makes this concreteness seem all the more necessary and significant. Since the ideal of unity bars nothing, Rilke can speculate rhapsodically on the possibilities of interaction with the absolute and make the sudden return to the simplicities of daily life seem like an overwhelmingly daring paradox. The persona he has chosen also makes the rhetoric more palatable: a monk is close to both God and nature, leading a simple life yet preoccupied with eternal things. Because Rilke has also distanced the poems from the reader's world, the rhetoric exists in a curious vacuum, a series of intellectual arabesques. These poems more than any others of Rilke have provoked the common charge of escapism, for they acknowledge no frame of reference outside the monk's consciousness.

The opening lines emphasize this point. The monk imagines himself as "gewachsen," a limb of nature happening to be endowed with consciousness. His days would be "leicht," the hours "schlank." Nothing is clearly focussed, but the thought of a vaguely desirable state is conveyed to the reader. At the first appearance of the hand theme, a leitmotif in the present poem, one senses the associative bond between the infinitely flexible "Du" and the second hand which is really a projection of the individual's own powers. The metaphor, heavily centered on "meine Hände" rather than "Du," recalls the diary entry quoted earlier of "die hart gewordenen Hände eines Verzweifelten" and their "krampf-

haften Falten."[12] Folded hands are a recurrent image of withdrawal for Rilke, and "halten," in the fourth and fifth lines, reads
like a transcription of this image into the terminology of the
rhetorical "Du."

The opening gesture of the second section, "vergeuden,"
matches the dissolution of the "Falten" in that same diary entry.
The hands reenter the world of "die Dinge," losing themselves in
order to find themselves. "Du" is still less definite in this stanza,
extending the absolute backward to the immediacy of childhood
("grenzenlose Gegenwart") and forward to a poetic essence
("Ding der Dinge") recognizable but unreachable for the austere
monk who thus imagines a wasteful way of life, an adult equivalent for childhood. This combination of reverence ("gewagt")
and playfulness reflect the confidence of the poet allowing his
hands full independence without fear of abandonment by the
second hand. The complicated rhyme scheme (*a b c a d c d d*) expresses the essential unity of the gesture of throwing and catching. Line six sets a regular beat with the very light stress on "ich"
both setting a forward impulse and throwing the emphasis on
"Dich"; "vergeuden" initiates the expansive gesture. Line seven
holds back the motion, as if in contemplation of "Du." Its words
are highly abstract, "Gegenwart" unrhymed. The concrete eighth
line restarts the forward movement, then the ninth line echoes
the rhythm of the first, this time with the light stress on "Dich"
and the central emphasis on "alle," as if to suggest the totality of
the gesture, dwarfing even "Du." The rhyme recalls the expansive
"vergeuden," but now there is no holding back. The rhythm
sweeps through to the climactic word "hineingeschleudert." The
unity of the lines is then cemented by the introduction of the
closing rhyme of "finge." At its peak the gesture already contains its end. Where line eight had emphasized both the con-

12. See above, p. 74.

creteness of the imagery and the dactylic rhythm, the balancing eleventh subtly turns attention back to the abstract values of the gesture ("Fall") while the retarding iambic rhythm reasserts itself. The twelfth line, though it describes energetic action, contains only one dactyl, and the ambivalence of "Fall" continues in the phrase "mit hohen Händen." Physical images are increasingly eclipsed by the sacramental nature of receiving "Du." In a sense the "catching" is already accomplished in line ten, and the three following lines merely enlarge on the effect of "Du" on the receiver. Line thirteen recalls the contemplative invocation of line seven while emphasizing the closing rhyme, associated with the active words "finge" and "springe." Abstract and concrete are welded together.

This is the best section of the poem. Yet comparison with "Solang du Selbstgeworfnes fängst" (1922), which Tubach regards as the final statement of the hand image,[13] reveals its subtle inadequacies. The first two lines of the late poem are indeed a kind of commentary on the image we have just analysed:

> Solang du Selbstgeworfnes fängst, ist alles
> Geschicklichkeit und lässlicher Gewinn. . . .
> [January 31, 1922; *Werke 2*, 132]

In the present poem Rilke really is exulting in his own creativity, throwing his own ball. He pretends not to be, confining his poetic impulse to the rhetoric of a monk attributing all to "God." The result is disturbingly out of focus. The "Du" seems simply a projection of the poet's own creativity, though at crucial points in the development of the imagery Rilke chooses to elevate it into something more, to turn away from concreteness towards a solemn generalization which dissolves the texture without increasing the reader's piety. Thus "alle wogenden Freuden" is al-

---

13. Tubach, pp. 245–46.

most a cliché. It deflects the reader from the concrete "Ball" and sets him puzzling after outside references, as does the biblical suggestiveness of "einer." Certainly the question of who receives the "Du" would seem important, but nothing indicates that "einer" is anything other than an anonymous figure. Instead of developing his image to a coherent conclusion, Rilke has retreated into the monk's persona and left us with something portentous yet ultimately empty.

The rhetorical tendency is still more apparent in the third section. Here it is not so much a loss of concreteness as a lack of direcness that undermines the imagery. Added to the basic subjunctive verb forms, the auxiliary "lassen" places the actions in a very remote realm. The first two lines consist of a cliché (glittering blades) wrapped in the enigmatic relationship between "ich" and "Du," which, impossible to imagine specifically, hardly relieves the cliché. There follows an extremely complex image rooted in the intensity of light and color: the verb "erfassen" suggests the other compound "einfassen." God's fire is enclosed like a jewel in the ring, and the intensity of the fire is brighter even than a white hand on which the ring is placed. The point of the two superlatives seems to be that fire partakes of both gold and white yet surpasses in intensity the extreme of both. But the image, presumably intended as the polar opposite of "vergeuden" in line six, is so contrived that one feels it is supposed not to be understood but felt like a psalmist's incantation. The uncertainty implicit in the subjunctive "müsste" does not impede the flow; rather the word seems chosen for its sound, to harmonize with "weisseste" in the next line: "Since the subjunctive necessitates the umlaut in many German verbs, it is probable that this determined Rilke's choice in some instances, for he often needed words with umlaut to fit them into his schemes of voweling."[14]

14. Belmore, p. 93.

Lines twenty to twenty-four attempt to inflate the already grandiloquent imagery through the crescendo of the repeated rhyme to the point where deflation will seem poetically necessary. The difficulty in using the imagery of the visual arts is that words like "malen" and "bilden" demand that the reader see what is being created. Rilke gives examples, but here his virtuosity understandably falters. After "Gigant" the phrase "Dich bilden würde" seems lame and over-explicit; and fires and mountains do not seem to be especially superhuman symbols of God. Sensing this weakness, perhaps, Rilke introduces the word "Samum," a term of Arabic origin meaning a desert storm. So obscure a word, however, turns the poem away from visualization and toward sonority. The fine phrase "wachsend aus Wüstensand" tends to compensate for this, making the reader feel he has seen more than he really has. It is a paradox both vivid and resounding. Like "Du Ding der Dinge" at the end of the second section it appears to sum up what has preceded it, but in fact only suggests what might have been.

Through the virtuosity of his rhyming, Rilke is able to link the final section not only with its resounding predecessor but with the closing image of the third section: subtly yet unmistakably "fand" echoes "Hand," seven lines earlier but more relevant to the last section than any of the intervening rhymes. The image of the hand developed here reverses the musical images discussed earlier. Instead of being an instrument in God's hand, suddenly the poet encloses God in his own hand. The paradoxical, multifaceted character of the human hand fascinated Rilke, as the present poem richly illustrates: the monk clutches God, throws him, catches him, dwells on the comparative whiteness of a hand and God's fire, and finally encloses the bird in the "Schale" of his own hand. The image is protective, but not self-protective like "das Falten"; rather, the open hand receives what is precious in nature.

The importance of the hand's role is clearly brought out in the letter of October 1900 describing the experience on which the present lines are apparently based:

> ... denn es geschieht nicht oft, dass sehr Grosses sich in ein Ding zusammendrängt, das man ganz in der Hand halten kann, in der eigenen ohnmächtigen Hand. Wie wenn man einen kleinen Vogel findet, der durstig ist. Man nimmt ihn fort vom Rande des Todes, und das kleine Herz schlägt wachsend an die warme zitternde Hand wie die äusserste Welle eines Riesenmeeres, dessen Strand du bist. Und du weisst plötzlich, mit diesem kleinen Tier, das sich erholt, erholt sich das Leben vom Tode. Und du hältst es empor. Geschlechter von Vögeln und alle Wälder, über welche sie ziehen, und alle Himmel, zu denen sie steigen werden. Und ist das alles so leicht? Nein: du bist sehr stark, Schwerstes zu tragen, in solcher Stunde.[15]

Mrs. Corcoran, with her psychologistic approach, stresses the references to death in the above passage (not present in the poem) and regards the fallen bird as a symbol of Rilke's *Todesangst*.[16] I find the tendency of both poem and letter to be in the other direction, toward *Lebensangst* if anything. In the letter Rilke is overwhelmed by the sheer amount of life contained in his hand. The paradox of the hand is that it is both an instrument of striving and one of receiving. Each of these positive gestures has its corresponding danger: striving can lead to the monk's anguished clutching with which the poem opens; and one may receive so much, by simply opening one's senses, that one's identity will be submerged under the sheer weight of reality past and present. This fear of being overwhelmed resonates behind the

15. An Otto Modersohn, October 23, 1900, *Briefe und Tagebücher aus der Frühzeit,* pp. 60–61.
16. Corcoran, p. 173.

last word in the present poem, although within the poem itself
it is hard to lend much existential weight to the word *Angst,*
which seems designed, rather, to restore an aesthetic balance between the particularity of the final section and the earlier generalities.

These lines resist evaluation precisely because of the contrast
with earlier imprecision. Rilke is being rather self-indulgent: the
theatricality of the stage setting with the friends, the near-senti-
mentality of "mit grossen Augen und tust mir leid," the clumsy
alliteration of "und lausche, ob Du ihn lechzend langst"—all
this exposes the poem's loose structure. The compelling image of
the bird expresses the mythical power of the human hand, but
the semi-theological framework counteracts the particularity of
the image, the intimacy of whose details are in conscious contrast
to the cosmic scope of the remainder of the poem. The conjunction "oder" that introduces the final section makes it clear that all
individual images are merely examples, illustrations of the central
idea of ecstatic unity to which all poetic values are subordinate.
Eight uses of the word "und" in as many lines suggest how little
Rilke has attempted to knit his lines together. While developing
the range of his themes, he has temporarily forgotten the primacy
of the unique poetic word.

> Das Lied vom Kehrreim hat auch Sinn für mich,—
> nach allen wahren Tagen fühle ich
> die stumme Unkraft über meinem Tun.
> Warum das Ruhn
> mich nicht erfreut,— 5
> warum ein Heut,
> das schlafen will, nicht, wie ein waches, halten?
> Weil Alles in mir *zittert zu gestalten,*—
> und weil der Tod vielleicht schon meinen Namen
> mit jenen andern Namen lernt, die er 10
> sich merken muss für seine nächste Fahrt.

O Nächte, Nächte, Nächte
möcht ich schreiben
und immer, immer über Blättern bleiben,
und sie erfüllen mit den leisen Zeichen,   15
die nicht von meiner müden Hand sind. Die
verraten dass ich selber Hand bin, Eines,
der mit mir wundersame Dinge tut.
So bauen sich ins Dunkel Dimensionen
und Kräfte, die mich, wenn ich diene, brauchen,   20
und Worte, deren letzte Silbe ich mit meinem Leben
rätselhaft verdecke,
und Schweigsamkeiten, die mir Rechte geben,
so tief in alle Stille mich zu tauchen,
dass ich mich unter aller Wellen strecke,   25
und keiner sieht es, dass ich mich bewege,
und selbst in einem stillen Teich
würden durch *mein* Bewegen keine Ringe rege,
so tief bin ich im dunklen Reich
des Grunds.   30
                [November 22, 1899; *Werke 3*, 667–68]

Written only two months after the poem just discussed, these
lines exhibit a remarkable change of emphasis. The image of God
which dominates *Das Buch vom mönchischen Leben* has been
torn aside, and behind it we see Rilke's preoccupation with his
own creativity. In the aftermath of the productive months of
September and October 1899, Rilke feels barren and empty. Instinctively he turns toward images of the creative act which have
been developing in his mind since childhood, in particular the
image of the hand. The relationship with the second hand is
formulated as a paradox. The moment of equilibrium and self-
confidence of the previous poem having passed, Rilke acknowledges that his own "müde Hand" is incapable of creation. It must
abandon itself totally to the second hand, move out of the sphere

of the poet's control. Yet this would not negate the poet's identity. Having surrendered his hand, he would become "selber Hand," the agent of the second hand, able to penetrate reality in ways the consciousness can only aspire to. In a letter of April 1903 Rilke formulates this condition more precisely as an interaction with nature. Mind and body are fulfilled by embracing their opposites, the mind by abandoning all independent categories and restrictions, the body or hand by accepting the isolation inherent in the task of formulating "die Dinge" as they speak directly through it. The letter focusses more actively on "die Arbeit," in contrast to the quasi-mystical sinking of the present poem, but the stress on the hands' independence transcends this difference of emphasis:

> Es liegt eine Art Reinheit und Jungfräulichkeit darin, in diesem Von-sich-selbst-Fortschauen; es ist, wie wenn man zeichnet, den Blick an das Ding gebunden, verwoben mit der Natur, und die Hand geht allein irgendwo unten ihren Weg, geht und geht, wird ängstlich, schwankt, wird wieder froh, geht und geht tief unter dem Gesicht, das wie ein Stern über ihr steht, das nicht schaut, nur scheint. Mir ist, als hätte ich immer so geschaffen: das Gesicht im Anschauen ferner Dinge, die Hände allein.[17]

Simenauer points out that this passage erupts spontaneously from a letter which is not about creation but about the artist's need to be alone with his work:

> Wie diese also nicht in der ursprünglichen Absicht des Briefschreibers gelegen hat, sondern plötzlich aus tieferen Schichten auf das Stichwort hin, der Künstler dürfe sich selber bei der Arbeit nicht zuschauen, in ihm emporgestiegen ist, so kommen die Hinweise auf die Hände aus noch ursprünglicheren Erlebnisschichten. Die Worte: "die Hand

17. An Clara Rilke, April 8, 1903, *Briefe 1903–06* (Leipzig, 1930), p. 83.

> geht allein irgendwo unten ihren Weg, geht und geht . . ."
> und nochmals "geht ängstlich . . . geht und geht tief unter
> dem Gesicht . . ." haben noch dazu eine fatale Ahnlichkeit
> mit der Beschreibung der angsterregenden Hand im *Malte,*
> die auch irgendwo unten, nämlich unter dem Tisch, geht
> und geht und unsagbares Grauen dem noch unerfahrenen
> Knaben einflösst.[18]

The key word "tief" provides a strong link between the *Malte*
episode (1908–09), the letter just quoted (1903), and the present poem (1899). The relationship with the second hand seems
often to be understood in the literal terms of a journey downwards.
For Malte the world under the table is a world beneath his own,
wholly foreign to him, perceived in aquatic terms (his hand is
like "ein Wassertier" investigating "den Grund"). In the present
poem, which welcomes the dependence on the second hand, similar imagery of water and depth is employed. The poet insists on
his being *below* all other people, so deep that he cannot be perceived. The metaphor can be interpreted in many ways. I would
emphasize the connection with the lines, "Worte, deren letzte
Silbe ich mit meinem Leben / rätselhaft verdecke." The second
hand brings into being words that are intimately dependent on
the poet, but the poet's own life both conditions these words and
obscures them. The conventional responses of daily life prevent
the "letzte Silbe" from being realized; hence the need for total
immersion in the "Grund," for isolation from outside influences.

These influences are summed up in the poem's opening line,
which is not readily comprehensible without reference to the
preceding poem, a *Rollengedicht* entitled "Chanson Orpheline,"
in which these lines appear:

> Wer rät mir: Wohin soll ich fliehn vor dem Schall?
> Sind diese Worte denn überall? . . .

18. Simenauer, p. 477.

auf den Wegen der Wiederkehr
kommt ein fremder Kehrreim, und der
macht mir das Leben leer.

[November 21, 1899; *Werke 3, 666*]

These poems were set down in a diary and never collected. Thus they never achieved the levels of self-sufficiency and impersonality Rilke considered necessary for publication. "Das Lied vom Kehrreim," especially, is all the more revealing of the poet's restless talent, his highly modern ability to create out of sterility. The "Kehrreim" in the orphan's song evokes the meaningless lives of the dead parents, returning to disrupt all the orphan's moments of deeper experience. In the present poem its resonance seems less specific. One might perhaps relate it to the rhetorical style Rilke has created for himself in *Das Buch vom mönchischen Leben;* it now burdens him. His perceptions have been released into new dimensions but he is still groping for a vocabulary to accommodate them. Meanwhile the paradoxical, self-intoxicated style which had seemed so valuable a month earlier now seems facile and false, "ein fremder Kehrreim."

The second line with a dominant *a* vowel and the third line with the *u* prominent set the tone for this uneasy stanza. Genuine experience ("wahren Tagen") coexists with sterility ("stumme Unkraft"), and the poem's form reflects this situation. These two model iambic pentameters are followed by a short line which, however, continues the rhyme, so that the very instrument of shapeliness, rhyme, draws attention to a certain formal dislocation. Lines five and six, following the rhythm of line four, appear to establish it as a new pattern. Line seven, jagged and discontinuous, cancels all feeling of flow. Formally it is a return to the iambic pentameter, the outward expression of "das Ruhn," but rhythmically it is a series of staccato bursts, heightening the tension of lines four through six. To call it a "synthesis" of the preceding lines would be to make it sound like a fulfilment, whereas it is hardly poetic at all, but a nervous self-questioning. In line eight the pentameter finally imposes itself again, and something like synthesis is at last achieved. The vowelling, with long stressed *a*'s framing the climactic "zittert," helps to achieve a unity between breadth and subjective tension. By answering the question about his restlessness Rilke seems to have freed some of his own creativity, matching his anguished "gestalten" with a perfectly formed line.

The last three lines recall the last lines of the 1896 poem, "Ich weiss, als Kind." Here as there the tension is dispersed as Rilke speculates on death. Rilke's attitude to death precludes the immediacy of a real confrontation with the void. His concern for "der eigene Tod" is undeniable, but the very phrase seems to imply an absorption in the style of death rather than its starkness. Not that Rilke shunned the horror of death; but when he dealt with it, as in *Malte,* the "Requiems," and the Tenth Elegy he invariably pursued it until death seems to point back toward life. Thus a conventional dualistic statement such as we read in these three lines sounds pale and forced from Rilke's pen. Significantly there is no link with the rhyme scheme of the first eight lines. Having hinted at his power in the line ending on "gestalten," Rilke must now enact his sterility as well by "finishing" the first section with lines that are in no sense a valid conclusion.

As if to sweep aside these pallid reflections, the second section erupts with controlled passion. The first two lines are really a single pentameter. Their separation only emphasizes the repetition of "Nächte," the insistence on existential urgency in contrast with the first section's images of barrenness. Perhaps too the rhyme "schreiben"/"bleiben" is de-emphasized by this irregularity, for there are no other rhymes in lines twelve to nineteen. These lines seem to embody the act of automatic writing they describe. Shorn of externals like rhyme they are the direct, unadorned result of the poet's submission to the second hand.

The outcry of the opening lines, the longing "möcht ich schreiben," is succeeded by an almost didactic description of the creative act in the indicative mode. Wish becomes reality as Rilke writes. The use of the metaphorical "erfüllen" is no accident. One can almost feel the transference from wish to fulfillment in line sixteen; built around the internal assonance "meiner müden," like the two preceding lines ("Blättern bleiben," "leisen Zeichen"), line sixteen stops on the nominally short syllable "sind." With the final "Die" we have moved from Rilke to the second hand to which he has surrendered. Line seventeen names the absolute in the only possible way, as a being perceived but not defined. The rather tortuous syntax leading to the word "Eines" expresses the strain of bringing so intimate a matter into the open. The following line is weak, as if the poet were momentarily withdrawing from the confrontation. In line nineteen, however, Rilke resolutely returns to the new poetic realm opened for him, with the combination of the abstract ("Dimensionen"), the concrete ("bauen") and the emotive ("Dunkel"). A consciously constructed line, it remains compressed and expectant of the imagery to come.

The last eleven lines have a complex rhyme relationship which resembles a fragmentary sonnet in reverse—*a b c, b a c, d e d e,*—until cut short by the finality of "des Grunds." The first "tercet" would consist of three iambic pentameters if the line division between lines twenty-one and twenty-two were made after "ich" instead of after "Leben." This irregularity places some extra emphasis on "ich," the expected last word of the middle line, and adds a dimension to "rätselhaft," a word expressing the whole mysterious event. With the second "tercet" the paradox intensifies. The "Schweigsamkeiten" are the ultimate reduction of the series consisting of the terms "Kräfte," "Worte," and "letzte Silbe." The active verb is still "sich bauen," and these silences are also the most *precise* of the forces building up into the darkness. For Rilke silence is more than the absence of noise. Silence is the positive state of a world ready to be transformed. Just as Rilke himself, by accepting release from subjectivity through the second hand, attains to a fuller awareness of the world, so nature itself, by accepting the deprivation of color and sound imposed by the night, becomes larger and more elemental.

Nature and poet are drawn together by the second hand, and the poet's words are freed from banality. He does not merge with nature; these lines are almost over emphatic on this point. He cannot be seen moving in the depths, yet he *is* moving. The extra length of line twenty-eight, centered on the italicized *"mein* Bewegen," places additional stress on the poet's identity at the very moment when he is insisting on his total invisibility. The shifting imagery of *Das Buch vom mönchischen Leben* was predicated on the elimination of all categorical distinctions, so that the poet could become whatever aspect of nature he chose. The paradox evolved in this poem from the workshop is that the deeper the poet plunges into the "Grund," the more he is responsible for his own identity, for the *Bewegen* without which his experience would have no meaning. By moving from the total autonomy of *Das Buch vom mönchischen Leben* to the conscious dependence of the present poem, Rilke is at last able to assimilate the childhood experience presented in "Ich weiss, als Kind" (1896). Loss of control over one's own hands does not mean loss of identity; rather it frees all other faculties for the maintenance of that identity, while the hands can at last fulfill their creative function without restriction.

Brautsegen

Es ist so seltsam: jung sein und zu segnen.
Und dennoch bin ich durstig es zu tun:
Am Rand von Worten Ihnen zu begegnen,
und mit den Händen, die in sehr entlegnen
Büchern blättern, . . .   5
in Ihren Händen abends auszuruhn.

  Das ist die Stunde, da die Hände reden:
des Tages Arbeit klingt in ihnen nach,

sie beben leise und erleben jeden
Gedanken wirklich, den der Mund nur sprach; 10
und wären Tasten unter ihnen, stiege
die Luft beladen mit dem Klang zur Nacht,
und wohnten sie am Rande einer Wiege,
so wäre lächelnd drin das Kind erwacht—
mit Augen, gross, als ob es das verschwiege, 15
was jeden Frühling mächtig macht.

Und nun die Hände in den Ihren sind,
belauschen Sie das Blut, das leise spricht,
erfinden Sie ein gutes Angesicht
zu diesen Händen, die in Ihren sind. 20
Ein weises, das des Lebens würdig ward,
ein stilles, welches Flüsterndes versteht,
ein tiefes, das, von seinem Bart umweht,
so ruhig bleibt, wie hinter Eichenkronen
durch die ein Sturm spricht, ein ganz stilles Haus, 25
in dem Sie sich nicht fürchteten zu wohnen.

Denn, sehn Sie, meine Hände sind viel *mehr*
als ich, in dieser Stunde da ich segne.
Da ich sie aufhob, waren beide leer,
und da ich mich, mit einer Angst, die lähmte, 30
für meine leichten leeren Hände schämte,
da, hart vor Ihnen, legte irgendwer
so schöne Dinge in die armen Schalen,
dass sie mir fast zu schwer
geworden sind und fast zu sehr, 35
mit grossem Glanze überladen, strahlen . . .

So nehmen Sie, was mir ein Überreicher
im letzten Augenblick verhüllt verlieh—
er kleidete mich, dass ich wie ein Gleicher
bei Bäumen bin: die Winde werden weicher 40
und rauschen in mir, und ich segne Sie.

Ich segne Sie mit jener Art zu segnen,
die man bei Abenden im Frühling sieht:
nach Tagen, welche flüstern, frösteln, regnen,
kommt eine Stille, einfach wie ein Lied.   45
 Die Bäume wissen schon, was sich bereitet,
die Felder schlafen ganz getröstet ein,
die nahen Himmel haben sich geweitet,
damit die Erde Raum hat, gross zu sein.
Kein Wort ist leis genug, um es zu sagen,   50
kein Traum ist tief genug, um ihn zu tun,
und alle Märchen sind wie leere Truhn,
weil alle Menschen jetzt die Kleider tragen,
die sonst in ihrem Dunkel duftend ruhn . . .
                [An Paula Becker-Modersohn,
                November 14, 1900; *Werke 3, 716*]

Since "Brautsegen" is the third successive longer poem to be considered in this chapter, a commonsense genre distinction between long and short poems in Rilke's work seems appropriate. Belmore distinguishes between "light" and "heavy" language:

> . . . whereas in a "light" poem the language is an open-work structure, something like a scaffolding, the "heavy" language resembles a very closely woven carpet. In the light style, each of the words used may be necessary, and their sequence and arrangement equally so, yet they will hardly be remembered as words: they float by, carrying the poetic meaning as a river carries flowers, swiftly, lightly, on its surface.[19]

Something in the human attention span and the makeup of human language sets a limit of length on the "heavy" style. The analogy with a carpet must not be pressed too far, for whereas a carpet is spatial (i.e., its totality is perceived in a single moment of time), language is linear, dependent on the retentive power of memory

19. Belmore, p. 120.

for its coherence. Although there is no given length for a "heavy" poem, a form as brief as the Japanese haiku is inherently enigmatic, with too few words for the weaving of even the smallest poetic carpet. Hence it depends on the reader to fill in the words' associations. For the full meaning of a poetic configuration to develop within the poem itself, a certain accumulation of detail is necessary, together with the rooting of that detail in a single imaginative reality. The historical development of the sonnet form doubtless reflects an instinctive sense that fourteen lines was something like the golden mean for a "heavy" poem. Beyond a certain point (it is impossible to specify an exact number of lines) the reader ceases to relate new words to the poem's first line; there ceases to be, as Belmore puts it, "an aura radiating from each word, connecting it in a sense other than that of logic or causality, to those that precede and follow." Instead the longer poem tends toward the "light" style, i.e., it is unified by an extra-verbal idea or image which the reader bears in mind as he reads.

I am thinking of Staiger's *Grundbegriffe* when I say that beyond a certain length a poem necessarily becomes "epic" rather than "lyric"—not that it therefore becomes an Epic poem, or even a ballad, although these are possibilities. But the words are linked by some force not contained within the poem itself. It may be an image which the poem constructs as it goes along, as in Rimbaud's "Bateau Ivre," or it may be a philosophical preoccupation which the poem approaches from different angles, recreating and developing the thought through imagery, as in Eliot's *Four Quartets*.

The long poem, oriented toward an extrinsic idea or event, will derive much of its significance from the actual thoughts it expresses. The short poem, by contrast, is itself both idea and event —the implicit associations of words are as important as explicit meaning. Since for Rilke the act of creation is intertwined with an urge towards the general statement, the mastery of "heavy" language is deepened by the constant impulse to break through it and present a poetry of ideas. The tension in Rilke's work is sum-

med up in the simultaneous production of the *Duineser Elegien*
and the *Sonette an Orpheus*. The sonnets force the poet's thoughts
into fourteen lines, with the strain constantly apparent in such
desperately enigmatic imperatives as "Wisse das Bild" or "Wolle
die Wandlung." The poems can be understood as self-contained
entities, but often with difficulty. Again and again an awareness of
Rilke's preoccupations permits a shortcut to a phrase's true resonance. On the other hand no one has ever regarded the *Elegies* as
lyric poems; neither is it possible to translate their rhetorical
style into intelligible prose. They are philosophical poems irre-
ducible to philosophical language, thoughts which live only in the
images that express them. They nonetheless overwhelm the intellect as well as the senses. Rilke's use of long and short forms
culminates in an attempt to infuse the one with the other's essence.

Rilke's earliest and poorest collection, *Leben und Lieder,* is
written in inherited stanza forms (most frequently of four lines),
as are most of the early collections until 1898. Parallel with this
continuing attempt to adapt traditional forms and stanzas to his
own needs and to discipline himself within them runs the urge
to develop as a man, to express ideas and imaginings so freely
that youthful experience will gradually crystallize into a personality. At times this activity seems almost schizophrenic—I have already mentioned E. M. Butler's comment on the discrepancy between the saccharine early verse and the morbid early stories. In
October 1896 Rilke writes the first three *Christus-Visionen* and
initiates a form that is to contain much of his anguished development towards poetic maturity, the long poem. These *Christus-
Visionen* are rambling and unfinished. They have something of
the epic in them, and a great deal of the adolescent preoccupation
with religion and death. In the midst of their ill-disciplined flow
are phrases that hint at a more mature ability to encompass
genuine experience in verse.

By 1899, when Rilke writes *Das Buch vom mönchischen Le-*

ben, he is able to use language in a wholly personal way. But the formal looseness, so valuable in the *Christus-Visionen,* has become a distinct liability, weakening the impact of individual images. The texture cries out for the discipline, the "heaviness" of which Rilke has already shown himself capable within the self-imposed limitations of the short poem, "Wenn ich manchmal in meinem Sinn" (1897). By the time of the *Neue Gedichte* the return to the shorter forms is completed and, with the exception of such highly subjective interludes as the "Requiems" and the "Gesänge" of August 1914, the short lyric remains Rilke's primary mode of expression for the rest of his life. Nevertheless prior to the Paris years Rilke continued to write long poems of an increasingly disciplined kind. As the climax of this process I regard "Brautsegen" and the "Requiem" for Gretel Kottmeyer written six days later. Both are openly concerned with matters external to the poetry, yet both are successfully unified by a single dominant image: in the "Requiem" it is Clara's wreath, "ein Ding mehr / auf Erden"; here it is the poet's hands.

Most of the aspects of the hand image so far discussed come together in "Brautsegen," unified by the gesture of blessing, a gesture symbolic of affirmation. As "Das Lied vom Kehrreim" (1899) utilized the poet's sense of sterility to penetrate the meaning of the creative act, so "Brautsegen" transforms a sense of exclusion into a sense of involvement. The first section expresses Rilke's paradoxical determination. Blessing implies experience of life, even fatherhood, and that Rilke feels very much an apprentice to life makes him assume fatherhood, as his awe before God in *Das Stundenbuch* gave him the paradoxical sense of being God's creator. The lines are full of the confrontation between life and the powerful dialectical urge through which Rilke makes life work for him.

The concrete notion of meeting Paula is juxtaposed with the abstract "Am Rand von Worten." The image of his own hand is clearly metaphorical—they are the instruments of creation at

work—yet Paula's hands are wholly natural, with the word
"abends" adding an especially homely touch. In this transformation the simplicities of actual life are synthesized with poetic am-
bition to create the new reality of the gesture. To be sure, the
gesture is merely adumbrated as yet. By uniting the strands of
life and imagination Rilke has already made it possible, indeed has
accomplished it. One is reminded of the mysterious lines in the
1922 poem, "Solang du Selbstgeworfnes fängst":

> Und wenn du gar
> zurückzuwerfen Kraft und Mut besässest,
> nein, wunderbarer: Mut und Kraft vergässest
> und schon geworfen *hättest* . . .
>
> [January 31, 1922; *Werke* 2, 132]

The first section of "Brautsegen" aspires to the gesture; the remainder describes it, in the indicative, as an accomplished fact.
Rilke has "forgotten" the daring hopes of the beginning—the
poem itself is his gesture.

The second section is almost symphonic in its exposition of
themes related to the hand. The musical imagery points in two
directions. Lines seven and eight evoke the "purity" of the 1902
essay on Rodin:

> Wie Parzifal heranwächst, so wuchs sein Werk in Reinheit
> heran, allein mit sich und mit einer grossen ewigen Natur.
> Nur seine Arbeit sprach zu ihm. Sie sprach zu ihm des Mor-
> gens beim Erwachen, und des Abends klang sie lange in sei-
> nen Händen nach wie in einem fortgelegten Instrumente.
>
> [*Werke* 5, 154]

Lines nine and ten are redolent of another world, the world of
melancholy and dream with which Rilke's diaries were suffused
a year earlier when he first arrived in Schmargendorf:

> . . . sie drängen den Jüngling mit den traurigen sinnenden
> Augen zu dem kleinen altmodischen Klavier und legen ihm

die heissen Hände auf die Tasten. Und der Jüngling fühlt in
dem fremden Zimmer, in dem sie, weiss Gott weshalb, bei-
sammen stehen, fühlt zwei Hände neben den seinen, wie
lehrend, aber so leise, und er ahnt auch das Gesicht zu diesen
zwei Händen. Ein Mädchengesicht, von leisen, zärtlichen
Linien begrenzt . . . Und Sascha spielt also willig das Lied
dieses Mädchens, wie die Tasten es wollen. Immer weiter,
immer weiter spielt er das Lied dieser Abwesenden, Fremden,
vielleicht schon Gestorbenen.

[November 3, 1899][20]

The passage reads like a much softened description of the union
with the second hand, but it is relevant to the present poem as
much by contrast as in verbal parallels. For the youth's hands,
merely agents that evoke the girl's "Lied," cooperate in a reality
that speaks through them. Similarly Rodin's hands, in the 1902
essay, are essentially agents, producers of his work.

The hands in the present poem are self-sufficient and pre-
eminent, their present gesture surpassing the work they have
done, their musicality contained within them. They have no need
of piano keys, let alone a stranger's song. The conditional mode of
lines eleven to fifteen thrusts towards the indicative. By simply
positing these actions as possibilities for the hands Rilke can make
them real, for gestures depend on the imagination for their existence. The verb "stiege" implies an imagining, but "die Luft
beladen mit dem Klang" is already real—the "Klang" has occurred. Similarly the child is only posited, but the vivid details
evoking him place him firmly in the sphere of reality. Indeed the
whole poem enacts what is implicit in this evocation of the child
image. The child contains within himself the rhythm of life which
the adult must recapture. The child understands instinctively the
power of nature's rebirth. Adults cannot regain this understanding, though by following the freedom of their hands in gesture

20. *Briefe und Tagebücher aus der Frühzeit*, pp. 204–05.

they can become again a part of the child's "Frühling." What is imagined strongly enough becomes real. Negatives and conditionals enlarge the range of the possible, and the verb "verschwiege" is both.

The third section introduces the important element of "das Angesicht." Once before it has been prominent in the poems studied—as the "Werktag . . . wie ein heiliges Gesicht / zu meinen dunklen Händen"—where its metaphorical nature and its link with "Arbeit" are already apparent. In "Brautsegen" the connection of the "Gesicht" motif with the problem of identity becomes clearer. In Rilke's overall development we have considered his initial struggle with the inherited language, the cliché, and his apparent solution in the *Rollengedicht* and the persona of the Russian monk. In the poems and letters of 1900 one can detect a new development, a struggle to move away from the ideals of unity and total flexibility towards the reassertion of a hard core of personal identity. Lacking our hindsight, he must have had difficulty seeing the emergence of his personality in his own early work, and the creative ideal expressed by the image of the second hand must have seemed replete with danger. If one surrenders one's creative force to the absolute, how will one attain independent identity?

The "Blick . . . verwoben mit der Natur," to quote again Rilke's letter of April 1903, is an essential complement to the hand which "geht allein irgendwo unten ihren Weg": but in such an involvement individuality could well be swallowed up in impotent attempts to reproduce nature. The pages in *Malte* about people exchanging their faces "unheimlich schnell" illustrate how genuinely terrified Rilke was of "das Nichtgesicht." His fear of such a void is well illustrated by lines nineteen to twenty-six of "Brautsegen," as he begs Paula to invent a face that could protect his hands' creativity against the forces to which they must expose themselves. Such an invention would not be arbitrary; it would bridge the gap Rilke so desperately felt between his

perception of nature and his ability to transform it, between his
sensitivity and his poetic identity.

Three weeks after the poem "Brautsegen" he wrote a prose
poem entitled "Das Antlitz," which is worth quoting in its en-
tirety for the continuity of thought and language evident between
it and "Brautsegen":

> Wäre ich als einfacher Bauer geboren, dann lebte ich mit
> einem grossen, geräumigen Gesicht: in meinen Zügen ver-
> riete ich nicht, was schwer zu denken und unmöglich ist zu
> sagen (oder: dass es schwer ist zu denken und was unmöglich
> ist zu sagen)....
>
> Und nur die Hände würden sich füllen mit meiner Liebe
> und meiner Geduld,—tags aber würden sie sich mit Arbeit
> bedecken, die Nacht würde sie im Beten verschliessen. Nie-
> mand ringsum würde erfahren,— wer ich bin. Ich bin alt
> geworden, und mein Kopf schwamm auf der Brust hinab,
> mit der Strömung. Er scheint weicher zu sein. Ich verstand,
> dass der Tag der Trennung nahe ist, und ich öffnete meine
> Hand wie ein Buch und legte beide auf Wangen, Mund und
> Stirn. Leer werde ich sie abnehmen, ich lege sie in den
> Sarg,—doch an meinem Gesicht werden die Enkel alles
> erkennen, was ich war . . . aber dennoch bin *ich* es nicht; in
> diesen Zügen sind sowohl Freuden als auch Qualen, ge-
> waltig und stärker als ich: ja, das ist das ewige Antlitz der
> Arbeit.
>
> [December 6, 1900; *Werke 4,* 962–63]

The face Rilke seeks would be both less and more than an "individual" face: less in that it would not reveal the process of creation, more in that it would register every accomplishment, every
emotion generated by the creative act. Such a face would both
"endure" and leave the hands unrestricted. It would be constructed
by the hands themselves. As his hands have not yet had the time

to do so, as he lacks both the simplicity and the age of his "ein-
facher Bauer," he begs Paula to invent such a face.

The plea has in a sense brought about the reality. Again Rilke
uses his own poem to establish the equilibrium he seeks. The
dimension of age is added by a simple change of tense: "Ein
weises, das des Lebens würdig ward." When the fourth section
begins with the words "Denn, sehn Sie . . . ," Rilke has already
established his "Antlitz der Arbeit." He is ready to bless, although
the only change since the poem's first line consists of the creation
of the poem itself. This act of "Arbeit" has redeemed the hands'
emptiness. Emptiness is not in itself a bad thing to Rilke. An
emptiness one can accept, in expectation of coming fullness, signals a developing sense of identity:

> Meine Gedanken gehen um Euere Häuser. Mein Herz
> hängt irgendwo im Wind und läutet. Meine Hände liegen
> offen und leer, wie halbe Muscheln, aus denen die Perle
> genommen ist. Aber haltet das nicht für Traurigkeit, sondern
> für eine Art Fest, mit welchem mein Winter leise anhebt.
>
> [An Paula Becker, October 25, 1900][21]

Simenauer identifies angels and women as essentially the same
to Rilke. Certainly the gesture of the second hand in filling Rilke's
empty hands (lines 32–36) is similar to that of "die reichende
Reiche" in "Wenn ich manchmal in meinem Sinn" (1897), as
she places her hand in the poet's "hingehaltne Schale." The identification of the act of receiving with the act of blessing expresses
Rilke's new ability to submit to the second hand while maintaining his own identity. The whole image is higly stylized. "Da ich
sie aufhob" suggests the conventional posture for a blessing, with
the palm of the hand turned outward. Without explanation the
hands turn into "Schalen," i.e., with the palms turned inward in
a receiving position. The act of blessing has become identical with

21. Ibid., pp. 66–67.

the creation of a poem, and the act of creation makes Rilke feel like an intermediary, a being whose identity is no longer separable from his own "Arbeit." The image outlined in Rilke's letter of April 1903 of the hand and the gaze in independent but complementary activity is enacted in this poem. With his gaze fixed on Paula and her marriage, his hand moves ahead and constructs a poem around the event and his relation to it. At the point of fulfillment, when he is ready to greet Paula, he finds that he has arrived on an altogether wider level of perception in which Paula's marriage, the "Ding" on which he has been concentrating, unlocks the door to the whole realm of "die Dinge." "Die Hände sind viel mehr / als ich": blessing is no longer a convention but a unique act of giving, or rather of passing on a gift.

There is a parallel between "Brautsegen" and a poem discussed in the previous chapter, "Ein einziges Gedicht" (1900). In both poems the act of creation itself produces a new harmony and clarity in the surrounding world. But in "Brautsegen" the reader witnesses the entire process, beginning before the poet even thinks of creating when he desires peace and personal communion. As this desire stimulates the imagination, the poem takes shape until by the end of the fourth section the act of blessing has become an all-embracing gesture.

The final section celebrates the achieved unity with "die Dinge." The governing image is that of clothing: the second hand dresses the poet in the costume of nature; the final mention of the word "ich" in the poem (line 42) coincides with the repeated act of blessing, as if the poet then becomes that blessing. The harmony is then described from nature's own point of view. Since the poet is "ein Gleicher / bei Bäumen," it seems no excessive anthropomorphism to write "Die Bäume wissen schon." The poet's own knowledge is as instinctual as that of the trees. Finally human beings reappear, free of life's complicating irrelevancies. They have donned the robes of fairly tales, which no longer need be considered allegories or dreams, since the poet's

blessing has covered all things with a single mode of reality.
The whole poem derives from the central theme of blessing and
its dependent hand imagery. There is nothing arbitrary about
the development of this theme, as there is so often in *Das Buch
vom mönchischen Leben.* Perhaps because the poem enacts the
process of creation, a perfect harmony subsists between the
whole and the individual words. Even phrases that border on
early clichés, like "einfach wie ein Lied" or "kein Wort ist leis
genug," seem entirely appropriate here in the poem centered on
the very hands that create it.

> Und wer hinausschaut in der Nacht
> sieht den an den er grad gedacht
> im Garten stehn.
> Er steht an einem Rosenbeet
> und wenn der Mond vorübergeht   5
> kann er es sehn.
>
> Ich sah mich stehn am Wegesrand
> still, von mir selber fortgewandt
> und noch ganz jung.
> Ich weiss nicht, ob ich wirklich war;   10
> ich schien gewoben wunderbar
> aus Dämmerung.
>
> Die stillen Bäume standen so,
> als wäre Einer irgendwo
> so still wie sie.   15
> Fern weinte es im Nachbarhaus,
> und alle Dinge waren aus
> Melancholie.
>
> Da dacht ich längst nichtmehr an mich,—
> aber aus unserm Garten wich   20
> der Knabe nicht.
> Jetzt hatte er sich umgewandt,

ich aber sah nur seine Hand,
nicht sein Gesicht.

Er hatte tief sein Haupt gesenkt   25
wie Einer, welcher Dinge denkt
gewaltig schwer—
doch seine Hand ging vor ihm her
und ging als wäre sie viel mehr
als er.   30

Da wusst ich alles gleich und sprach:
man geht nur seinen Händen nach,
die alles tun.
Wir sind nur Hände, Antlitz nicht,
Gott aber ist das Angesicht,   35
darin wir ruhn.

        [September 21, 1901; *Werke 3,* 751–52]

After a reading of "Brautsegen" one is struck, in the present poem, by such consistencies of imagery as the merging of a human figure with "die Bäume" and the virtually identical phraseology of the hand's role, "als wäre sie viel mehr / als er." This poem is no mere footnote to "Brautsegen." Written nearly a year later, as part of the original *Buch von der Pilgerschaft,* it treats identical preoccupations very differently. Whereas "Brautsegen" is wholly inward, the present work is objective in both its narrative inclination and its presentation of theme. It begins and ends with general statements arising from shifting time patterns. The first stanza is in the present tense, but all the others are in the past, including the last, which presents the "message" of the poet-in-the-past, not necessarily that of the poet-in-the-present. Above all, the hands' independence is presented in a radical yet unruffled way, as if Rilke were using the detached perspective to say things that otherwise could not easily be said.

Three years earlier, in a short piece entitled "Generationen"

(1898), he had described hands in a similar way, but at an even
further remove from life as subjectively lived, through the medium of ancestors' portraits:

> Es wären keine Porträts geworden ohne diese Hände, hinter
> denen sie leise und bescheiden hingelebt haben, alle Tage
> lang. Diese Hände hatten das Leben gehabt und die Arbeit,
> die Sehnsucht und die Sorge, waren mutig und jung gewesen
> und sind müde und alt geworden, während sie selbst nur
> fromme, ehrfürchtige Zuschauer dieser Geschicke waren.
> [Autumn 1898; *Werke 4,* 509]

Words like "leise," "bescheiden," "fromm," "ehrfürchtig" beg
the question in an important sense. This is very much an impression of art rather than life. One may contrast with this the passage
in *Malte* (1908–09) about "das Entsetzliche." Here too Rilke
uses an indirect perspective, the "Du" form, but as the flimsiest
of shields to protect himself from his own anguish:

> Besser vielleicht, du wärest in der Dunkelheit geblieben
> und dein unabgegrenztes Herz hätte versucht, all des Un-
> unterscheidbaren schweres Herz zu sein. Nun hast du dich
> zusammengenommen in dich, siehst dich vor dir aufhören
> in deinen Händen, ziehst von Zeit zu Zeit mit einer unge-
> nauen Bewegung dein Gesicht nach.
> [*Werke 6,* 776–77]

The present poem stands, in attitude as well as date of composition, somewhere between the two prose passages quoted. The
fundamental problem, the relation between hands (creativity)
and face (personal identity), is hidden, in "Generationem"
(1898), behind pieties and narrative distancing. In *Malte* (1908–
09) it is out in the open, raw and frightening. The poem attempts
to solve it by means of a parable designed to remove its problematic character.

The first stanza assumes a reading of the poem immediately

preceding it (in *Das Buch von der Pilgerschaft* they would have been in sequence):

> Da sitz ich in dem schwarzen Haus
> in meinem langen Nachtgewand
> mit meinem Blut in meiner Hand
> und schau hinaus.
>
> [September 21, 1901; *Werke 3, 751*]

The hand theme is resonant before the poem starts, as is the image of the poet gazing into the night, but these lines are in the first person and the present tense. The bridge to the past narrative is provided by the generalizing first stanza, with its shift of perspective: the "er" who sees the rose bed is imagined by the viewer, who is merely a poetic postulate. Such diffusion verges on the bewildering. This together with the inappropriate pedantry of the second line may have left Rilke dissatisfied. But if the aim of this blurring is to dissolve the meaning of the verb "sehen," the tendency of the eyes to classify, that aim is well achieved.

The treatment of the *Doppelgänger* motif lacks the horror one might expect from its literary connotations or from the comparable scene of Malte dressed up in front of the mirror. The double removal in time suggests Rilke's purpose, with the incident described in the past and the vision of himself as a youth ("noch ganz jung"). Space as well as time is dissolved: the youth seems formed out of the natural background, itself merging in the dusk. This quest for a dimension at once immediate and remote suggests that the youth will symbolize the creative act in its purer form. He is not a child, as the fifth stanza stresses, yet he is not burdened with the adult's need for an identity, a "Gesicht." The poem loosens the bonds that bind the "ich" together: only in the second stanza does the poet speak of both self and *Doppelgänger* in the first person. Evolving from the word "Dämmerung," the third stanza turns away from subjectivity altogether, first towards the trees whom the *Doppelgänger* resembles, then to-

wards a distant house which is not perceived, merely heard. Finally the scenery dissolves altogether into "Melancholie."

The time dimension is again invoked at the beginning of the
fourth stanza, but the physical scene is no longer felt. As a result,
the figure in the garden seems more remote, more obviously symbolic. The first line, by a last reference to the opening "Spruch,"
separates what is to follow from what precedes. The figure established as a *Doppelgänger* has now outlasted his reason for
being there. He is both the poet and more than the poet. He has
turned to confront the poet—clearly he has something to com-
municate. After the dissolution of the physical background, we
are prepared for the rest of the poem to move on a purely symbolic level: the verb "ich sah" is not the same as it was in the
second stanza, because there is nothing incidental now in what
the poet "sees." The stanza form places an automatic stress on
the third and sixth lines, as a kind of summation of the preceding
couplet. Rilke has made good use of this effect. In the first stanza,
introductory in both material and rhythm, the third and sixth
lines have no special significance. But in the second stanza "und
noch ganz jung" is a line with its own point to make. From then
on, through the parallel stanza endings "aus Dämmerung" and
"Melancholie," these lines are given increasing weight. The
rhythm tells us that the unpretentious statement "nicht sein
Gesicht" has great importance: the hand is seen, while the face,
in symbolic contrast, is invisible. In the fifth stanza it becomes
apparent that Rilke has used the romantic elements of the poem,
the narrative style, the nocturnal atmosphere, the *Doppelgänger*
motif, to prepare for an unambiguous statement, to take sides
on the issue of the "Gesicht" in relation to the "Hände." Thus
the figure is not contemplating, he is thinking, and thinking like
an introvert. His gaze is not upwards and outwards but turned in
on himself. The image seems to imply the inherited dichotomy of
reason and passion, with the hands as man's living center.

One could accept this as a heightened image of the hands' importance in a purely narrative context. But Rilke is not content

to leave his story alone. His didactic tendencies are well known, from both works and correspondence. Here, as elsewhere, he feels compelled to develop the truth of his own imagery explicitly, to relate the concrete to the abstract. The result only emphasizes the impossibility of easy solutions to the problem of identity. In the fifth stanza the figure's hand is "viel mehr / als er," but in the sixth "Wir sind nur Hände." The statements cannot be reconciled. If our hands are more than we are, there must exist a contrasting human dimension. That dimension is "das Gesicht," image of our subjectivity. Rilke, using his strict form as a means of making the statement appear inevitable, incorporates "das Gesicht" in a final elusive paradox in the manner of *Das Buch vom mönchischen Leben.*

These last two lines convey very little in concrete terms. It seems that Rilke has telescoped three strongly felt impulses into a single image in the hope that their contradictions would thus appear resolved. He is conscious of a powerful force from which he draws his creativity, a force often pictured as a hand, but also felt in religious terms. There is, further, a firm underlying harmony in the world which Rilke needs to perceive and affirm. He also needs to give his work a personal stamp which can only be gained by committing himself to the second hand in the hope that "Gottes Angesicht" will be revealed in the creative act. This is the paradoxical meaning of the phrase "das Antlitz der Arbeit": an identity that emerges from acceptance of one's instrumentality.

This complex situation Rilke has attempted to compress into the last two lines. Apprehensive of the difficulties of achieving an "Antlitz der Arbeit," he resorts to a facile piety, to an assertion that mere recognition of the problem can lead to its solution: if we renounce our subjectivity the world's unity will be comfortably evident and the conflict between our need to respond to the second hand and our need to develop a personal identity will simply vanish. For personal identity, he implies, is an unnecessary illusion. The final "ruhn" is deeply felt, but such peace, like the ideal of childhood, is something to which Rilke constantly aspired while

he knew that the dynamics of human creativity would never let
him attain it.

Herbst

> Die Blätter fallen, fallen wie von weit,
> als welkten in den Himmeln ferne Gärten;
> sie fallen mit verneinender Gebärde.
>
> Und in den Nächten fällt die schwere Erde
> aus allen Sternen in die Einsamkeit.
>
> Wir alle fallen. Diese Hand da fällt.
> Und sieh dir andre an: es ist in allen.
>
> Und doch ist Einer, welcher dieses Fallen
> unendlich sanft in seinen Händen hält.
>
> [September 11, 1902; *Werke 1, 400*]

This is one of Rilke's perfect poems. It deals, directly or by
implication, with all the problematical aspects of the hand image.
The leaves themselves prepare us for the metaphors to come;
their "Gebärde" places them in a human context. In his essay
"Worpswede," written earlier in 1902, Rilke has developed his
ability to integrate the natural with the human through a study of
landscape art:

> [Das Licht] fiel nichtmehr breit durch das grossmaschige
> Netz zählbarer Äste auf die Wiesen; die Blätter, die Blüten,
> die Früchte, die Flächen von tausend aneinander-gedrängten
> Dingen fingen es wie kleine Hände auf und spielten damit,
> glänzten, dunkelten und glühten.
>
> [*Werke 5, 132*]

In "Herbst" Rilke seems to use language as a painter uses
colors, to convey an effect of varied but sustained light. The harmoniousness of the vowelling is extraordinary: the vowel *o*
appears just once, in the penultimate line, like a tinge of a darker
color to prepare us for the new element, namely "Einer"; the

vowel *u* is not used in the poem, nor are any diphthongs except *ei* and *ie*. The whole poem is organized round the vowels *a-ä-e,* and these often in conjunction with the labials *l* and *r*. As a result of such fusions it seems that a constant soft chant, "fallen"-"fällt"-"fern," expressive of the falling leaves, continues behind the actual words, sometimes merging with them. The dominant word "fallen" remains enigmatic despite its repetition. Theophil Spoerri, an early interpreter, sees the imagery in terms of dramatic contrast:

> Siebenmal erklingt dieses Wort und jedesmal mit schwererem Klang. Zuerst ist es ein ganz irdischer Blätterfall, der den Blick an sich zieht und an einen gewöhnlichen Herbst erinnert. Aber sofort erweitert sich die Anschauung zu unendlichen Massen . . . Und in der Bewegung der fallenden Blätter sehen wir nun das schicksalsschwere Nein des Sterbens.[22]

In this stress on "fallen" as "fallen in den Tod" he would be joined by Mrs. Corcoran.[23] It is in the reading of the third section that this view diverges most from my own. Spoerri writes:

> Das Angstgefühl dringt nun zum Herzen. Ein Schrei: "Wir alle fallen!" Diese Hand, die ich dir entgegenstrecke, sie fällt. Schau um dich, siehst du nicht, wie alle untergehen?

Spoerri claims to have heard Rilke read the poem. But there is in fact no exclamation mark after "Wir alle fallen."

Rilke did not conceive the natural cycle in terms of a life-versus-death dualism, and the phrase "mit verneinender Gebärde" suggests willing renunciation of life rather than a "schicksalsschweres Nein." For him "fallen" was a positive, indeed essential attribute of life, as the following lines from *Das Buch Von der Pilgerschaft,* written a year earlier in equally autumnal mood, il-

22. Theophil Spoerri, *Präludium zur Poesie* (Berlin, 1929), p. 312.
23. Corcoran, p. 181.

lustrate. Falling is a metaphor for the self-containment of "die Dinge," the child's instinctive antidote to adult striving:

> Da muss er lernen von den Dingen,
> anfangen wieder wie ein Kind,
> weil sie, die Gott am Herzen hingen,
> nicht von ihm fortgegangen sind.
> Eins muss er wieder können: *fallen,*   5
> geduldig in der Schwere ruhn,
> der sich vermass, den Vögeln allen
> im Fliegen es zuvorzutun.
>
> [September 19, 1901; *Werke 1, 321*]

The structure of "Herbst" seems to me to divide after the second section rather than the third. The rhyme scheme links the sections in this way, and the content reflects the rhyme. The first section presents a concrete image of nature which yet includes both the human world and the wider cosmos. The second section moves throughout on a cosmic level, generalizing the falling motion to the extreme of "Einsamkeit," which contains both limitless space and a simple human feeling. It is as if the very words a poet uses compel his imagination simultaneously towards the exalted and remote, and the simple and everyday. Rilke shows that he has "learned to fall" in this poem about falling. The step from "Einsamkeit" to "Wir alle" is both contrast and continuation, for the only way to give a meaning to loneliness is to return to mankind.

The third section, with its nervous pauses, expresses both man's lack of rhythm and his bewildering multiplicity of perception. There is the generalized first person plural "wir," the detached contemplation of one's own "Hand," the second person dimension of communicated experience, and finally the awareness of an impersonal force, "es," governing all the other perceptual levels. The fourth section again offers both contrast and continuation. The contrast is in the newly flowing rhythm, the explicit and noticeable "doch," and the return to the cosmic level. The continuation is in the simple transition from "es" to "Einer"; the impersonal falling of nature is in complete harmony with the force that sustains it, just as the loneliness of the cosmos exemplifies that of the individual. Man must learn how to fall in order to be sustained. The second hand is pictured as below man, recalling both the emphasis on "Tiefe" in "Das Lied vom Kehrreim" (November 1899) and the image of "Ruhe" at the end of "Und wer hinausschaut" (September 1901). Here at last Rilke has achieved a synthesis of the ideals of peaceful harmony and dynamic creativity by adding the concepts of "fallen" and "das Schwere." The hands no longer have to be constantly active to prevent an intolerable sense of emptiness. Rather, by accepting "das Fallen" they rejoin the rest of one's being and work toward a personal identity instead of against it. The paradox of falling is that it unites all the faculties. Creativity and inactivity become complementary movements whether clasping the second hand or falling towards it.

That these questions do indeed lie beneath the poem's delicate surface is suggested by the following lines written a few days later. They ask again, in similar vocabulary, the questions to which "Herbst" has provided a symbolic answer:

> Wer hat die Welt, die dämmert, in der Hand?
> Wer hält sie so unendlich sanft an sich?
> (Bin ich allein? Merkt keiner denn als ich,
> dass jemand die gefallne Erde fand,
> dass er sie unter seinen Mantel tat.)   5
> Im Schauen welches Auges lebe ich
> den ganzen Tag, ein Wesen ohne Wände,—
> und wenn es Abend wird, in wessen Hände,
> zu wasfür andern Dingen leg ich mich?
>
> [September 21, 1902; *Werke 3,* 761]

That Rilke has accepted the authority of the second hand does not solve his problems, it merely makes possible momentary glimpses of a solution, as in "Herbst." For the initial horror of the

hand experience for the child is constantly in the background, and
the lines in parentheses ("Bin ich allein?") suggest that an awareness of harmony is inseparable from an awareness of the grotesque, that there is no peace in a relationship with the second
hand. Both poems contain the words "unendlich sanft," but in all
other respects their tone is different. To perceive this underlying
harmony is to be involved with it. To be involved with it is to be
aware that others are not involved, that the enigmas of daily living
persist, and that the fragile balance of one's own psyche ("ein
Wesen ohne Wände") can be lost at any moment.

If the child represents the ideal way of life to which the
adult must aspire, the hand image stands for the elements in
adult life that cannot be accommodated within the child's self-
contained, timeless world. The hand is the image of relationship,
of the individual's unavoidable connection with outside forces
and other wills. It is also the image of temporality, of man's involvement in time. Rilke's fascination with the hands of old
people in portraits and in life expresses this sense of the hand as
embodying a whole lifetime of accumulated experience, as opposed to the pure essence of childhood. Just as with the child
image Rilke developed the inherited notion of the child wrapped
in dreams for some years before introducing elements from his
own childhood, so in the poems of the present chapter the second hand dominates the first four poems (1896–98), with the
poet's own hand in an essentially passive role. The second hand
stands for relationship in its pure form, for involvement in time
and linear development. The second hand insists that the way
back can only be the way forward, that the pure gesture of the
child can never be recaptured, only recreated in the fullness of
maturity. Thus the next three poems (1899–1900) are almost
obsessively concerned with the poet's own hand and its self-
assertion in relation to the second hand. In the last two poems
(1901–02) Rilke attempts to distance himself from the situation,

to find equivalents in the external world for a subjective relationship that is inherently and permanently unstable. He can never achieve harmony with the second hand, for a relationship constantly generates new situations. But the constant articulation of his longing for such a harmony does in fact give birth to moments of fulfillment in which temporality is briefly suspended.

The dominance of the second hand is immediately apparent in "Ich weiss, als Kind" (1896). A significant difference between the poem and the recreation of the same incident in *Malte* (1908–09) is that the child's hand plays no role at all in the poem. The comparison of the second hand with "die Totenhand" illustrates how wholly negative the incident appears to the Rilke of 1896. The hand disrupts his childhood without putting anything in its place. "Zwei weisse Nonnenhände" (1897) reads like an instinctive reaction to this event: the poet's ambivalence is suggested by the distanced portrayal of the hands blooming autonomously, followed by the sudden closeness and nervousness of the line "müssen sich fest zusammenfalten." The attempt to create something organic and growing out of the image of folded hands, an image expressing the rejection of all relationships, fails before Rilke's compulsive awareness of the hands' static loneliness.

In "Wenn ich manchmal in meinem Sinn" (1897) Rilke finds a momentary solution to the problem of relationship. The second hand becomes identical with the beloved, and the poet's own passivity no longer excludes him from the living world. The beloved raises her hand, then places it in the "Schale" of the poet's hands. In a woman's shape the second hand no longer seems so intrusive. This gesture of receiving is a small but crucial step away from the nuns' folded hands. The hands are still inactive, still protectively close together, but the fingers have become untwined, the hands are open to the world, an entrance rather than a barrier. This openness is the essence of "Aus Nächten" (1898), where the image of the poet's whole being as a "Teich" seems like an extension of the hands as a "Schale." The positive aspects of passivity are carried in this poem as far as, or perhaps farther than, the imagination will allow.

The transition from "Aus Nächten" to "Wenn ich gewachsen wäre irgendwo" (1899) is abrupt. Suddenly the poet's hand is involved in all its aspects, with the second hand an apparently willing tool. The prevalent subjective mode provides an element of distance in the imagery. Indeed the images in the indicative are already familiar ones of anguished clutching ("wie sie Dich manchmal halten, bang und hart") and the cupped receiving of the fallen bird. Nevertheless the apparently infinite potentiality of the poet's hands leaves a disquieting as well as an exhilarating impression. From fear of involvement with the second hand Rilke seems to have plunged to the opposite extreme of underestimating its autonomy. The persistent power of the second hand is the theme of the much more mature poem "Das Lied vom Kehrreim" (also 1899), in which the central connection is made between the second hand and man's creativity. The self-confidence of *Das Buch vom mönchischen Leben* prevented this connection from becoming clear to the poet, but the new feeling of sterility leads him to concentrate on the instrument of creation, his hand, and to realize that the hand is both the essence of his being and also not his own at all. Without the second hand he is powerless, with it he ceases to be himself. Paradoxically this awareness of a lack of firm identity lays the foundation of a genuine self-acceptance rooted in functionality.

"Brautsegen" (1900) contains all the dimensions of the hand image: the concentrated longing to make a ritual gesture rewarded by the filling of "die armen Schalen" by "ein Überreicher"; the independent life of the hands arising from their daily "Arbeit" and conveying the harmonies to which man's consciousness vainly aspires; and the transformation of the gesture of blessing into a cosmic fulfillment within which the poet's identity, his function in the natural world, instantly and effortlessly appears to him. Such moments must be paid for by a constant sense of being without a normal identity, a secure foundation when creativity falters. By means of an indirect perspective, Rilke expresses very plainly his sense of nonexistence in "Und wer hinausschaut in der Nacht" (1901). His identity ("das Angesicht") derives solely from the relationship with the second hand here portrayed as sustaining man from underneath. Man's position is that of a caryatid; the second hand both maintains his existence and stays permanently above him, a hand which he must grasp in order to realize the personal identity always implicit in his situation. This situation is concentrated into the brevity of "Herbst" (1902). That the falling hand is used to illustrate the general statement "Wir alle fallen" expresses the hand's natural tendency to rise and strive. *Even* the hand falls. Just as springtime is so often used as an image of creativity, so the falling leaves of autumn naturally express artistic sterility. Such sterility resembles the emptiness of the hands prior to the gesture in "Brautsegen"—the eventual fulfillment, the poetic identity, is implicit in its apparent negation. Rilke has to learn to "fall," to accept the anonymous dependence on the second hand beneath him instead of either striving to maintain an identity no longer valid or despairing at his own emptiness.

4   Das Ding

"Das Kind" and "die Hand" are recurring motifs in Rilke's poetry, expressing, not necessarily on a fully conscious level, his view of the world and the artist's place in it. Only occasionally, as in "Brautsegen" (1900) or "Kindheit" (1905–06), do they emerge as the actual theme of a poem. "Das Ding," in contrast is one of the major themes of Rilke's middle and late periods. All critics who write comprehensively about Rilke must concern themselves with it, and the familiar distinction among "Naturding," "Gebrauchsding," and "Kunstding has been analyzed to the point where there can be little more to add.

Since the critics are not unanimous it is not difficult to juxtapose two diametrically opposed interpretations of the same Rilkean symbol:

> Dieses Gesammeltsein, dieses Ganzsein eines Dinges aber sieht er vor allem an einem besonderen und eigentümlichen Ding, das halb als Naturding genommen wird und doch andererseits ein Ding des Gebrauchs und zwar des kindlichen Spiels ist. Es ist die Puppe. Im Wesen der Puppe findet Rilke am reinsten ausgeprägt, was alle Dinge insgesamt kennzeichnet, und was alle Dinge ihrem innersten Wesen nach sind: gesammeltes Dasein.[1]

> Denn die Puppe ist im strengen Sinn kein Ding. Sie ist "weniger als ein Ding" . . . In der Puppe . . . geschieht das Unheimliche, dass das von uns Gemachte aus dem Kreis der Vertrautheit heraustritt und sich uns als ein Fremdes gegenüberstellt, eben durch die Paradoxie, dass in ihr etwas ge-

---

1. Eberhard Kretschmar, *Die Weisheit Rainer Maria Rilkes* (Weimar, 1936), p. 132.

macht ist, ein Ding, das sich als ein nicht gemachtes Natur-
wesen, als Kind, ausgibt.[2]

I feel Bollnow is much closer to the Rilkean implications, but
the disagreement raises the issues I intend to deal with in the
present chapter. For although the critics have extracted and codi-
fied a "philosophy" of things from Rilke's poems, Rilke himself
never enunciated such a philosophy. The word "Ding" had different connotations for him at different periods of his life and in
different emotional contexts. Thus, in the example we have
chosen, Kretschmar is perfectly aware of the essay "Puppen"
(1914), which seemingly contradicts his view, but he contends
that Rilke is illustrating, in that essay, "wie das eisige Schweigen
des Schicksals geradezu selber zum Ding geworden ist." Kretschmar says this partly because he wants to present Rilke as a
seer who has solved life's problems instead of the self-lacerating
human being he actually was, also because Rilke really does
set no limits on a "Ding." Emotions, memories, periods of time—
all these intangibles may be so described. I intend to avoid the
perils of categorization and examine the levels of meaning present
in specific poetic contexts.

Another factor differentiating "das Ding" from "das Kind" or
"die Hand" (one that further complicates attempts at a definition
of it) is that the word does not seem to have subconscious roots
but was "discovered" by Rilke when he was on the verge of maturity. Bollnow has noticed that the word does not occur at all in
Rilke's early poetry before the meeting with Lou Salomé in 1897,
with the solitary exception of a wholly conventional line—
"Nächte, / drin alle Dinge Silber sind"—from *Traumgekrönt*
(1896; *Werke 1,* 84).[3] Despite the much wider range of early
poetry made accessible by the third volume of the new collected
edition (1959), Bollnow's observation still holds true. Perhaps

2. O. F. Bollnow, *Rilke* (Stuttgart 1951), p. 118.
3. Ibid., p. 111.

it helps to explain the diverse yet highly personal ways Rilke employed the word "Ding" from 1898 onward. As an extremely ordinary word, it was not demeaned for him by the clichés of his earliest writings. Rilke used it as a bridge between the ordinary life with which he wanted to remain in contact and the new poetic voice he felt developing within him. During the spring and summer of 1898 he grappled with the problem of the artist's mission in a series of formal and informal prose writings. For the Rilke of 1898, the artist has to function in two different dimensions: time, which obliges him to attempt to retrieve his own past (an idea gained from or strongly reinforced by his 1897 reading of Jacobsen); and space, which compels him to seek his inspiration in the realities surrounding him, to abandon his own ego in favor of a wider identity. The key to a synthesis of these contradictory impulses lies in Rilke's emerging use of the word "Ding," for "die Dinge" exist in both time and space, linking the experiences and rhythms of the past with the simplicities as well as the grandeur of everyday spatial living. The poet can thus only enrich his inner life by identifying himself with them. The first, somewhat vague formulation of this view of art is found in the lecture on "Moderne Lyrik" which Rilke gave in Prague on March 5, 1898:

> Kunst erscheint mir als das Bestreben eines Einzelnen, über das Enge und Dunkle hin, eine Verständigung zu finden mit allen Dingen, mit den kleinsten, wie mit den grössten, und in solchen beständigen Zwiegesprächen näher zu kommen zu den letzten leisen Quellen alles Lebens. Die Geheimnisse der Dinge verschmelzen in seinem Innern mit seinen eigenen tiefsten Empfindungen und werden ihm, so als ob es eigene Sehnsüchte wären, laut. Die reiche Sprache dieser intimen Geständnisse ist die Schönheit.

> [*Werke 5, 365*]

Arguably the language of this definition is so loose that Rilke has not said very much beyond what Romantics have always

said; but the question of poetic identity, although presented as
solved, occurs in the context in which it will remain, namely
the relationship with "die Dinge." The term is used here in the
broadest possible sense, but the important thing is *that* it is
used.

A more concrete approach to "die Dinge" begins to appear in
Rilke's writing at the time of his journey to Italy, a confrontation with genuinely great art that placed the self-conscious theories
of the Prague lecture in a living perspective. The buildings of
Florence can be seen as necessary intermediaries between the
vague and refined "Dinge" of the March lecture and the impartial,
nonaesthetic approach Rilke was to develop later. The products
of a truly aristocratic art, these buildings were yet entirely at ease
in the everyday world, beckoning to the onlooker rather than demanding his aesthetic credentials. The opening pages of the *Florenzer Tagebuch* consist of florid passages possibly designed to im-
press Lou Salomé; yet one can almost feel, in the elaborate prose,
the poet's vision of the world quickening and sharpening. There
is a shift from the notion of things as having exotic *Geheimnisse*
to a feeling that the sensitive observer is *necessary* to the objective
world, and that his "possession" of things makes them complete.
Thus Rilke writes of the Renaissance buildings in Florence:

> Aber die abweisende Verschlossenheit ist dem verständigen
> und bewussten Sich-Anvertrauen trefflicher Menschen ge-
> wichen, welche ohne Pose und ohne Angstlichkeit geben,
> im Gefühl, dass doch nur der Beste ihr Bestes empfängt;
> denn nur ihm kann es durch das Begreifen zum Besitze
> werden.
>
> [April 1898][4]

Rilke cannot immediately assimilate the lesson of this joyously
spatial art. He seems almost to react against it, reaffirming defi-

4. *Tagebücher aus der Frühzeit*, p. 27.

antly his theory of art as rooted in time and asserting the total
primacy of the subjective over the objective:

> Wisset denn, dass der Künstler für sich schafft—einzig für
> sich. Was bei euch Lachen wird oder Weinen, muss er mit
> ringenden Händen formen und aus sich hinausheben. Er
> hat im Innern nicht Raum für seine Vergangenheit, darum
> gibt er ihr in Werken ein losgelöstes, eigenmächtiges Dasein.
> Aber nur weil er keine andere Materie weiss als die eurer
> Welt, stellt er sie in eure Tage. Sie sind nicht für euch.
> Rühret nicht daran, und habet Ehrfurcht vor ihnen.
>
> [May? 1898][5]

Rilke is trying to have it both ways, to present the artist both as
an anguished sufferer and as an Olympian being from whom
works effortlessly flow. The whole tone of the passage is petulant
and pretentious. Nevertheless; as the Florentine spring moved
towards summer Rilke seems to have developed a mystical analogy between Renaissance art as the art of spring and his own as
the art of summer and fulfillment. The rhythm of nature and the
historical dimension of Italian art combined with the concrete
perfection of Florence to give Rilke an ecstatic sense of unity between the temporal and the spatial, the ego and the external
world. In one of the few dated entries in his diary, that of Sunday,
May 22, 1898, he writes:

> Und mein schauerndes Schweigen war ein tief erzitterndes
> Gebet zu dem heiligen Leben, dem ich so nahe war in den
> seligen Schaffensstunden. Dass ich würdig werden möchte,
> in Treue und Vertrauen in seine Erfüllungen einzugehen.
> . . .[6]

From aristocratic disdain Rilke now plunges to the opposite extreme, worshipful humility. Although the rhapsodic extrava-

5. Ibid., p. 37.
6. Ibid., pp. 79–80.

gance of the language prevents any precise definition of "die Dinge," the poet delights in the cardinal realization that self-expression and self-identification with the world of objects are one and the same activity:

> Und dabei wird es mir immer klarer, dass ich gar nicht von den Dingen rede, sondern davon, was ich durch sie geworden bin. Und dieses, welches ganz unwillkürlich geschieht, macht mich froh und hebt mich hinauf; denn ich empfinde, dass ich auf dem Wege bin, ein Vertrauter alles dessen zu werden, was Schönheit verkündet; dass ich nicht mehr bloss ihr Lauschender bin, der ihre Offenbarungen wie stumme Gnaden empfängt, dass ich den Dingen immer mehr ein Jünger werde, der ihre Antworten und Geständnisse durch verständige Fragen steigert, der ihnen Weisheiten und Winke entlockt und ihre grossmütige Liebe mit der Demut des Schülers leise lohnen lernt.[7]

During the remainder of the summer Rilke continues to elucidate exactly what "die Dinge" mean to him. His premise is still aesthetic: the assumption that both they and he are subordinate to something higher, namely "die Schönheit"; and that the central concern of art is man. In "Zur Melodie der Dinge," written during the summer and autumn of 1898, he develops a dualism whereby human concerns should occupy the foreground but remain essentially secondary to the macrocosm governing "die Dinge" (understood again in a very imprecise sense, as if the Florentine experience were receding). The idea is basically a dramatic one, reminiscent of Nietzsche's *Geburt der Tragödie,* which Rilke was to annotate in March 1900 (*Werke 6,* 1163):

> Wollen wir also Eingeweihte des Lebens sein, müssen wir zweierlei bedenken:
> Einmal die grosse Melodie, in der Dinge und Düfte, Ge-

7. Ibid., pp. 88–89.

fühle and Vergangenheiten, Dämmerungen und Sehnsüchte
mitwirken,—und dann: die einzelnen Stimmen, welche
diesen vollen Chor ergänzen und vollenden.

[*Werke* 5, 418]

Rilke is still seeking a generalized solution, an appreciation of
"die Dinge" that will enhance rather than negate the conventional
view of man's role in the world:

> Aller Zwiespalt und Irrtum kommt davon her, dass die
> Menschen das Gemeinsame *in* sich, statt in den Dingen
> *hinter* sich im Licht, in der Landschaft im Beginn und im
> Tode, suchen. Sie verlieren dadurch sich selbst und ge-
> winnen nichts dafür. Sie vermischen sich, weil sie sich doch
> nicht vereinen können.

[*Werke* 5, 124]

At the same time Rilke's terminology is shedding its vagueness.
The insistence on isolating human beings must soon be followed
by a comparable clarity of approach to their "background"—the
"verschmelzende Dinge" of the March lecture are at last to be
brought into focus. This is finally done in the second part of "Über
Kunst" (January 1899). By means of the child image Rilke now
brings his ideas of artist and "Dinge" into more intimate contact
with each other.

The identification of the artist's outlook with the child's allows
Rilke to emancipate himself from the dramatic preoccupations of
1896–97. The problem of human relations, of "das Gemeinsame," ceases to be important once the spontaneity of the child is
posited as the ideal, and aesthetic differentiation also becomes irrelevant:

> Kein Ding ist wichtiger als ein anderes in den Händen des
> Kindes . . . es empfindet als sein Eigentum Alles, was es
> einmal gesehen, gefühlt oder gehört hat. Alles, was ihm ein-
> mal begegnet ist. Es zwingt die Dinge nicht, sich anzusie-

deln. Eine Schar dunkler Nomaden wandern sie durch
seine heiligen Hände wie durch ein Triumphtor. Werden
eine Weile licht in seiner Liebe und verdämmern wieder
dahinter; aber sie müssen alle durch diese Liebe durch. Und
was einmal in der Liebe aufleuchtete, das bleibt darin im
Bilde und lässt sich nie mehr verlieren. Und das Bild ist
Besitz. Darum sind Kinder so reich.

[*Werke* 5, 429–30]

The temporal, Jacobsenesque dimension, the preserved past, is
welded to the unending spatial present of the child's vision
through the concept of "Bild." The things that pass through the
child's hands become "Bild," a spatial image that exists permanently in the memory.

The three central motifs of "Kind," "Hand," and "Ding" are all
present in this early formulation of the idea of the creative process.
In a letter written four months later to Frieda von Bülow the
concept of "Bild" is the essential element in the natural world
as well as the human; the ecstatic union with "die Dinge" expressed in the *Florenzer Tagebuch* is superseded by a sober working relationship. The artist must combine the child's casual spontaneity with a distance dictated by his subjective needs. He no longer
needs to surrender himself to "die Dinge," for they need him as
much as he needs them. His "Bilder" fulfill the natural order,
which has no meaning without them:

> Im Grunde sucht man in jedem Neuem (Land oder Mensch
> oder Ding) nur einen Ausdruck, der irgendeinem persön-
> lichen Geständnis zu grösserer Macht und Mündigkeit ver-
> hilft. Alle Dinge sind ja dazu da, damit sie uns Bilder wer-
> den in irgendeinem Sinn. Und sie leiden nicht dadurch,
> denn während sie uns immer klarer aussprechen, senkt
> unsere Seele sich in dem selben Masse über sie.

[May 27, 1899][8]

8. *Briefe und Tagebücher aus der Frühzeit*, p. 17.

"Die Dinge" are thus as much the subject of Rilke's thoughts as they are the subject of his poems. My purpose will be not so much to read these ideas into the poems as to find out the direction in which the poems themselves seem to lead, and to analyze the relation between Rilke the creator and Rilke the thinker, or rather, rationalizer of his creative urge.

> Ich möchte Purpurstreifen spannen
> und möchte füllen bis zum Rand
> mit Balsamöl aus Onyxkannen
> die Blumenlampen, die entbrannt
> im Mittag flammen, und verbrennen   5
> bis wir uns mit dem Namen nennen,
> der Sterne ruft und Tage bricht;
> die Täler taun, die Winde fallen
> den Dingen in den Schooss und allen
> ist bang nach deinem Angesicht.   10
> [June 10, 1897; *Werke 3, 174*]

At first reading this poem seems typical of Rilke's ornate style, with cliché imagery inflated by exoticisms above a fundamental emptiness of meaning. In fact the exotic vocabulary is largely confined to the first half. The last four lines, within the limitations of the poetic diction of the time, are unusually simple and direct. In other poems of *Dir zur Feier* Rilke seeks to unify lines by the device of repetition, either framing a poem with similar-sounding lines ("Leise ruft der Buchenwald . . . wie der rufende Buchenwald," *Werke 3, 175*) or repeating a short phrase continuously, like a leitmotif ("Ich geh dir nach," *Werke 3, 176*). Here he strives for something more, the binding together of diverse styles and moods through sheer virtuosity of rhythm. The rhyme scheme, for example, can be read in two ways: *a b a b, c c d, e e d,* or *a b a b, c c, d e e d.* The first of these is favored by the punctuation, which posits a pause after the seventh line. The second, however, fits the consonant structure of the poem—from the seventh line the recurring dentals tend to dominate the labials which prevailed earlier. The seventh line is thus both an end and a beginning; and the fourth and fifth lines, nominally divided by the rhyme scheme, are so tightly connected by enjambement, assonance, and near-repetition ("entbrannt"/"verbrennen"), that the seam in the center of the poem is completely invisible. Rilke has thus achieved a series of transitions while blurring the point at which the transitions take place. Such continuity supports the poem's effort to compress passing time from morning to evening.

One of the few quotations given by Grimm (vol. 7, p. 2275) for "Purpurstreifen" derives from Platen: "Aurorens Purpurstreifen,"[9] and a comparable image of the dawn seems intended here. The first and following lines are consciously artful, associating the high ambitions of the speaker with metaphors appropriate to *l'art nouveau,* The repetition of "möchte" reminds us almost unnecessarily that the imagery is not supposed to be descriptive. Rilke's dawn is wholly decorative, as remote as possible from, say, Goethe's "Mailied." But the artifice is not aimless; the action evoked by the verb "füllen" is enacted in the heaping up of exoticisms toward the word "Blumenlampen."

At this point Rilke uses a technique noted in other contexts, that of treating what is merely imagined as an established reality. From infinitives depending on "möchte" ("spannen," "füllen") he abruptly changes to the indicative mood, and inundates the reader with verbs describing burning and flaming. The actual passing of time, from the full force to the dying down of the "Blumenlampen," is compressed into a line and a half ("entbrannt"-"flammen"-"verbrennen"), creating a highly charged atmosphere for the "wie" of the sixth line. The ambivalence between given and arranged natural occurrences is sustained throughout the poem, which is gradually revealed as a love poem.

9. Jacob and Wilhelm Grimm, *Deutsches Wörterbuch,* ed. Matthias von Lexer, 7 (Leipzig, 1889), 2275.

The perspective moves from "ich" through "wir" to "deinem Angesicht," as if the poet wanted to illustrate his love's power by first creating an atmosphere, then becoming a part of it together with the beloved, and finally effacing himself from it. He surrenders the power he has summoned up to the force that emanates from the beloved's face.

This power persists, but has been transferred from the "ich," which could only approach nature through artifice, to the "Name," which automatically subdues nature. Either the sixth or the seventh line can be read as concluding the second section, which consists of either two or three lines. Here we witness the transference from the day willed by the poet to the night which flows from the "Name." The power of love is invoked in the sixth line, and its omnipotence in preparing the lovers' night is sweepingly announced in the seventh line. Unfortunately, "Sterne ruft" seems ill adapted to the poem's increasingly intimate tone, while "Tage bricht" is too sharply dramatic a phrase to emphasize continuity.

The last three lines broaden the imagery to the point where universal nature seems to act on behalf of the poet's love. This early use of "Dinge" reinforces this feeling. As in the prose piece "Zur Melodie der Dinge" (1898), "die Dinge" are understood as a collective phenomenon. The plural form is inseparable from Rilke's earliest usage of the term to connote wholeness or the aesthetic totality of nature which the artist apprehends. "Dinge" include all aspects of the external world as well as those elements of the artist's subjectivity which he brings to his perception of the scene. To use the epistemological terminology recently brought to bear on Rilke by Käte Hamburger, the poet is here the very opposite of a phenomenologist.[10] "Die Dinge" have no existence, no meaning, apart from their place within the poet's imagination.

The image of the winds falling into the lap of "die Dinge"

10. Käte Hamburger, *Philosophie der Dichter* (Stuttgart, 1966), pp. 179–268.

evokes the union of the male and female principles and provides
a basis in nature for the final cosmic image of the beloved. Certainly the reintroduction of "dein" at the end does not obstruct
the general broadening of the lines from the individual to the
universal. Simenauer makes clear how close in Rilke's mind were
the images of woman and absolute.[11] Especially in *Dir zur Feier*
there is a constant blurring between the invocation of Lou
Salomé and some higher principle. Frau Lou embodied, for Rilke,
the ability to combine complete openness with a highly developed
individuality. She could seem utterly at one with her surroundings
while maintaining her own unmistakable "Angesicht." Rilke
strives to emulate this quality in the present poem. He is too self-
conscious. The objects evoked are too intricately contrived to
achieve a genuine life of their own. But the poem's organization is
in itself impressive. All Rilke needs is the experience to match his
technique, the involvement that will bring "die Dinge" into focus.

> Ich fürchte mich so vor der Menschen Wort.
> Sie sprechen alles so deutlich aus:
> Und dieses heisst Hund und jenes heisst Haus,
> Und hier ist Beginn, und das Ende ist dort.
>
> Mich bangt auch ihr Sinn, ihr Spiel mit dem Spott,   5
> sie wissen alles, was wird und war
> kein Berg ist ihnen mehr wunderbar;
> ihr Garten und Gut grenzt grade an Gott.
>
> Ich will immer warnen und wehren: Bleibt fern.
> Die Dinge singen hör ich so gern.   10
> Ihr rührt sie an: sie sind starr und stumm.
> Ihr bringt mir alle die Dinge um.
>
> [November 21, 1897; *Werke 3*, 257]

The poem recalled most vividly by these stanzas is the earliest

11. Simenauer, p. 534.

evocation of the second hand, written exactly a year earlier ("Ich weiss, als Kind: Mein Spielzeug fiel," November 20, 1896). Both poems give the impression of powerful emotion transcribed directly into verse, without the poeticizing Rilke customarily applied at this period. The poems stand out from their contexts because they are very close to everyday expression, to direct enunciation of the poet's most intimate feelings. Both describe extremely negative, even horrible, experiences. Through their very immediacy they bring to the surface problems Rilke will have to confront in the future. In the earlier poem the enigma of the second hand is that it is both the destroyer of childhood innocence and the source of adult creativity. Here the attack on soulless humanity leads the poet back to the problem of his own subjectivity. For the closing line is about himself, not "die Dinge"; they do not die, but they die *for the poet.*

The implication Rilke makes is that he must reject human society with its corrupting and utilitarian perceptions, and seek an isolated existence oriented solely towards "die Dinge." This attitude, which Simenauer regards as a symptom of a defective personality,[12] was crystallized in the poet's diary two years after the present poem: "Denn da Menschen und Verhältnisse eigenmächtig sind und sich ewig verwirren, woran soll man sich messen dürfen, wenn nicht an den willigen Dingen?" (December 4, 1899).[13] Controversial though such an outlook may be, it is implicit in everything Rilke wrote and must, I feel, be accepted before one can begin to appreciate his poetry. The more difficult question to which the present poem gives rise is how the poet differs from other people. What kind of relationship is possible with "die Dinge" apart from the categories of language?

In the diary entry just quoted (December 4, 1899) Rilke describes a fulfilled relationship with "die Dinge":

12. Simenauer, pp. 153–69.
13. *Briefe und Tagebücher aus der Frühzeit*, p. 242.

Hast Du noch nie bemerkt, wie verachtete, geringe Dinge
sich erholen, wenn sie in die bereiten zärtlichen Hände eines
Einsamen geraten? Wie kleine Vögel sind sie, denen die
Wärme wiederkehrt, sie rühren sich, wachen auf, und ein
Herz beginnt in ihnen zu schlagen, das wie die äusserste
Welle eines mächtigen Meeres in den horchenden Händen
steigt und fällt.[14]

This passage reads like a direct answer to the poem of two years
earlier. The insistence on "Einsamkeit" as a precondition of connecting with "die Dinge," the image of their return to life from
the death of the poem's final stanza, and the verb "horchen"
echoing the "singen" of the poem's tenth line—all this suggests a constant frame of reference for "die Dinge" in Rilke's
mind. But there is an important change in the emphasis on "die
Hände" in the diary entry. Hands recur as Rilke's image for the
creative faculty, and the act described in the diary is clearly a
metaphor for the poet's "possession" of "die Dinge." Far from
draining them of life, this act renews and enhances "die Dinge"
and thus represents reciprocal fulfillment. The poet is necessarily
an active partner, as a passage quoted earlier from "Über Kunst"
("Und das Bild ist Besitz") underlines. Hence Berger misses the
point when he says the present poem rejects all active contact with
"die Dinge" and advocates total passivity in listening for the eternal truths transmitted through them.[15] The question is not
whether or not "die Dinge" should be touched, but *how* contact
can best be established.

During the following year (1898) Rilke frequently returned
to the problem of combating the irresistible human urge to transform an object through possession and in effect kill it by denying
its independence. He described the urge even more sharply than in

14. Ibid.
15. Berger, p. 118.

the poem of November 1897 in a short story "Im Gespräch" (1898/99):

> Wurden die Dinge nicht wertlos im Augenblick, da Sie erkannten, dass sie nicht Ihnen allein gehörten, sondern so herumstehen, dass ein jeder sie anfassen und benutzen kann nach Laune? Überlegen Sie das, bitte. Ob man nicht alles echte Gold, welches man hat, langsam in Scheine umwechselt. Wie? Und endlich hat man lauter Anweisungen statt der Werte.
>
> [*Werke 4,* 226]

Rilke evolves a concept of possession that has nothing in common with this devaluating tendency, a possession that is temporary and in no way diminishes the freedom of "die Dinge"—a kind of confrontation. In an article entitled "Der Wert des Monologes" (September 1898), a critique of the monologue as the apotheosis of "der Menschen Wort," Rilke coins a striking image for the essential freedom of "die Dinge": [Der Monolog] Zwingt das, was über den Dingen ist, in die Dinge hinein und vergisst, dass der Duft eben nur besteht, weil er sich von der Rose befreit und allen Winden willig ist" (*Werke 5,* 436–7).

In a diary entry a few months later Rilke correlates this image of the independent "Duft" with the whole notion of the artist's non-possessive possession of "die Dinge":

> Bei jedem Ding will ich einmal schlafen, von seiner Wärme müd werden, auf seinen Atemzügen auf und nieder träumen, seine liebe gelöste nackte Nachbarschaft an allen meinen Gliedern spüren und stark werden durch den Duft seines Schlafes und dann am Morgen früh, eh es erwacht, vor allem Abschied, weitergehen, weitergehen. . . .
> [March? 1899][16]

16. *Tagebücher aus der Frühzeit,* p. 154.

Clearly this "Duft" is a metaphor for the essential element man shares with "die Dinge." It is in the air, around them both, and can only be perceived by the "Einsamer" whose senses are open to it. Man can possess it without infringing on the independence of "die Dinge," for if "die Dinge" are not independent they lose their meaning and hence their intrinsic value for man. Rilke's cry, "Bleibt fern," is clearly designed to protect "die Dinge," not himself. Man must withdraw from "die Dinge," allow them to breathe and sing, before he can hope to approach them with understanding.

This process of reverent withdrawal followed by an increasingly clear vision of the individuality of "die Dinge" is described by Rilke, in terms of art history, in a 1902 essay, "Von der Landschaft":

> Und so musste man auch die Dinge von sich fortdrängen, damit man später fähig wäre, sich ihnen in gerechterer und ruhiger Weise, mit weniger Vertraulichkeit und in ehrfürchtigem Abstand zu nähern. Denn man begann die Natur erst zu begreifen, als man sie nichtmehr begriff.
>
> [April 1902; *Werke 5*, 521]

As the last phrase suggests, the process is basically dialectical. The last state of understanding will outwardly resemble the first, but it will be infused with a truth born of the rejection of verbal categories. Thus it is not irreverent to juxtapose the sarcastic third line of the poem—"Und dieses heisst Hund und jenes heisst Haus"—with the famous list of "Dinge" in the Ninth Elegy:

> Sind wir vielleicht *hier,* um zu sagen: Haus,
> Brücke, Brunnen, Tor, Krug, Obstbaum, Fenster . . .

It is surely no coincidence that "Haus" occurs in both contexts, or that "Hund" is the most frequently invoked of the "Tiere" to whom the Eighth Elegy is devoted. Their very importance to him causes Rilke to protest against their crude categorization.

The first stanza of the present poem cries out against the false
clarity with which men perceive the spatial world. The second at-
tacks their refusal to admit the existence of any other dimension.
Rilke's sarcasm, so very rare in his writing, has a curious effect,
because the lines in which he employs it gain an interest of their
own. The third line, as we have seen, has a resonance born of the
juxtaposition of "Hund" and "Haus": the familiarity coupled
with the dissimilarity of the two objects suggests the future development of the idea of "die Dinge." The sixth line, again, while
explicitly ridiculing human arrogance, has a breadth of its own.
"Alles, was wird und war"—the phrase evokes Rilke's fascination
with the web of the past that controls a human destiny, the dimension explored in the Third Elegy. Finally the eighth line, although
weighted with alliteration, contains a most striking image. The
notion of proximity to God is not only the main theme of *Das
Stundenbuch,* but also suggests the cosmic intimacy of the first
Elegy. These strange resonances reflect the power of the dialectical
process Rilke himself described. Simply by naming the categories
he finds especially absurd, Rilke hints at the direction in which
he himself will ultimately move. What is important to a man is
within him from the start, and through the dialectic of withdrawal he learns how to approach it. Rilke's gradual return to "die
Dinge" was predicated on their absolute independence and autonomy.

The third stanza exchanges the more critical tone of the first
two for an expression of anguish. The poet has prepared his way
by the opening words of the earlier stanzas, "Ich fürchte mich"
and "Mich bangt." Now his distress is evoked by abrupt changes
of rhythm and shifts of perspective between the poet and those
he is addressing. The alliterated verbs in the first lines express
emotion rather than purpose. "Wehren" denotes presumably the
action of warding people off, guarding the "Dinge" so threatened
by their familiarity. With "warnen" the poet warns the people

against touching "die Dinge," and warns the latter of danger from the people. The act of warning links the poet's personal problem to the wider implication that society as a whole is in danger of atrophied responses. The simple folk rhythm of the second line enhances the wider perspective. It is like an incantation of a lost Schubertian dream, but its context turns it into an insistence that the dream need not be lost, that men need not meekly accept the death of their adolescent perceptions. In the final couplet combat is joined. The cry of "Bleibt fern" is now followed by a direct challenge to the humanity attacked hitherto in the third person. Rilke's social criticism consists essentially of the Romantic complaint that the bourgeois have lost all sense of wonder. Characteristically he is unable to separate himself from this situation, to adopt the superior posture of the "artist." He seeks "Einsamkeit" not because he cares too little for people but because he cares too much. His involvement with the whole web of existence is so intense that jarring elements threaten to destroy his creativity. The important word in the final line is "mir": the bourgeois, with their categories, threaten neither themselves nor "die Dinge" but they threaten the poet, for whom the problem of approaching "die Dinge" is difficult enough without the debasement of his only weapon, language. The very immediacy and sinuous energy of his language in this poem, the complete absence of cliché represent a decisive step forward in Rilke's ability to approach "die Dinge," even as he proclaims the need to withdraw and listen in humility.

> Wenn die Uhren so nah
> wie im eigenen Herzen schlagen,
> und die Dinge mit zagen
> Stimmen sich fragen:
> Bist du da?—: 5
> Dann bin ich nicht der, der am Morgen erwacht,

einen Namen schenkt mir die Nacht,
den keiner, den ich am Tage sprach,
ohne tiefes Fürchten erführe—

Jede Türe   10
in mir giebt nach . . . .

Und da weiss ich, dass nichts vergeht,
Keine Geste und kein Gebet,—
dazu sind die Dinge zu schwer,—
meine ganze Kindheit steht   15
immer um mich her.
Niemals bin ich allein.
Viele, die vor mir lebten
und fort von mir strebten,
webten,   20
webten
an meinem Sein.

Und setz ich mich zu dir her
und sage dir leise: "Ich litt—"
hörst du?   25
         Wer weiss wer
      murmelt es mit . . . .

                    [September 20, 1898; *Werke 3,* 262]

Although written nearly a year later, this work is placed very
close to the poem "Ich fürchte mich so vor der Menschen Wort"
in both editions of the collection *Mir zur Feier.* If the latter represents the beginning of a profound involvement with "die Dinge,"
the present poem is a summation of their meaning for Rilke at
this stage in his development. Berger treats the work as an apotheosis of Rilke's early period, discussing it in a chapter entitled,
typically, "Das unmittelbare Erfahren der Ewigkeit."[17] Bollnow,

17. Berger, p. 119.

on the other hand, notices the statistically pertinent fact that at the very end of *Mir zur Feier* there is a sudden recurrence of the word "die Dinge," always in the plural. I intend to keep both aspects of this poem in mind when discussing it: its unique expression of Rilke's outlook at this period, and its position within a group of poems Rilke seems purposefully to have gathered because of the centrality of the theme "die Dinge."

At this time Rilke was writing the prose pieces already mentioned ("Zur Melodie der Dinge," "Der Wert des Monologes"), and the governing idea outlined there is expressed in an otherwise rather weak poem written the day after "Wenn die Uhren so nah," but not included in *Mir zur Feier:*

> Schau, die Dinge sind klug und klar.
> Dein Garten, dein Haus, dein Gott, dein Jahr—
> stell sie alle um dich herum
> sie bleiben nicht stumm,
> Aber du bist nicht zufrieden mit ihnen: 5
> und horchst dem Klingen,
> das die Winde dir bringen,
> und musst dich sehnen:
>> hinter den Dingen   10
>> singen
>> Sirenen. . . .
>>
>>   [September 21, 1898; *Werke 3*, 630]

Where the names of things in "Ich fürchte mich so" had been cerebral distortions of the living reality, the catalogue in this poem is not presented in an adverse light. It is more subjective than the earlier bare statement of "Tier" and "Haus." Possession is not a barrier to perception. Indeed the possessive pronoun has a peculiarly Rilkean ring, and the concept of "Dinge" now includes anything *felt* as such, a breadth already announced in a diary entry a few months earlier: ". . . dass Sehnsucht und Seligkeit nur wie Dinge waren neben den anderen Dingen, nur wie

Farben neben den vielen Farben" (June 1898).[18] Nevertheless
"die Dinge," even when defined so loosely, are not the true goal
of man's perception. They are damned with faint praise: it is not
enough to be "klug und klar." Rilke has developed the theory of
a "Melodie" which is the order behind "die Dinge," joining them
together but not contained within them.

"Wenn die Uhren so nah" appears loosely and spontaneously
constructed, but in fact the progression of the poet's openness falls
into distinct stages. The poem begins with eleven lines in which
the rhymes are dominated by the vowel *a*. Then follow eleven
more lines in which *e* dominates. Each of these sections can be
divided in two, the first of five, the second of six lines. Rilke has
concealed these relations by the irregular numbers of lines and the
varied order of rhyming words, but a schema brings out the structure. The first five lines have one rhyme three times, another
twice: *a b b b a*. The next six lines have one rhyme four times,
another twice (if one accepts the impurity of "Nacht"/"sprach,"
which the flow of the lines demands): *c c c d d c*. The next five
lines have one rhyme three times, another twice: *a a b a b;* the
next six lines have one rhyme four times, another twice:
c d d d d c. The final five lines seem to begin the pattern again,
except that the word "du" stands out unrhymed. This expresses
the pattern's meaning, for the five sections thus established reflect what is happening within the poet. In the first section he
begins to hear "die Dinge," in the second he opens himself to
night's melody, in the third he feels his identity surging with the
weight of a past given significance and permanence by the melody.
In the fourth it becomes doubtful whether, after the falling of
all barriers, the ego can be credited with any independent existence; and in the fifth he turns towards "du," as if seeking a guarantee of his own reality in the awareness of the beloved. The
cultivation of subjectivity causes all certainty, all clear-cut de-
marcations, to dissolve.

18. *Tagebücher aus der Frühzeit*, p. 132.

The two images of the first section balance each other by contrast. The clocks, so unobtrusive in daytime, seem to grow and dominate at night. Their persistent presence deprives man of that sense of an ordered world in which they have a place. Because of the void in his perceptions, the clocks' ticking, the only constant left, invades and obsesses what remains "im eigenen Herzen." The word "eigen" quietly establishes the poet's presence as a witness to the contrasting image of "die Dinge" which, like the poet himself, seem to lose their identity at night. The rhyming of "so nah" and "bist du da?" underlines the contrast. What was imperceptible in the day looms close, and what was concrete and in the foreground withdraws and dissolves. The notion of a whispered conversation among "die Dinge" after dark was developed by Rilke in a poem written many months earlier but placed very close to the present poem in the sequence of *Mir zur Feier:*

> . . . bis sich die Dinge nichtmehr unterscheiden.
> Und halb im Traume hauchen sie sich zu:
> "Wie wir uns alle heimlich verkleiden,
> in graue Seiden
> alle uns kleiden,— 5
> wer von uns beiden
> bist jetzt du?"
> [February 4, 1898; *Werke 3*, 261]

What is explicit in these lines has been concentrated and made implicit in "Wenn die Uhren so nah." The slightly whimsical stress on clothing has been eliminated, and with it the self-consciousness that turns the conversation into a game played by "Dinge" who merely simulate ignorance. It is no longer a question of identity change between "uns beiden." The question is rather whether any kind of identity at all persists, not "wer bist du?" but "bist du da?"

In the February poem the imagined dialogue is placed at the end as a culmination of a vaguely disquieting mood picture, but by September Rilke is no longer standing outside. He uses the

scene as a prelude to extended self-questioning. The unobtrusive-
ness of "eigen" and the terse prominence of "bist du da?" impart
the strong impression that the poet himself is a part of the dissolving "Dinge," subject to the same question they put to each other.

This interchange of background and foreground and falling
of the barriers between subject and object become explicit in the
next four lines. They are weak lines because they introduce an
element of posturing, as if Rilke were proclaiming in advance that
his inherently uncertain and frightening situation entitled him to a
special dignity. The poet has, as it were, consciously grasped the
second hand without knowing where it will lead him, to poetry or
to chaos. Having discarded all conventional identification he does
not know whether to exult or to bewail his new situation, to assert
or deny his own identity. Thus he claims here that night has
endowed him with a new name, and that this name would terrify
his daytime acquaintances. The portentousness is circular—we
cannot imagine what the name would be because we are by definition excluded from the poet's state.

Lines ten and eleven, printed separately, are typical of a device common in these poems, the bridge passage between self-
preparation and revelation. In the previous chapter I discussed a
comparable passage in "Aus Nächten," written on the same day:

> Und wir schauen, was um uns begann;—
> nur noch eine Weile Angst und dann:

The image of doors opening in the present poem conveys simultaneously the feeling that the poet has become part of "die Dinge"
and that he has retained some control of his consciousness. The
doors may open of themselves, but at least they are doors, entry
ways that can be observed.

Lines twelve to sixteen articulate ideas of great importance for
the future. There is an exhilarating certainty, expressed by "da
weiss ich," in the way Rilke makes the connections between idea
and experience. In 1897 he read Jacobsen and absorbed the no-

tion of the permanently existent past, the childhood truth that persists through adult decadence. In the spring of 1898 he visited Italy and was overwhelmed by the permanence of its objects. Now, in this creative autumn of 1898, he is formulating the concept of "die Dinge" which can unite these two experiences. "Die Dinge" are "schwer" because they absorb man's subjectivity. Jacobsen is externalized: man's childhood and emotions are not dead, but neither are they within him. They are absorbed by the objects that surround him, and that is why the path to one's own identity lies through its dissolution. To realize oneself one has to open the doors to everything that is in the atmosphere around one.

The lines on childhood have a parallel in a poem written a week later entitled "Kindheit." It rambles sentimentally, but the opening lines are closely related to "Wenn die Uhren so nah":

> Auf einmal ist Alles so
> wie auf *einem* Blatt.
> Auch das, was kein Recht mehr hat,
> schläft nicht ein.
> Ich bin allein,   5
> und die Kindheit ist irgendwo
> und ist eine Stadt. . . .
>
> [September 29, 1898; *Werke 3, 631*]

The unity of experience which is a prerequisite of creation is here evoked. "Die Dinge" and the "Melodie" behind them are "auf einem Blatt," the barriers of identity have fallen. The subconscious decides which element of the past achieves priority, and it may well be "das, was kein Recht mehr hat" which the consciousness has repressed. The comparison of "Kindheit" and "Stadt" is possible because the imagery is "auf einem Blatt." Both childhood and city stand for that larger reality which always surrounds the individual, from which his existence is inseparable. He is limited by them, but they are not limited by him. As one part of a city merges with another in a chain of reality of which the individual can perceive only a small segment, so childhood opens up areas of the past which threaten to engulf the individual altogether.

The seeming paradoxes in the wording of the two poems of September 1898 actually express the same sensation on two different levels. Childhood is "immer um mich her," and it is "irgendwo." The poet is "niemals allein," yet also "allein." In the earlier poem, "Wenn die Uhren so nah," the poet describes the revelation from within. It is actually happening to him and he is surrounded by figures from the past. In the poem of a week later the same phenomenon is seen as if from outside: the poet is indubitably alone, but he can perceive the reality of his childhood as one senses the spatial immensity of a city from behind closed curtains. The depths to which a fascination with childhood can lead are hinted at by this imagery. The word "Stadt" cannot but be ambivalent, and something of its repetitive impersonality is resonant in the comparison with "Kindheit."

Lines seventeen to twenty-two of "Wenn die Uhren so nah" suggest a theme that eventually leads to the Third Elegy. If the identity is not within the individual but in the past contained by "die Dinge," what is "personal" about such an identity? It is reached through the subconscious—yet the subconscious is the side of man's nature most subject to heredity, to involuntary impulse, to the accidents of personal relationship. Can a man sustain being both "allein" and "niemals allein," preoccupied with the self yet aware that the self is but the tip of the iceberg of the past? Curiously enough, Rilke does not yet seem anguished by his own analysis. There is even something loving about the repeated "webten, / webten."

The final section of the poem is similarly ambivalent about the theme of anonymity. Rilke uses a technique familiar from other poems, the posing of a hypothetical question which, simply by being posed, becomes a real situation. The phrase "hörst du?" represents the moment of transition from hypothesis to reality and adds a dimension of naïve excitement to the last two lines. Rilke has willed this situation and seems to welcome it. The phrase "Wer weiss wer / murmelt es mit . . ." is followed by no question mark; the hypothetical condition has become a kind of affirmation.

In 1898 Rilke can perceive intellectually the hazards of self-dissolution. Emotionally he is involved with the immense spatial and temporal vistas opened up by such images as "Kindheit" and "Stadt." His formulation of the theory of a "Melodie der Dinge" protected him from the consequences of his own thinking: however many barriers fall, the "Melodie" is a constant to which all individual existences are subject, a harmony which is merely obscured by such categories as "identity." Moreover this notion of harmonious continuity seems to solve the problem of inherited language. The elaborate framework Rilke builds around the words "Ich litt" suggests his feeling that so banal a statement can somehow be reborn. The situation is an imagined conversation with the beloved, the tense is the past, and the poet's ancestors speak the words with him. Such an atmosphere, Rilke implies, endows the familiar words with resonance. It is a short step from this conclusion to some of the more pedestrian religious phrasing in *Das Buch vom mönchischen Leben* (1899), where Rilke similarly intends the aura of the monk's cell to imbue old truths with new meaning. The technique does not succeed. The conclusion of "Wenn die Uhren so nah" seems all the more faded and ephemeral because the remainder of the poem contains so much that is enduringly Rilkean.

Du dunkelnder Grund, geduldig erträgst Du die Mauern
und vielleicht erlaubst Du noch eine Stunde, den
           Städten zu dauern
und gewährst noch zwei Stunden den Kirchen und
           einsamen Klöstern

und lässest fünf Stunden noch Schönheit allen Erlöstern
und siehst noch sieben Stunden das Tagwerk des Bauern—   5
eh Du wieder Wald wirst und Wasser und wachsende Wildnis
in der Stunde der unerfasslichen Angst,—
da Du Dein unvollendetes Bildnis
von allen Dingen zurückverlangst.

Gieb mir noch eine kleine Weile Zeit: ich will die
                    Dinge so wie keiner lieben   10
bis sie Dir alle würdig sind und weit.
Ich will nur sieben Tage, sieben—
auf die sich keiner noch geschrieben,
nur sieben Seiten Einsamkeit.

Wem Du das Buch giebst, welches die unfasst,   15
der wird gebückt über den Blättern bleiben,—
es sei denn, dass Du ihn in Händen hast,
um selbst zu schreiben.

                    [October 4, 1899; *Werke 3,* 359–60]

In the final version of this poem Rilke substitutes "Mühsal" for
"Schönheit" in the fourth line, and the change indicates his developing attitude towards "die Dinge." In "Wenn die Uhren so
nah" (1898) we observed a certain luxuriant passivity, a welcoming of anonymity, of the "Melodie der Dinge" embodied in the
imagery of "Stadt," and "Kindheit." In the present poem, by
contrast, the artist vows to express his individuality "so wie
keiner," on a scale great enough to redeem the unfulfilled past.
The transition from "Schönheit" to "Muhsal" is indeed accomplished, and the "Arbeit" of the Paris years foreshadowed. Rilke
implies here the working relationship between artist and "Dinge,"
their interdependence, which I have described in the introduction
to this chapter. He does so, however, in the context of the macrocosm so dominant in the autumn of 1898. "Die Dinge" remain
subordinate to the great "Melodie" that envelops them, yet the

poet seems determined to emancipate them from this position. Despite adjectives like "würdig" the tone here is not one of reverence. By the end the reader feels the relevance of the question about all of Rilke's Russia-inspired writing, "ob hier nicht vielmehr die Vernichtung Gottes vermittelst der Kunst beabsichtigt sei."[19]

The poem "Kindheit" (September 29, 1898), once again, says: "und die Kindheit ist irgendwo / und ist eine Stadt," but in the important letter to Charlotte Scholtz (April 7, 1899), already quoted in the chapter on "Das Kind," Rilke writes: "Die Kindheit ist das Bild der Kunst." In 1898 childhood is associated with the past. It is an image of the "Melodie der Dinge" enveloping both the individual and the objects he has lived with. But in the course of 1899 Rilke emancipates the idea of childhood from time and presents it instead as a mode of perception, a model for the artist to follow. Art, the act of creation, implies a return to the child's way of seeing the world. "Die Dinge" need no longer be examined for the traces of a specific childhood, but can instead be celebrated and enhanced as ends in themselves, as the idols of a new and universal childhood, the poet's. Instead of waiting solemnly for the doors of his being to open, the poet must simply speak as a poet, and his voice will mingle with that of "die Dinge." The macrocosm still exists as the principle of harmony between man and nature, but where it was amorphous, all-enveloping, something to be *perceived,* it is now both immanent and distinct, something to be *achieved* by the poet and "die Dinge" in concert.

The important poem of January 12, 1900, discussed in the chapter on "Das Kind," can be read as a paradigm of this achievement of a higher harmony:

> Ein einziges Gedicht, das mir gelingt,
> und meine Grenzen fallen wie im Winde;
> es gibt kein Ding, darin ich mich nicht finde:

19. Kohlschmidt, p. 57.

> nicht *meine* Stimme singt allein:—es klingt.
> Die Dinge werden heller und metallen,
> und wie sie atmend sich im Raum berühren,
> sind sie wie Glocken, die mit seidnen Schnüren
> spielenden Kindern in die Finger fallen. . . .
>
> [*Werke 3,* 674]

Possibly the airy lightness and open self-absorption of these lines seem to have little to do with the cosmic resonances of "Du dunkelnder Grund." The poems are in fact only three months apart (October 1899, January 1900), and their very dissimilarity provides the clue to their fundamental common theme. For in the course of *Das Buch vom mönchischen Leben* Rilke submits the concept of "God" or "Du" to so many and varied paradoxes that it is left without any specific attributes whatever. It is best described as the absolute, an intangible goal to which the poet aspires. But, in a refinement of Angelus Silesius, it has no meaning outside of his creativity: "Was wirst Du tun, Gott, wenn ich sterbe?" (*Werke 3,* 334).

The abstractness of the absolute is illustrated by the opening words of the present poem. "Grund" recalls many metaphors discussed in connection with the hand, that central metaphor for the absolute: hands cupped beneath the world, depths into which the poet must plunge. But it is not immutable. Rilke plays with the image in the manner of the seventeenth-century mystics in a poem written on October 1, 1899:

> Du bist der Tiefste, welcher ragte,
> der Taucher und der Türme Neid.
>
> [*Werke 3,* 344]

He puts the matter as plainly as he can a few lines later in the same poem: "Du bist der Wald der Widersprüche." Even "Dunkelheit," which Ruth Mövius considers the basic attribute of God as opposed to the soulless categories of "Licht," imposes certain restrictions Rilke refuses to maintain:

> Oft wenn ich Dich in Sinnen sehe,
> verteilt sich Deine Allgestalt:
> Du gehst wie lauter Lichte Rehe
> und ich bin dunkel und bin Wald.
>
> [October 1, 1899; *Werke 3*, 343]

Nevertheless "Dunkelheit" is in fact a common attribute of the absolute in these poems. Its pervasiveness derives from the previous enshrining of the "Melodie der Dinge" in "die Nacht," but the word is subtly changing its resonances. In 1898 darkness suggested the romantic opposition to daytime categories; in 1899 it connotes the remote and impenetrable, that which is by definition inaccessible to man.

The exhilarating aspect of *Das Buch vom mönchischen Leben* is that the artist can and does change all previous definitions. The absolute always *is*—the artist can never reach it—but he can conquer more and more of its positions, force it to retreat further and further. This is the significance of the dynamic "dunkelnder" as opposed to the static "dunkel": the absolute grows darker all the time because the poet claims all the intermediate shades. By the same token it also grows lighter. In the end only absolute darkness and absolute lightness, the negations of color as it is found in nature, represent the secure realm of the unattainable. The connection between the present poem and that of January 12, 1900 becomes clearer:

> die Kinder ziehn zugleich an allen Strängen,
> die sie erstaunt in ihren Händen spüren,
> so dass die Töne vor des Himmels Türen,
> die viel zu langsam aufgehn,—schon sich drängen.

Heaven's doors never will open fully, for heaven is the realm of absolute light; but the artist-child forever pushes against these doors, just as he thrusts into the darkening depths.

The poem "Du dunkelnder Grund" also has something in common with the representative work of autumn 1898, "Wenn die Uhren so nah." Both are cogent evocations of a process going on in the poet's mind. The similarity is suggested by the internal structure of the lines. "Wenn die Uhren so nah" consisted of twenty-seven lines divided 5-6-5-6-5, or alternatively 11-11-5. The present work is divided 5-4-5-4 (in the final version of *Das Stundenbuch*), or alternatively 9-9. The irregularity of the "stanzas" makes one aware of poetic blocks with a self-contained momentum as opposed to a rounded and "objective" lyric. At the same time the overall symmetry draws the reader's attention to the central point of transition in the poem, where the first two blocks are succeeded by the second two. In "Wenn die Uhren so nah" at this point the poet's "doors" opened and his identity merged with his past (lines 10–11). Here at this point the poet turns from the cosmic task imposed by the absolute to his own determination to fulfill it.

"Du dunkelnder Grund" stands out in *Das Buch vom mönchischen Leben* because it does not play with the technique of paradox. Instead it articulates the mood underlying a paradoxical world-view: a sense of personal capacity, of freedom from a restrictive past, and simultaneously, a preoccupation with death and loss. The existential situation resembles, that of the baroque poets, but whereas Gryphius will list the glories of this world in order to arrive at the nothingness of the temporal, Rilke evokes the majesty and power of God to end in a passionate endorsement of the temporal. Gryphius is a believer attempting to cut through the world's illusions; Rilke is an unbeliever seeking to legitimize the world of "die Dinge" by imagining the worst that can happen to it, the withdrawal of the absolute. Gryphius' poetry tends to grow ever more agonized in its repetition of the static central theme; Rilke's poem, with its dynamic shifting of fundamental categories, constructs an image of coming catastrophe but leads back to a basic sense of harmony and fullness in the present.

The inversion of the seventeenth-century outlook is apparent in the fluent dactylic pentameters of the opening lines. The concentration of worldly imagery as a prelude to death is typical of the baroque, but everything else is different, as a comparison with Gryphius' famous sonnet, "Es ist alles Eitel," illustrates. Gryphius' lines are either jagged and disrupted ("Nichts ist, das ewig sei, kein Erz, kein Marmorstein") or continuous but predicated on a rise and a fall ("Der hohen Taten Ruhm muss wie ein Traum vergehn"). Always they are heavily accented to emphasize the immediacy of the horror, and filled with negatives, as if to prevent the reader from being seduced by an attractive image ("Als eine Wiesenblum, die man nicht wiederfind't!"). In Rilke's lines, by contrast, there is virtually no punctuation at all. Each line rises toward the end, as if to exalt worldly things ever higher. The rhythm floats freely, as if to envelop the imagery in a reassuring incantation, and every verb suggests persistence, duration, continuity, without a hint of a negative ("erträgst," "erlaubst," "gewährst," "lässest," "siehst").

An additional point of contrast is the emphasis on time. Gryphius constantly proclaims the unpredictability of the future ("heute"/"morgen," "jetzund"/"bald," "jetzt"/"morgen," "jetzt"/"bald"). Rilke also seems to stress the temporal limits of the present, but the repetition of the word "Stunden" and the numerals that grow ever larger ("eine . . . sieben") create quite the opposite impression. Time becomes a reality instead of an illusion, the future is contained in the present. The reader is led away from any sense of finite disaster. Furthermore, instead of indicting pomps and vanities, Rilke orders his "targets" in such a way that the impersonal images ("Mauern," "Städte") come first, and the lines build up through ever more personal and deserving realities until we reach the "Bauer," whose activities are the most essential and durable of all. The very line "und siehst noch sieben

Stunden das Tagwerk des Bauern" reads like Genesis, with the
little word "noch" much blunted by unstressed repetition.

The alliterative sixth line both rounds off the sequence of de-
clamatory images and introduces the second section, the catastrophe itself. It now becomes clear just how radical Rilke's inversion of his baroque theme is. There is no such thing as destruction in Rilke's world: the catastrophe, as expressed by the dynamic
imagery of this line ("wirst . . . wachsende"), is unrestricted, di-
rectionless growth. Life that simply continues, without any relation to the absolute, is the ultimate horror for Rilke. Many factors are at work here. The imagery of unrestrained growth is
connected with the poet's feeling, set out in the "Worpswede" essay (1902), that landscape is basically "fremd," the enemy of
man-made things—the "Dinge" of line nine are clearly man-
made, in contradistinction to the "Wildnis."

The theme of the withdrawal of the absolute is especially
meaningful to Rilke because of his sense of being overwhelmed
by the sheer mass of life. For him life is a continuum, swirling
and recurring without beginning or end. In "Wenn die Uhren so
nah" (1898) he welcomed the comforting aspect of this thought:
"Und da weiss ich, dass nichts vergeht." But there is also a distinctly uncomfortable side to it. Rilke rejects conventional categories and seeks life's underlying meaning. What if life has no
meaning, or worse, if the meaning it seems to have is suddenly
withdrawn? Since there is no retreat for Rilke, no certainties to
which he can turn for explanation, the religious imagery seemingly misused in this poem becomes appropriate after all. The believer in life, as much as the believer in God, has his "Stunde der
unerfasslichen Angst."

In *Malte Laurids Brigge* there is a scene that fulfills almost exactly the horror adumbrated in this poem: the "Leere" of the street
terrifies the woman with her face in her hands, as if the withdrawal of the absolute were suddenly perceptible. When she

jerks up, her face remains in her hands (*Werke 6,* 712). The face is the "unvollendetes Bildnis," the guarantee that past, present, and future can be meaningfully coordinated—the guarantee that is now withdrawn. Yet the unimaginable horror is that life could continue without that face: "Mir graute, ein Gesicht von innen zu sehen, aber ich fürchtete mich doch noch viel mehr vor dem blossen wunden Kopf ohne Gesicht."

And life *would* continue. This catastrophe will simply not be perceived by the many, because nothing apparently will happen. It is this nothing that is the catastrophe. If I may permit myself an image that is, I think, close to the spirit of *Das Stundenbuch:* the absolute is in life like a temple in the jungle. The temple can never be complete, though for centuries men have been building it higher and higher; but the jungle grows too, and it is a long time since anyone has seen the floor of the temple. Very few people can comprehend what the temple as a whole would look like. They lose interest in what can still be seen of the temple; the effort of continuing it no longer seems worthwhile. But the jungle never stops growing, and the time is fast approaching when it will completely cover the temple. The absolute will be submerged in the chaos of life.

Rilke places increasing stress on the importance of the artist only because he perceives the urgency of the artist's task. This poem about *Weltuntergang* is rooted in Rilke's awareness both of himself and his historical situation. Thus in one sense the absolute is nothing more than a metaphor, which Rilke mixes (e.g., "Grund" into "Bildnis") to suit the needs of his imagery. In another sense it is real. It is the mystery of man's relation to the world, a mystery lying dormant in the "Dinge" redolent of the past, a mystery no one tries to understand any more. Another famous passage in *Malte* indicates the issue, and suggests why the artist's hubris is no problem for him once he has understood what he must do:

> Ist es möglich, zu glauben, man könne einen Gott haben,
> ohne ihn zu gebrauchen?
> Ja, es ist möglich.
> Wenn aber dieses alles möglich ist, auch nur einen Schein
> von Möglichkeit hat,—dann muss ja, um alles in der Welt,
> etwas geschehen. Der Nächstbeste, der, welcher diesen
> beunruhigenden Gedanken gehabt hat, muss anfangen, etwas
> von dem Versäumten zu tun; wenn es auch nur irgend einer
> ist, durchaus nicht der Geeignetste: es ist eben kein anderer
> da.
>
> [*Werke 6,* 728]

This quotation takes us beyond the range of Rilke in 1899. The imposing rhetoric of the present poem's first nine lines is a fine example of the successful blending of style and theme. But although the logic of the phrase "unvollendetes Bildnis" demands a return to the theme of the artist, Rilke cannot yet articulate that theme convincingly. The kind of intimacy and understanding of detail that were his in the Paris years are what the situation calls for. Rilke can only give us the rhetoric of self-exaltation undermined by his fatal fluency. The language becomes vague, over-assonant. The diphthong *ei* is obtrusive. Two phrases which should be important by virtue of their content and their position in the stanza—"eine kleine Weile Zeit" and "sieben Seiten Einsamkeit"—are vitiated by their mellifluous flow. Similarly the repeated rhyme, both external and internal, of *-ieb* and *-ieben* makes what is supposed to be an intense process appear facile. Words like "lieben" and "weit" are an inadequate response to the resounding challenge of "zurückverlangst."

The stress on the "seven days" of creation makes it appear that the poet is toying with the Christian myths, yet the creation myth is inappropriate when the poet is trying to insist on his responsibility towards the existent world, not his innovatory powers. He does not increase his stature merely by invoking it. The involved image of the last stanza carries the awkward intimacy with the absolute even further. By making God imitate what the poet has done, Rilke is, as Kohlschmidt suggests, seeking "die Vernichtung Gottes vermittelst der Kunst."[20] The absolute silently withdraws from the situation, while the all-conquering art becomes hollow and smug. The second half of the poem is like so much of *Das Buch vom mönchischen Leben* in that no limit is placed on the imagery; as a result few images achieve concreteness or conviction. The first nine lines of the poem *do* posit limits: there is a "Bildnis" that must be "vollendet." Rilke is attempting to dissolve the portents of the first half of the poem in the self-confidence of his own aspirations. But the reverse happens, and he is indicted by the power of his own rhetoric.

Hermann Kunisch is puzzled by this poem, which he regards as exceptional in the context of *Das Stundenbuch:*

> Hier sind die apokalyptischen Töne der Sonette und Elegien, das Urteil über den Zeitgeist und die Maschinen vorweggenommen. Diese Ablehnung hat noch nicht den vollen Sinn der späteren Lehre von der Verwandlung des Hiesigen ins Unsichtbare, wenn sie auch auf unbegreifliche Weise über den Bereich der sonst im *Stundenbuch* umschriebenen Probleme hinausgehen. Selbst die Absicht, den Dingen als Verwandelnder gegenüber zu stehen, wird schon hier ausgesprochen; jedoch ohne dass die genaue Haltung der späteren Dichtungen innerlich begriffen ist.[21]

The very tentativeness with which Kunisch expresses these judgments suggests that he has been misled by the poem's unevenness. The radical presentation of the artist's problem leads Kunisch to anticipate an equally radical answer. Actually the adjective "weit" is very common in Das Stundenbuch, and its application to "die Dinge" hardly implies "Verwandlung." While the first half of

20. Ibid.
21. Hermann Kunisch, *Rilke und die Dinge* (Cologne, 1946), pp. 19–20.

the poem is indeed apocalyptic, it is not really concerned with indicting anything so specific as the "Zeitgeist." The juxtaposition
of such dissimilar entities as cities, cloisters, and farmers precludes any implication that he is attacking the world as it is.

The poem is essentially concerned with *affirmation*. What terrifies Rilke is the thought that the existent world will lose its
meaning because men have ceased to affirm that meaning. His
apocalypse extends in two directions: backward to the baroque
view, which he carefully inverts, and forward to the problems of
the Paris years and the need to reconstitute the concrete world.
"Die Dinge" are becoming the primary reality and the artist's
task is to serve them, to restore their relationship with the absolute. The poem is about the tangible world Rilke is seeking to
embrace, not the metaphysical quest for values of the *Elegies*. "Du
dunkelnder Grund" impels the poet towards future development.
The very inadequacy of its second half must have suggested to
him that the urgency of his mission called for more than the expansive but ill-disciplined imagery of *Das Buch vom mönchischen
Leben*.

> Am Rande der Nacht
> Meine Stube und diese Weite,
> wach über nachtendem Land,—
> ist Eines. Ich bin eine Saite,
> über rauschende breite
> Resonanzen gespannt.   5
>
> Die Dinge sind Geigenleiber,
> von murrendem Dunkel voll;
> drin träumt das Weinen der Weiber,
> drin rührt sich im Schlafe der Groll
> ganzer Geschlechter   10
> Ich soll
> silbern erzittern: dann wird
> Alles unter mir leben,

und was in den Dingen irrt,
wird nach dem Lichte streben,   15
das von meinem tanzenden Tone,
um welchen der Himmel wellt,
durch schmale, schmachtende Spalten
in die alten
Abgründe ohne   20
Ende fällt. . . .

[January 12, 1900; *Werke 1, 400*]

This poem was written on the same day as "Ein einziges Gedicht,
das mir gelingt," discussed in the chapter on "Das Kind." The
two poems, with one other brief stanza, are the only ones Rilke
wrote during this month of January, and belong together in many
ways. Indeed I find it hard to explain why Rilke should have incorporated this poem and not the other into *Das Buch der Bilder;*
both are of high quality. "Am Rande der Nacht" can be read
as a thematic prelude to "Ein einziges Gedicht." While the latter
describes the effects of creation, "Am Rande der Nacht" evokes
the process of creation itself—it is surely the "Gedicht" mentioned
in the other's first line. Both poems are dominated by musical
imagery, and together they adumbrate an increasingly personal
world structured by the motifs "das Kind," "die Hand," and "das
Ding." The spontaneous act of children in "Ein einziges Gedicht"
stands for artistic creation. In the present work the poet's childhood has by implication filled "die Dinge" with the past generations that speak through him (cf. "Wenn die Uhren so nah,"
September 1898). The motif of the hand is not stressed in either
poem, but it is the children's hands which bring the "Glocken" to
life in "Ein einziges Gedicht." Here, although it is not directly
stated, the sense of the musical image is incomplete without hands
that pluck the string that is the poet.

For Rilke the presence of the absolute in the shape of the
second hand is so instinctive a part of his poetic universe that the

preparedness of the string automatically implies a response by the "hand." Again, the string will not respond to anything less. The image pervades his writing at this time, and is most simply expressed on an actual musical occasion two months later, in lines written before a performance of Beethoven's *Missa Solemnis* in March 1900. The act of creation and the effect of a mighty work are part of the same process—as is suggested also by the creative state of the world after the completion of "Ein einziges Gedicht, das mir gelingt":

> Lass dich von den Lauten nicht verleiten,
> die dir fallen aus dem vollen Wind.
> Warte wachsam, ob zu deinen Saiten
> Hände kommen, welche ewig sind.
> [March 24, 1900; *Werke 3, 677*]

The combination of selectivity and generalization, intimacy and universality, implied in these lines, characterizes the poems of January 1900 and suggests a subtle shift in Rilke's attitude towards "die Dinge" since the completion of *Das Buch vom mönchischen Leben*. This shift is the result not of any new revelation, but rather of a stabilization of the poet's relationship with the absolute.

The consistent use of musical imagery during the early months of 1900 is in striking contrast to the bewildering variety of metaphors employed to evoke the absolute the previous autumn. In the context of *Das Buch vom mönchischen Leben* "die Dinge" were necessarily subordinate to such metaphorical abundance. "Du dunkelnder Grund" shows that they were increasingly important to the poet ("ich will die Dinge so wie keiner lieben"), but they were not yet at the center of his imagery. As I suggested earlier, the very variety of images with which the Russian monk invokes the absolute tend to cancel each other out and leave the absolute indistinguishable from the monk's own soul. By the time of the *Neue Gedichte* (1907), in contrast, the absolute has become implicit in the poet's universe, rarely mentioned yet endowing the *Dinggedichte* with an indefinable tension, a sense that the poet's recreation of the external world is also a bid to compete with its perfection. In *Das Buch vom mönchischen Leben* the absolute is everywhere yet nowhere; in *Neue Gedichte* it is seldom explicit but everywhere implicit. These poems of early 1900 are in this respect transitional from the one world to the other. The dominance of the musical imagery suggests on the one hand an abstraction appropriate to the essential remoteness of the absolute and on the other hand the persistent identification of the absolute with the intimate second hand:

> Du hast mich wie eine Laute gemacht:
> so sei wie eine Hand.
>
> [March 21, 1900; *Werke 3, 676*]

Rilke cannot be said to have distanced himself very far from the absolute, but the essential impersonality of the musical image permits him, as in "Am Rande der Nacht," to endow "die Dinge" with the significance to which his theories entitle them. As early as the summer of 1899, in the article "Ein Prager Künstler," Rilke has developed his intellectual understanding of "die Dinge" to a point which he is only now, six months later, beginning to approach in practice:

> Aus allen Wandlungen und Wirrnissen und Übergängen soll die Kunst den "Extrakt der Dinge," welcher ihre Seele ist, retten; sie soll jedes einzelne Ding isolieren aus dem zufälligan Nebeneinander heraus, um es in die grösseren Zusammenhänge einzuschalten, längs welcher die Ereignisse, die wirklichen Ereignisse, sich vollziehen.
>
> [July 1899; *Werke 5, 474*]

The concept of "Extrakt der Dinge" is a fascinating example of Rilke's theories in transition from the plural "die Dinge" to the singular "das Ding." For what is posited here is a dual process:

things should be isolated *in order that* they may be reunited in an overall harmony. "Die Dinge" are ends in themselves, yet not self-sufficient: it is their "essence" the artist seeks, an essence somehow distinguishable from them. Although the passage concerns the Prague painter Emil Orlik, one can feel the dominating influences of the Worpswede period: the breadth of the North German landscape and the resultant artistic ideal of combining a simple life with immersion in a particular landscape.

If the symbolic art form of the *Neue Gedichte* is the still life, the concentration on single forms, the art-form characteristic of the period 1899–1901 is the landscape. Rilke's idea of the landscape is thoroughly emancipated from realism, in that the component "Dinge" are presented not for any anecdotal or picturesque quality but for their essence as the artist sees it. "Die Dinge" are only fulfilled within the form of the picture, the underlying pattern through which the artist tries to approach the absolute. Epistemologically, Rilke accepts that he cannot have direct knowledge of "die Dinge." But as an artist he claims an insight into the "grössere Zusammenhänge" to which they belong. By aligning his images of the individual "Dinge" (and hence their essence) with these "Zusammenhänge," perceived a priori, he can bring about the "Ereignis" of aesthetic fulfillment. These poems of January 1900 illustrate this process vividly. In "Ein einziges Gedicht," "die Dinge werden heller und metallen": in striking contrast to the "Verschmelzung" of an earlier period of Rilke's writing, the prelude to final harmony is a hardening, a greater clarity in "die Dinge." They then touch each other, "im Raum," divorced from the irrelevant, and become like "Glocken"—a poetic *Extrakt* which has nothing to do with refined purity but rather with the careless spontaneity of children playing.

The "Ereignis" of "Ein einziges Gedicht" is an overwhelming evocation of light and gaiety. "Am Rande der Nacht," written the same day (January 12, 1900), seeks the opposite effect, the sonorities of darkness and depth. It is equally an "Ereignis," an expression of the harmony between man and "die Dinge" becoming a reality, a "poem about a poem." Here too an image is found for "die Dinge" which is as concrete and as resonant as the "Glocken" of the other poem, "Geigenleiber." Indeed the shape of the two poems is very similar: an initial section about the poetic "Ich" and its immersion in an overall harmony; the introduction of "die Dinge" and their governing image, in conjunction with the human element naturally associated with that image, the eternal present of the children or the enduring past of the human race; finally the artist and "die Dinge" come together to produce an aesthetic "Ereignis." In the case of the children, their act is so complete an expression of the creative instinct that the artist himself does not need to reappear—he is at one with them.

At the beginning of "Am Rande der Nacht" Rilke sketches the system of relationships from which the rest of the poem flows in five economical lines. The "Ich" is no passive observer to be absorbed by his environment; he is the artist whose subjectivity controls the scene described, indeed brings it into existence in the first place. Yet he is also indistinguishable from it. The image of the artist as a violin string is so satisfying because the position of the absolute is unambiguous without being obtrusive and the mutual dependence of artist and "Dinge" is made crystal clear. These relationships are rooted in the very rhythm of the lines. The first line links the concrete "Stube" with the undefined "Weite"—"meine" implies the artist's controlling presence and hints that "diese Weite" is no more independent of him than his "Stube." At the same time the line has a simplicity and a dactylic lilt that make this complex situation appear utterly natural. The lilt is more prominent still in the second line, while the words themselves swiftly add further dimensions to the scene: the room and the poetic "Weite" are awake, and thus distinguished from nature, which is withdrawing from them. "Über nachtendem Land" has a resonance like that of "Du dunkelnder Grund," as if the absolute were present both above and below the scene, plucking the poet's string with one hand and holding the other cupped beneath the darkening world outside. The scene is dependent on this retreating darkness in that only now does the adjective "wach" become meaningful, but it is not part of the darkness. The relationship with the night is thus a striking inversion of that evoked in "Wenn die Uhren so nah" (September 1898). There Rilke "opened his doors" to the night, here the night brings into clear focus that which is distinct from it, the things that are "wach."

The significance of the title is thus abundantly clear by the end of the second line: it is on the edge of night, not within it, that creation takes place. The centre of that creation is presented in the abrupt rhythms of the third line. There are strong accents on "Eines," "Ich," and "bin," whereupon the dactylic rhythm resumes, and the next accent, on "Saite," leads back into the harmonious fourth and fifth lines. The unexpected singular "ist" is emblematic of the transition from plural "Dinge" to singular "Ding." The scene as a whole is one "Ding," just as the poetic "Ich" is another, albeit of a very special kind. The similes of *Das Buch vom mönchischen Leben* have been superseded, the poet really "is" the violin string, with no need to "become" one or to imagine himself into the situation. The arrival of night has simply created the situation, not by drawing the poet into itself but by making him aware of his own distinctness and the distinctness of his environment. The fourth and fifth lines do not conflict with this distinctness but fulfill it. For these "Resonanzen" are those of the "Stube" and the "Weite," of the circumscribed body of reality to which the poetic violin string is attached. One cannot give a precise meaning to "Weite," any more than to the "Raum" of "Ein einziges Gedicht." They have a similar resonance, expressing an inner space which is yet located in the objective world, an area in the poet's environment in which "die Dinge" respond to his image of them.

Rilke has here transferred his sense of being "Im All-Einen" to a specific segment of the world in which he, the poet, holds sway. He is not thereby negating his awareness of an overall harmony, but defining his relationship to it. He is now a master of "die Dinge" as well as their disciple, a poet competing with the perfection of the absolute as well as receiving sustenance from it. It is hard to resist the symbolism of the fact that these lines were written in the first days of the new century. After the fluidity of *Das Buch vom mönchischen Leben* they represent the solid base on which Rilke's mature poetry is to be built.

The second five lines evoke the dionysiac complement to the apolline purity of the notion of the poet as a violin string. To maintain a strictly consistent image, Rilke should perhaps have written the singular "Geigenleib" rather the plural. That we have to imagine the poetic "Ich," as a violin string, spanning numerous violin bodies, emphasizes the almost superhuman tension of poetic mastery. The themes which, in "Wenn die Uhren so nah" (1898), had caused the poet's identity to dissolve in time and in space are here literally encompassed by an image which enables the poet to absorb them and to retain his identity. The key lines of "Wenn die Uhren so nah" suggest immobility: "Meine ganze Kindheit steht / immer um mich her." By contrast the perfect synaesthesia of "von murrendem Dunkel voll" gives a dynamic effect. The darkness within "die Dinge" is not simply the spatial mystery of night, drawing the poet out of himself, it is also something *heard* and therefore temporal, a querulous discontent which needs the poet's identity in time, his ability to lend it meaning. The violin image limits darkness. The darkness does not "emanate" from "die Dinge," but is sealed in them and cannot encroach on the poet's identity. The almost playful word "murren" suggests a new distance in Rilke's relationship with "die Dinge." From his vantage point as a violin string their movement can be registered and defined.

What was inchoate darkness is now subject to total particulari-
zation. Emotions ("das Weinen," "der Groll") have acquired
concrete form, as "Dinge within Dinge." Having existed in time,
they linger on in that dimension as "musical" sounds. They are
"Dinge" in the sense that a piece of music is "ein Ding." The dual
nature of the violin image presupposes the existence of "die
Dinge" in time as well as space, and it presupposes the presence
of the artist as the string necessary to evoke the temporal dimension. For while a violin has a spatial existence, its shape and
purpose are enigmatic without the sounds it can produce.

The brief line "Ich soll" belongs rhythmically to the line before. If it were placed there, the poem would fall into four symmetrical sections governed by the rhyme scheme of five, five, four,
and six lines respectively. The isolation of the two words reflects
a method used elsewhere by Rilke for marking the point of transition in a poem (cf. "Wenn die Uhren so nah, 1898). In this case,
he suggests the transition from describing the relationships to en-
acting their consequences. The two words also firmly indicate the
poet's position: he is the master of the situation yet also obliged
to participate in it; he exists independently of "die Dinge" but is
not free to deny the bonds which link him to them. Lines twelve
to fifteen, the third section, show the poet drawing the *Extrakt*
from "die Dinge." In lines six to ten we have seen the process of
isolating the individual elements within "die Dinge." Now the
Zusammenhänge are created for a new fusion of these elements.
The lines testify again to the value of the violin image. A phrase
like "silbern erzittern" still echoes the clichés of his earlier years
but it is perfectly in place here as a way of reminding us that the
poetic "Ich" is a violin string. The simplicity of the action, a light
touch on a string, brings the image into accord with Rilke's view
of the artist as a child at play. The poem comes very close at this
point to "Ein einziges Gedicht," wherein the children blithely
pull the ropes of bells and cause the sound to press against
heaven's gates.

The last six lines of "Am Rande der Nacht" enact an exultant synthesis between the artist and "die Dinge" in motion towards each other. It becomes clear at this point to what extent this poem is in a complementary relationship to "Ein einziges Gedicht." In the latter poem the absolute, as the concept of perfection, is assaulted by the "Töne" of the child artist. Here the absolute, as the second hand sustaining the artist, endows the artist with the "Licht" whereby the assault on perfection can be mounted. The line "um welchen der Himmel wellt" implies this relationship— in the context of the violin metaphor it is the second hand that plucks the string and sets the artist's "Ton" vibrating. The synaesthesia of "meinem tanzenden Tone" suggests a delightful counterpart to the "murrendes Dunkel" of line seven, and makes it clear that the dual nature of the violin metaphor is to be maintained to the very end. In the first half of the poem intangible emotions became sound, the resonances within the violin's body. Now the pure sound of the violin-string becomes concrete, tumbling alliteratively into the "Abgründe" of the violin-body.

The synthesis of these two dimensions is the "Extrakt der Dinge," and the "schmale Spalten" of the violin's body, through which the sound must pass, suggest the simultaneous processes of purification and enlargement which constitute the act of creation, or the aesthetic "Ereignis." Of course, if one is too precise about this metaphor, one notices that it distorts somewhat the nature of the violin. One cannot really conceive of a separation between the plucking of the string and the arrival of the sound from the body —the sound has no real existence apart from the string. But Rilke's poetry is not weakened by such objections. Dr. Gray has pointed out a comparable inadequacy in the metaphor of the arrow in the First Elegy ("wie der Pfeil die Sehne besteht"),[22] yet his demonstration seems beside the point. In both cases Rilke has

22. Ronald Gray, *The German Tradition in Literature* (Cambridge, 1965), p. 242.

so filled the image with his own meaning that one is quite prepared to suspend disbelief.

> Der Schauende
> Ich sehe den Bäumen die Stürme an,
> die aus laugewordenen Tagen
> an meine ängstlichen Fenster schlagen,
> und höre die Fernen Dinge sagen,
> die ich nicht ohne Freund ertragen,   5
> nicht ohne Schwester lieben kann.
>
> Da geht der Sturm, ein Umgestalter,
> geht durch den Wald und durch die Zeit,
> und alles ist wie ohne Alter:
> die Landschaft, wie ein Vers im Psalter,   10
> ist Ernst und Wucht und Ewigkeit.
>
> Wie ist das klein, womit wir ringen,
> was mit uns ringt, wie ist das gross;
> liessen wir, ähnlicher den Dingen,
> uns *so* vom grossen Sturm bezwingen,—   15
> wir würden weit und namenlos.
>
> Was wir besiegen, ist das Kleine,
> und der Erfolg selbst macht uns klein.
> Das Ewige und Ungemeine
> *will* nicht von uns gebogen sein.   20
> Das ist der Engel, der den Ringern
> des Alten Testaments erschien:
> wenn seiner Widersacher Sehnen
> im Kampfe sich metallen dehnen,
> fühlt er sie unter seinen Fingern   25
> wie Saiten tiefer Melodien.
>
> Wen dieser Engel überwand,
> welcher so oft auf Kampf verzichtet,
> *der* geht gerecht und aufgerichtet

und gross aus jener harten Hand,   30
die sich, wie formend, an ihn schmiegte.
Die Siege laden ihn nicht ein.
Sein Wachstum ist: der Tiefbesiegte
von immer Grösserem zu sein.

[January 21, 1901; *Werke I*, 459]

In the first volume of the new *Sämtliche Werke* this poem is
dated "Mitte Januar." In the third volume, the first version of the
same poem is dated January 21, which correlates it more precisely
with the series "Aus einer Sturmnacht," written on the same day
and placed immediately after it in *Das Buch der Bilder*. Presumably Zinn came upon new information between the publication
of the two volumes. Whatever the precise date, "Der Schauende"
was written almost exactly a year after "Am Rande der Nacht,"
and the differences are striking. The latter poem has a hermetic
quality, a sense that the poet has mastered the world's complexi-
ties by means of flexible yet self-contained images. Here, in contrast, the focus is constantly shifting. Exultant and belittling
images follow each other abruptly. The poet appears exposed,
uncertain of himself. At the same time the realities of the daytime
world do not seem excluded as they are from "Am Rande der
Nacht." Technically the poem is not nearly so well unified as its
predecessor, but it contains some of Rilke's most frequently
quoted lines. In discussing the poem I should like to introduce
biographical matter of a personal as well as an artistic kind, but
I hope the results will lead toward the poem, not away from it.

One extremely important development in Rilke's thinking at
this time is well described by Bollnow, although he defines the
time of the change as September 1901, the time of *Das Buch von
der Pilgerschaft*—an odd error, in that he quotes "Der Schauende"
in his analysis:

Die neue Wendung lässt sich am leichtesten so bezeichnen,
dass jetzt das Vorbildhafte nicht mehr im richtigen Umgang

des Menschen mit den Dingen liegt, sondern dass jetzt die
Dinge selber als solche für den Menschen eine vorbildhafte
Bedeutung gewinnen, weil nämlich in ihnen eine Weise des
Seins in ihrer Reinheit verwirklicht ist, die auch für den
Menschen massgebend ist, von der sich die Menschen aber
in ihrer Eigenmächtigkeit gelöst haben und an der sie sich
jetzt neu orientieren müssen. Darum wird es seine Aufgabe,
"ähnlicher den Dingen" zu werden.[23]

At this same time, however, another central notion has been growing in Rilke's mind, the notion of the "Kunstding," the roots of
which Bollnow accurately detects in Rilke's diary entry of November 20, 1900:

> Wie spricht [Clara Westhoff] von diesem schweren schwar-
> zen Kranz, den sie ahnungslos vom Giebel ihres Hauses aus
> der grauen Novemberluft geholt hat und der nun in der
> Stube so ungeheuer ernst wird, ein Ding mehr plötzlich und
> ein Ding, das immer schwerer zu werden scheint, gleichsam
> alle Trauer auftrinkend, die in der Luft des Zimmers und in
> der frühen Dämmerung ist.[24]

The traditional process of becoming a "Ding" through the accumulation of time and emotion has been violently accelerated in
this image. Simply by being created, the artist's "Ding" sucks into
itself the emotional reality of its surroundings.

There is something sinister, even frightening, about the wreath
which is made the subject of the long "Requiem" for Gretel Kottmeyer written the same day (*Werke 1*, 469). He imagines the
wreath, heavy with emotion, breaking down the lid of the coffin
and in some way absorbing the dead child's body. Recoiling from
his own fantasy the poet reassures himself:

23. Bollnow, p. 114.
24. *Briefe und Tagebücher aus der Frühzeit*, p. 393.

> Aber dieser Kranz ist schwer
> nur im Licht,
> nur unter Lebenden, hier bei mir. . . .

There remains something anguished in the poet's urge to rid himself of the wreath, as if it were a kind of monster:

> Nimm ihn zu dir, denn er ist dein
> seit er ganz fertig ist.
> Nimm ihn von mir.
> Lass mich allein! Er ist wie ein Gast. . . .

Later, of course, under Rodin's influence, Rilke fitted the "Kunstding" easily enough into the brotherhood of "die Dinge." At this stage an object like the wreath is a usurper, upsetting the established relationship between man and "die Dinge." Its implications are especially disturbing when Rilke is consciously tilting that relationship towards "die Dinge," surrendering the artist's proud mastery in favour of humble emulation. Combining the need to create with the need to abandon what is distinctively human is already a difficult feat intellectually. The reminder, in the shape of the wreath, that man is innately alien to "die Dinge," bending nature to his own ends without intending to do so, must have left Rilke deeply confused.

The chief testimony to his confusion can be found in the harrowing pages near the end of the *Schmargendorfer Tagebuch* about the "Zwischenland," the horror of wasted days:

> Wenn man das "ich" nennen müsste, dieses unsäglich zusammenhanglose, ratlos vereinsamte, von den Stimmen der Stille abgeschiedene Bewusstsein, das in sich hineinfällt wie in einen leeren Brunnen, wie in die Tiefe eines Teiches mit stehendem Wasser und Tieren, welche aus Fäulnis geboren werden. Was ist man dann? Wer weiss, wie viele solche mit dem Zwischensein Behaftete in den Irrenhäusern leben und

zugrunde gehen. Und es ist furchtbar leicht zugrunde zu gehen.

[December 13, 1900]²⁵

The confident synthesis of "Am Rande der Nacht" (January 1900) has broken down completely, because it rested on a premise of the poet's earlier years: that "die Dinge" *need* man, and are fulfilled in his "Bilder" of them. In a sense this premise is restored in the Ninth Elegy (1922): "Erde, ist es nicht dies, was du willst: *unsichtbar* / in uns erstehn?" Meanwhile the over-simple epistemology of the idea's early version must be ruthlessly swept aside. "Die Dinge" exist, the absolute exists, and they have no need of the artist's mediation.

The violin image in "Am Rande der Nacht" expresses the artist's view of himself, but it has no functional relationship to the real world it metaphorically embraces. It is this real world that is breaking in on Rilke. For a man who has staked his poetic beliefs on the relationship to "die Dinge," the sense that they are permanently separate and indifferent to him must have been intolerable (Hofmannsthal describes a perhaps comparable crisis in the "Chandos Letter," 1902). The two germinal ideas we have discussed can be seen as responses to the difficult challenge: man can abandon his humanness altogether and become part of the world of "die Dinge," or he can pour his subjectivity into "Dinge" created by himself. Apart from the tendency of these solutions to contradict each other, they are as yet essentially no more than metaphors. They posit the disappearance of the independent "ich," of whose continued stubborn and enigmatic existence Rilke shows himself agonizingly aware in the diary entry of December 13, 1900. Being a poet as well as a courageous man who faced existential problems squarely, Rilke grappled with the situation in verse, particularly in "Der Schauende."

The title reminds one of "das Schauen" in the Paris years, the

25. Ibid, p. 405.

concept Käte Hamburger has shown to be the foundation of the
Rilkean *Dinggedicht*. But the word is used here in a strikingly
negative sense, implying the poet's exclusion and helplessness in
the face of the natural world. Rilke's inward desolation, his
"Zwischensein," imbues the very first line, which expresses the
extreme separateness of "der Schauende." We know from the
essay "Worpswede" (1902) that Rilke was not at home in a
wholly natural landscape ("man ist furchtbar allein unter Bäumen, die blühen . . ."), and the combination of this least intimate
kind of "Dinge" with the savage strangeness of the storm provides a powerful negation of the world Rilke had sought to build
for himself. The absolute, so often approached through musical
and other images, manifests itself as meaningless destructive energy. "Die Dinge" respond to it, seem to receive new life from it,
while the poet is so weak that he cannot even expose himself to
it—he sees the storm only "den Bäumen an," through the medium
of the "Dinge" in its grasp. He who had presumed to mediate between "die Dinge" and the absolute cannot face this higher force
when it is most tangibly present. He must rely on the enduring
"Dinge" themselves for his glimpses of it.

The total obliteration of the human by the storm is expressed
even more sharply in the first poem of the series "Aus einer
Sturmnacht," written on the same day (January 21, 1901):

> Die Lampen stammeln und wissen nicht:
> *lügen* wir Licht?
> Ist die Nacht die einzige Wirklichkeit
> seit Jahrtausenden. . . .
>
> [*Werke 1, 460*]

In these lines, however, there is a theatrical element, a sense that
the imagination at least can be protected and can respond to the
"Sturmnacht." "Der Schauende," by contrast, has no internal escape route. His storm takes place in the daytime, forcing him to
witness his own irrelevance. The days are "laugeworden"; there

are potential moral overtones in this description of the lull
before a storm, and perhaps a sense of the storm's destructiveness
as a response to a human void. Similarly the windows are "ängst-
lich" not just in face of the storm but because the poet has imbued
them with his fears. The symbolic implication of the fragile win-
dow cutting off, "protecting" human consciousness from the reality of a storm is the subject of some terrifying lines in a poem
entitled "Fragmente aus verlorenen Tagen." Written several
weeks before the diary entry of December 13, 1900, it testifies to
Rilke's growing absorption in themes of sickness and alienation:

> wie Morgen im April
> vor allen vielen Fenstern des Spitales:
> die Kranken drängen sich am Saum des Saales
> und schaun: die Gnade eines frühen Strahles
> macht alle Gassen frühlinglich und weit;
> sie sehen nur die helle Herrlichkeit,
> welche die Häuser jung und lachend macht,
> und wissen nicht, dass schon die ganze Nacht
> ein Sturm die Kleider von den Himmeln reisse,
> ein Sturm von Wässern, wo die Welt noch eist,
> ein Sturm, der jetzt noch durch die Gassen braust
> und der den Dingen alle Bürde
> von ihren Schultern nimmt,—
> dass Etwas draussen gross ist und ergrimmt,
> dass draussen die Gewalt geht, eine Faust,
> die jeden von den Kranken würgen würde
> inmitten dieses Glanzes, dem sie glauben.
>
> [November 7, 1900; *Werke 1,* 445–46]

"Der Schauende" himself is not deceived by the storm, not reduced to the false optimism of the sick. But his exclusion from
reality is as real as theirs, and he is no longer certain if there is
any tangible distinction between himself and those in "Irren-

haüser," as the December 13 diary entry makes clear: "es ist furchtbar leicht zugrunde zu gehen." It must be thoughts like these that constitute the "Dinge" of line four, wafted to him by the storm. The use of the concrete term is not accidental, as the application to it of "leben" in line six illustrates. That thoughts and feelings can become "Dinge" is a premise of the idea of the "Kunstding" towards which Rilke is moving. At the moment he can see only horror in the growing tangibility and impersonality of his fantasies: the lurid series of images, "Aus einer Sturmnacht," may represent examples of these imaginings become "Dinge." Lines five and six express a withdrawal from an artist's exposed level. The artist must be isolated, but Rilke cannot bear the strain of being excluded from natural as well as human society. As if to echo this withdrawal, the lines are of lesser quality than their predecessors. The repetition of "nicht ohne" is clumsy, the verb "lieben" seems inappropriate to its context, and the self-conscious terms "Freund" and "Schwester" embody their own strangeness in Rilke's artistic world.

Having become momentarily detached from the scene's implications for himself, Rilke gives, in the second section, a verbal equivalent of the storm's effect. These five lines represent a miniature "Kunstding" in themselves, an attempt to transcribe the storm in words. It is a singular "Sturm," as opposed to the existential "Stürme" of the first section. They are not weak lines, but neither are they really adequate to their subject. The neutral verb "gehen," especially when repeated, reduces the storm's stature, while the parallel use of "durch" seems too pat, rooted in intellectual categories rather than sense-perceptions. The storm does not pass "durch die Zeit" of its own accord, for the concept of time is irrelevant to it. Rather it is forced through this dimension by the observing poet. The third of the five lines has an impressive starkness, marred only by the little word "wie." Its intrusion reminds us of "der Schauende" behind the windowpane

searching for similes instead of being truly open to the reality outside. From now on the language tends towards the abstract. As if
to compensate for this and at the same time to assert the dignity
of the human word, Rilke introduces the simile "wie ein Vers im
Psalter." I feel Rilke has here again withdrawn behind his windowpane, trying to reduce the overwhelming "Dasein" of the
landscape while perhaps too cunningly enlisting the religious
connotations that will bolster the abstract "Ewigkeit." The
imagery is just too neat and well ordered to evoke a storm.

There is another dimension to these lines, concentrated in the
word "Umgestalter." The word is surprisingly precise, especially
in this context, and it expresses the realm of the "Kunstding" revealed to Rilke by Clara Westhoff's wreath the previous November. Moreover, "Ernst" and "Wucht" also fit the wreath in its
final state. Rilke actually describes the wreath as "ungeheuer
ernst," and in the poem "Requiem" the wreath is so heavy with
emotion that it is imagined as breaking the coffin lid. The storm,
in the light of these verbal analogies, can be seen as a creator. It
is the manifestation of the absolute force with which Rilke is
competing, a force whose mastery of the material world exposes
the poet's images as pale and irrelevant. Rilke reaches here a
mood at the opposite extreme from the self-exaltation of "Am
Rande der Nacht."

I am aware that the "Kunstding" is nowhere mentioned in this
poem, that it is possible to read the work as a straightforward contrast between inflexible man and flexible "Dinge." But the critique
of the human condition in the third section is not phrased in
either / or terminology. Rilke uses "ringen" to describe not only
the forces of nature but also the essential activity of man. If he
were designating man's activities as vain he would surely not
dignify them with the verb "ringen." Lines twelve and thirteen
depict not alternative possibilities but a fundamental situation
which cannot really be changed. The problem lies in man's instinctive withdrawal from "das Offene," his quest for analogies

from his own experience, his need to change reality into words before he can assimilate it. By the time of the Eighth Elegy (1922) Rilke can accept these limitations:

> Der Schöpfung immer zugewendet, sehn
> wir nur auf ihr die Spiegelung des Frein,
> von uns verdunkelt.

> [*Werke I*, 715]

In January 1901 things must have looked very different. Nourished for years on assumptions like the centrality of art and the harmony between man and nature, Rilke must have found the harsh otherness of the storm difficult to absorb. The storm, as I have suggested, symbolizes the independent power of the absolute. In January 1900 Rilke was exultantly challenging the absolute with "Ein einziges Gedicht." Now in 1901 he feels excluded from the whole realm of things. The way back is through "die Dinge," not through imitating them but through *learning* from them, becoming "more like" them. As he put it in a poem of September 1901, already quoted in connection with "Herbst"; "Da muss er lernen von den Dingen . . . Eins muss er wieder können: *fallen*." In other words, "sich bezwingen" is not the opposite of "ringen" but an essential supplement to it. "Das Ringen" is man's inalienable nature and vocation, but without the ability to "fall," to involve himself totally in "das Offene," he is condemned to waste his struggle in the production of "das Kleine."

The wreath, with its overtones of introversion and isolation, is again in Rilke's mind in lines seventeen to twenty. The word "gebogen" evokes the last lines of the "Requiem" for Gretel Kottmeyer:

> Efeulaub holt ich am Abend und wands
> und bog es zusammen, bis es ganz gehorchte,
> Noch glänzt es mit schwarzem Glanz.

Und meine Kraft
kreis in dem Kranz.

[Werke 1, 476]

The words "ganz gehorchte" suggest why Rilke has, in "Der Schauende," turned against the poetic ambiance of the "Requiem." For such total obedience is an illusion, man's way of cutting himself off from "das Offene" and imagining "das Kleine" to be of equal validity: "Und der Erfolg selbst macht uns klein" (line 18). By pouring his "Kraft" into the wreath man drains himself of power and becomes a fascinated spectator of his own craft (I am not suggesting that this is implied in the "Requiem" itself, but in the existential situation from which the poem derived).

What we witness in the dialectic developed in "Der Schauende" is a radical reordering of Rilke's fundamental concepts, a conscious movement from the world of Jacobsen towards the world of Rodin. For the Rilke of "Wenn die Uhren so nah" (1898) or even of "Am Rande der Nacht" (1900) the time dimension was of great importance. "Die Dinge" gain their identity through the absorption of time, and emotions live on in them. They are in harmony with the absolute, which is intimately present in and around them, a "Melodie" speaking through them. Man's role is also in harmony with both realities—through his emotions he nourishes "die Dinge," and through his "Bilder" he crystallizes the bond between "Dinge" and absolute, bringing the underlying "Melodie" into the open.

All these relationships are broken apart by the storm image. The storm negates time, forcing "die Dinge" into a perpetual present. No longer is the absolute mirrored in a passive "Melodie." Its image now is that of an "Umgestalter," an imperious force reshaping the world at will, and it mocks at man's pretensions to being essential in the scheme of things. Through the storm image the absolute becomes both more concrete and immediate and yet more remote and unattainable. The musical imagery of "Am

Rande der Nacht" (1900) tended in this direction, away from the confusing intimacy of *Das Buch vom mönchischen Leben* (1899). Still it presupposed a continuum in which man had a vital role. Now he is rudely excluded, and the only way for Rilke to regain valid relationships with both the absolute and "die Dinge" is to acknowledge that exclusion and build a new identity based on man's fundamental median position as a value *in itself* without being "necessary" to the framework of reality. In other words the poet must begin again and learn—learn from "die Dinge" how to fall beneath the force of the absolute, and from the absolute how to recreate "die Dinge," to give them time-less existence.

The ultimate outcome of Rilke's earlier assumptions about creativity had been the wreath in the "Requiem" of November 1900, an object so swollen and distorted by its creator's emotion that it became almost horrifying. Rilke's new idea of the "Kunst-ding" is grounded in an insistence that artist, absolute, and "Dinge" do *not* merge with each other. Product of his confron-tation with the absolute, this "Ding" will stand beside the "Dinge" of nature and testify that a lesser but none the less existent creator is at work. A "Kunstding" is valid not because it expresses the poet but because it contains something of the same force that created the "Dinge" in nature. Such an attitude is the opposite of *l'art pour l'art*. It implies that art is condemned to perpetual imper-fection, with Sisyphean self-discipline as the only goal. The concepts of Rilke's Paris years, "die Arbeit" and "das Schauen," arise naturally from this view. Subjectivity is not eliminated from such an art, but is rather absorbed in it. For as the dialectic of "Der Schauende" shows, the subject must confront the absolute before a "Kunstding" becomes possible.

It is not necessary to pursue the ramifications of the angel image in Rilke's work in order to grasp the essential characteristics of the angel who dominates the latter part of "Der Schauende." This angel has the intimacy, the physical contact implicit in the story of Jacob, and it has the remoteness, the fundamental "otherness" of the figure in the *Elegies*. Such a paradox corresponds exactly to the image of the absolute as a second hand discussed in the previous chapter. Its importance to Rilke at this stage is shown by the intricacy with which the dualism is worked out in "Der Schauende." In lines twenty-three to twenty-six the separateness of man and angel is established by a mixed metaphor. Man is preparing for battle, while the angel is in an altogether different world, a harmonious world in which the very notion of conflict is out of place. The musical imagery of "Am Rande der Nacht" (1900) returns exactly as before to evoke the angel's perspective. Music remains a basic image of the absolute's relation to man. It no longer suffices for the perspective of man himself. The image of a battle, of victory and defeat, is also not wholly apposite, as Rilke shows in his development of it; but it does suggest the fundamentals of the human condition, the unmusical conflicts which he is trying to encompass. There are the overwhelming forces, storm and angel, which demand submission but there is also Goethe's "Wer immer strebend sich bemüht," the impulse toward self-assertion without which man is not man, and the artist certainly not an artist. Such a situation is not harmonious. It is rooted in the paradox of the absolute which both sustains man and withdraws from him. In "der Schauende" Rilke seeks a comparable and complementary paradox for man himself, the warrior who fights in order to be defeated.

The final section of the poem develops the intimacy of the relationship between man and the angel, the second hand. If lines twenty-three to twenty-six contain two consciously ill-matched metaphors in distinctly separate couplets, lines twenty-seven to thirty-one lock the combatants so closely into a single metaphoric and syntactical unit that one must read closely to distinguish one from the other. The importance of the fight itself is established, and implicitly, the special place of the artist. For the option of entering into combat with the absolute depends on the absolute as well as on man. One could grope eternally for the second hand

and never make contact if the hand did not choose to participate. Having established the struggle itself as a privilege, Rilke attempts to compress its paradoxical nature into lines twenty-nine to thirty-one. The hand is "hart" but somehow flexible. In the act of smiting man down it seems to caress him and mold him (how easy it must have been for Rilke to regard Rodin as a virtual incarnation of the absolute, here so like a sculptor!). The final paradox is that this gentle defeat is no defeat at all. In three different adjectives Rilke emphasizes the independence, indeed the "hardness" of man's final state. The very intimacy of the contact communicates to man something of the absolute's essential remoteness and strength. The connection between the images of the angel and the storm is now apparent. By learning to *act* like "die Dinge," to bend before the storm, man also learns to *be* more like the storm itself, the force that destroys time and the accretions of intellectual categories and recreates the underlying timelessness of "die Dinge."

Rilke had difficulty formulating this final section. It is the only part that differs greatly in the first version, and a comparison is instructive:

Final version:

> Wen dieser Engel überwand,
> welcher so oft auf Kampf verzichtet,
> *der* geht gerecht und aufgerichtet
> und gross aus jener harten Hand,
> die sich, wie formend, an ihn schmiegte.   5
> Die Siege laden ihn nicht ein.
> Sein Wachstum ist: der Tiefbesiegte
> von immer Grösserem zu sein.

First version:

> Und der Besiegte von den Beiden
> (der Sieg macht leicht verwöhnt und klein)
> der wie der Sieger ist—und rein,—

verlangt, aus Demut unbescheiden,
von immer Grösserem zu leiden   5
das grosse Überwältigtsein. . . .
[Both versions January 21, 1901; *Werke 3*, 726–27]

As the nature of the conflict is not described in the earlier version, the paradox is left in a naked state. It is unclear just why
man, in defeat, is like the victor. As a result too many compli-
ments are paid him, and the meaning veers back toward the
image of the all-powerful artist of "Am Rande der Nacht"
(1900). It is implied that he can virtually stage the conflicts
when he pleases, and that he is *exactly* like the angel—the word
"rein" further minimizes the motivation of the conflict. As if to
offset the seeming arbitrariness of the confrontation, Rilke maintains the image of a battle and exalts it at the end into a kind
of cosmic event, "das grosse Überwältigtsein." In the final version the struggle ceases to be a straightforward conflict long before
the end. It becomes, through the sculptural use of the hand
motif, a new kind of aesthetic event, and we see that this "defeat"
is likely to be a daily occurrence, much as the trees are bent daily
in the winds. The artist's task is to summon more frequent storms
and absorb their power into himself.

I have offended against the stricter doctrines of immanent interpretation by introducing such extraneous elements as the wreath
(November 1900) and Rilke's state of mind as revealed in his
diary (December 1900). In the case of "Der Schauende" I consider my procedure justified, because it is a very important poem
without being a really good one. In its initial stages, before the
emergence of the angel, the dialectic between "gross" and "klein"
is almost labored, and the concreteness of the storm dissolves as
the scene is consciously transformed into allegory. Rilke seems to
be moralizing, and doing so rather enigmatically. Lines twelve and
thirteen, in particular, are mysterious: what is "das, womit wir
ringen"? Rilke has not placed his protagonist in a "struggling"
situation, nor is it clear in what sense the storm is "struggling"

with him. Eventually this is clarified by the introduction of the angel and the repetition of the word "Ringer." But the relationship between the two parts of the poem, the images of the angel and the storm, is not fully realized on a strictly poetic level. Thus the weak line "wir würden weit und namenlos" implies an identification between man and "die Dinge," a dissolution of humanness, which is belied by the reappearance and affirmation of man as a "Ringer." To understand the poem fully, the reader must be aware that Rilke is striving to reconcile the need to yield to higher forces with the need to gain mastery as an artist. "Der Schauende" (1901) is inferior to "Am Rande der Nacht" (1900) as a work of art, and the latter displays a technical mastery not present here. Nevertheless the problems that emerge from a study of "Der Schauende" are the problems which, in various guises, preoccupy Rilke for many years to come.

Pont du Carrousel

Der blinde Mann, der auf der Brücke steht,
grau wie ein Markstein namenloser Reiche,
er ist vielleicht das Ding, das immer gleiche,
um das von fern die Sternenstunde geht,
und der Gestirne stiller Mittelpunkt.   5
Denn alles um ihn irrt und rinnt und prunkt.

Er ist der unbewegliche Gerechte,
in viele wirre Wege hingestellt;
der dunkle Eingang in die Unterwelt
bei einem oberflächlichen Geschlechte.   10

[1902–03; Werke 1, 393]

This is the third successive poem chosen from *Das Buch der Bilder,* a collection covering a very extensive formative period in Rilke's writing (1899–1906). "Pont du Carrousel" is in one sense a culmination of the trends from plural "Dinge" to singular "Ding," from "Künstler" to "Kunstding," from the dominance of the poetic "ich" to its reabsorption in the poetic subject matter. In another sense it is itself transitional, as a comparison with Rilke's two other poems about blind people illustrates. The first, "Die Blinde" (November 25, 1900; *Werke I,* 465), arises from the same subjective ambiance as "Der Schauende." Written in dialogue form, it is concerned entirely with the blind woman's way of seeing the world, her gradual acceptance of her isolation: "Ich bin von allem verlassen— / Ich bin eine Insel." This image of an island could stand as the motto for all three poems. In the third, "Der Blinde" (August 21, 1907; *Werke I,* 590), the island is viewed wholly from outside. The blind man's social context is established in the first line and thereafter he is seen purely in terms of his exterior. The "reality" of the surrounding sea of humanity is concentrated in his person, or rather *on* his person. For the blind man's feelings are also externalized; they can be *seen,* just as the world they are drawing to them can be seen: "Nur sein Fühlen rührt sich, so als finge / es die Welt in kleinen Wellen ein." The blind man does not "absorb" the world. Rather, in the third stanza, Rilke ventures the image of a marriage between the blind man's externalized feelings and the patterns which form around him in isolation from the flux. Insofar as his feelings cannot be perceived from outside, Rilke is not concerned with them.

The present poem stands, in theme as well as in time, somewhere between these two extremes. The blind man is viewed from outside, but he is not the center of the poet's attention. Despite the reiteration of his centrality in the universe, we never really see him the way we see the blind man of the *Neue Gedichte.* He is presented more emblematically, as the starting point from which the reader can perceive the underlying order concealed by the flux. He is a beginning, not an end. Kunisch writes of Rilke's themes in the Paris years:

> . . . menschliche Gestalten, nicht Einzelwesen, sondern Typen (noch immer herrscht der Zug zu den Abseitigen, Entrechteten vor, die gegenüber den Glücklichen dunkel,

> namenlos und darum dem Ding und Gott näher sind):
> Die Bettler, Die Irren, Der Blinde....[26]

It is the special quality of the *Neue Gedichte* to transform these "types" into "individuals," to make the reader feel the unique, inevitable outline of the person or thing described. In "Pont du Carrousel," on the other hand, we are well aware of the typological function of the outsider theme.

The blind man is not yet an object divorced from the subjectivity of "Die Blinde" (1900). In "Die Blinde" clear analogies exist between the blind woman's heightened sensitivity and her acceptance of her isolation and the artist's needs. These analogies persist in the language of the present poem. The lesson of "Der Schauende" is that the artist must become more like "die Dinge" in order to retain his creativity. The blind man in this poem represents an attempt at rendering the artist himself as an object, because for Rilke the obvious way to move from the ideal of the controlling "Künstler" to that of the pliant "Kunstding" is through objectification of the self, by seeking an image like the blind man, which is both part of the external world and suggestive of the artist's relations with the absolute. That is why the blind man, in "Pont du Carrousel," is placed symbolically on a bridge and relates, not to the real world around him, but to the cosmos, the "Gestirne."

"Pont du Carrousel" is not so much a "Kunstding" in itself as a poem *about* a "Kunstding," or rather about the marriage between "Künstler" and "Ding" which Rilke hoped would produce a "Kunstding." There are striking linguistic parallels between this poem and the short prose piece from this period, "Kunstwerke," in which Rilke consciously separate the "Kunstding" from the objects surrounding it:

> Denn das, was die Kunstwerke unterscheidet von allen
> anderen Dingen, ist der Umstand, dass sie gleichsam zu-

26. Kunisch, p. 22.

künftige Dinge sind, Dinge, deren Zeit noch nicht gekommen ist. Die Zukunft, aus der sie stammen, ist fern; sie sind die Dinge jenes letzten Jahrhunderts, mit welchem einmal der grosse Kreis der Wege und Entwicklungen sich schliesst, sie sind die vollkommenen Dinge und Zeitgenossen des Gottes, an dem die Menschen seit Anbeginn bauen und den sie noch lange nicht vollenden werden. Wenn es trotzdem scheint, als ob die grossen Kunstdinge vergangener Epochen mitten im Rauschen ihrer Zeiten gestanden hätten, so mag man dies damit erklären, dass den entfernten Tagen (von denen wir so wenig wissen) jene letzte und wunderbare Zukunft, welche die Heimat der Kunstwerke ist, näher war als uns.

[January 1903; *Werke 5, 634*]

One could almost substitute the blind man for the "Kunstwerke" without doing damage to the sense of either the poem or the prose passage. There is the same use of cosmic circular imagery, the same apartness from the "Rauschen der Zeiten," above all the same insistence on an order above and beyond the world of "die Dinge." In 1902–03 Rilke is still reluctant to accept the sheer concreteness of "die Dinge" as an end in itself. The "Kunstding" is not yet a simple partner to the things of the objective world.

One should not reproach a poem with not being what it does not set out to be. "Pont du Carrousel" succeeds as a poetic structure in its own right. The first five lines are tightly organized around the central third line in which the blind man's permanence is explicitly stated, albeit with a qualifying "vielleicht." The first and fifth lines frame this permanence with static imagery: the man's position on the bridge, with people moving past him and water flowing beneath him as if to bisect the human flow, establishes him at the center of a cross through which the flux of reality pours. His position at the centre of the "Gestirne" suggests the same kind of stillness-within-motion on a cosmic scale. The second and fourth lines connect these images with the explicit third line. Subtly the second line repeats the implications of the first: a "Markstein" suggests a meeting point, and its alignment with "Reiche" evokes time as well as space. People pour over the boundary from one empire to another. At the same time the empires themselves change, disappear, leaving the meaning of the "Markstein" obscure to later generations, an enigmatic intersection of time and space. The time dimension is again present in the fourth line, and again it is inseparable from the spatial imagery of the fifth. For the stars' orbits are so remote that their motion is imperceptible to the eye. What is in fact moving seems static. Like the stars, the "Markstein" appears to bespeak a spatial order, while in fact it reflects the ceaseless motion of the temporal.

Another feature of the "Markstein" which foreshadows the poem's penultimate line is its rootedness in the earth. By its obstinate persistence on the earth's surface it reminds one of the dead beneath it, the occupants of the "namenlose Reiche." The blind man is thus the meeting point of a subterranean and a stellar cosmos as well as the center of a constant horizontal flow. He unites in himself, as Rilke thought a work of art should do, "der grosse Kreis der Wege und Entwicklungen." But, to repeat, it is the idea of the blind man, like the idea of a work of art, that gives rise to these metaphors. Nothing in the poem distinguishes the blind man from the "Markstein" with which he is compared. The word "vielleicht" emphasizes his secondary status. The poet is primarily aware of the macroscosm and its need for a center, then deduces that the blind man is that center.

The word "Denn," in sharp contrast with "vielleicht," illuminates these causal relationships. The blind man has to be the nodal point, the intersection, precisely because he is the only stable feature in a swirling, chaotic landscape. The three verbs in line six evoke three different aspects of this ceaseless movement. "Irrt" suggests individual human beings, their paths crisscrossing as they establish and dissolve new spatial relationships every moment; "rinnt" recalls rather the water beneath the bridge, the flow from which no individual components can be isolated, the homogenized motion so long a *topos* for the movement of life towards death; and "prunkt" evokes a further contrasting image of the ephemeral splendor, the meaningless self-confidence of humanity in public. The three varied verbs are in deliberate contrast to the controlled order of the first five lines and the greyness of the blind man. They dissolve the macrocosm into a kaleidoscopic immediacy.

The second stanza then systematically rebuilds the order of the whole scene by developing the contrasts of the first stanza. The essence of the first five lines is presented again in line seven with the added dimension of the adjective "gerecht," which establishes a contrast with the human world. It is the same contrast as in the first stanza, presented in more concrete terms. The last three lines take up each of the three verbs from line six in turn. The "wirre Wege" recall the aimless individualism of "irrt"; the ninth line brings out both the implications of "rinnt," the fact that the water flows silently beneath the bridge as well as its metaphorical link with death; and "prunkt" is clearly resonant behind the final indictment of superficial humanity. Moreover we now see why "rinnt" was placed second of the three verbs. Its connotation of continuity provides a bridge between the chaotic motion of the concrete world and the invisible motion of the cosmos around the blind man. Thus the blind man implicitly returns at the center of the last three lines, and "Eingang" suggests the possibility that the gap between him and the rest of humanity can be bridged.

Not only are the last three lines thus centered again on the blind man; the stanza as a whole gains an indissoluble unity. Lines seven and nine are bound by their reference to the blind man, while lines eight and ten stand out in contrast. The rhyme scheme links lines seven and ten in a frame around lines eight and nine. The intersection of dimensions described in the first stanza is given poetic reality in the second. Both the contrast between the blind man and his surroundings and the possibility of reuniting these two orders of reality are embodied in the structure of the lines.

The poem's title suggests yet another structural element. A carousel seen from a distance is a colorful image of disorderly life. Close to, it is a stable generator of repetitive motion around a central nodal point. The two levels of reality embodied in the carousel are the basic components of Rilke's bridge, with the blind man at its center: visible "Prunk," invisible stability. Form as well as structure reflects the title. The first five lines are like a circle of images describing the blind man. These images are then concentrated, as if by unseen spokes in a wheel, into the summation of the seventh line. Conversely, the world around the blind man is compressed into the sixth line, while each of the three verbs, again as if through spokes, expands to claim a line for itself at the end.

Yet the poem is not wholly satisfactory. The circular construction implies a danger Rilke does not entirely avoid, the danger of repetition. The meaning is essentially present in the first two lines, and the remainder of the poem merely amplifies it, building concentric circles around it. The root of the matter is that the blind man is not really a part of "die Dinge." Rilke *wills* him to be "ein Ding," but the source of inspiration remains the analogy between blindness and creativity established in "Die Blinde" (1900). The emotive force in the very idea of the blind man is intended to sustain him as an image, while the poet constructs around him his role as a "Ding." The poem is a "Kunstding" in a very literal sense: a "Ding" built up through "Kunst," a symbol of the overriding aesthetic order centered on the figure of the artist-blind man. The mature concept of a "Kunstding" implies a poem built on the concreteness of an external phenomenon and aspiring to a validity comparable to that of its model. "Pont du Carrousel" is a poem still in transition from the primacy of "Kunst," with the associated aesthetic values of "die Dinge," to the unambiguous primacy of "das Ding" in its singularity and in its freedom from aesthetic prerequisites. Rilke displays here much of the formal mastery of *Neue Gedichte,* but at the core of his concentric circles is the hollowness of an image not fully realized.

The word "Ding" hardly occurs in Rilke's poetry before 1897. By 1902 it is perhaps the central motif in both his theory and his practice. The term undergoes constant shifts of meaning in the poems I have chosen from these five years. The basic situation is an interaction between the poetic "Ich" and "die Dinge," and this interaction—although this can be seen only in retrospect—tends toward increased independence for "die Dinge." In the first poem, "Ich möchte Purpurstreifen spannen" (June 1897), "die Dinge" are a passive component of a unified natural order. True, they are an important element—the winds "fall into their lap" —but only as receivers; they exude no aura, no strength of their own. The poem is wholly anthropocentric: the whole natural scene "ist bang nach deinem Angesicht," and the time period projected in the poem is conceived and controlled by the poetic "ich." The second poem, "Ich fürchte mich so vor der Menschen Wort" (November 1897), in contrast, pursues the implications of such anthropocentricity and protests against them. If man really "creates" nature, he has done a poor job of it, because he has replaced direct perceptions by empty verbal categories. The poet pleads for the independence of "die Dinge" from such philistinism, but the last stanza makes clear how relative this independence is. "Die Dinge" still have no solidity, they become lifeless at the philistine's touch; and the "life" which the poet attributes to them is essentially the art of pleasing himself: "Die Dinge singen hör ich so gern." The shift in perspective between these two early poems lies in the position of the poetic "ich" rather than in "die Dinge" themselves.

In "Wenn die Uhren so nah" (September 1898), "die Dinge" have acquired reality on two distinct levels. They become independently alive at night, when vulgar intruders cannot touch them, but their independence is sharply circumscribed by its relationship with the night. Rilke seeks "das Gemeinsame," and "die Dinge" present themselves, as individuals, only very tentatively, "mit zagen Stimmen." On the other hand they have also gained great importance as repositories for the poet's subjectivity. There is no conflict here with Rilke's view of himself as "creator" of "die Dinge." Once he has "created" them they become essential to him, preservers of a past that otherwise could not be recalled. They gain a kind of independence through time: created by the poet but not contained by him, they live a life of their own from the segments of his life, and suggest the total fluidity of personal identity. The poet's focus shifts from the "Naturdinge" of the first two poems to the "Gebrauchsdinge" of his immediate surroundings—but such labels should be used very sparingly. Rilke himself made no such distinctions, and the more intimate vision of this poem reflects the theme of the night rather than any arbitrary division within "die Dinge."

All such differentiations are irrelevant to "Du dunkelnder Grund" (October 1899). Indeed they are superseded by the important contrast between "die Dinge" and "Wasser und Wachsende Wildnis," between shape and shapelessness. At this time, as *Geschichten vom lieben Gott* (November 1899) testifies also, Rilke was seeking comprehensive myths which would give permanent meaning to the artist's life, would render the artist as indispensable to the absolute as he already is to "die Dinge." "Die Dinge" have an essential but secondary role. In May 1899 Rilke writes the letter to Frieda von Bulow in which he says: "Alle Dinge sind ja dazu da, damit sie uns Bilder werden in irgendeinem Sinn." They are the artist's raw material, the theater in which the drama of his relationship with the absolute is played out. In "Du dunkelnder Grund," "die Dinge" have become an independent entity, but they are seen *as a whole*. Once again the shift in perspective lies primarily in the poet's view of himself and his cosmic role. The social theme of "Ich fürchte mich so vor der Menschen Wort" has combined with the theme of personal fluidity in "Wenn die Uhren so nah" to produce a new theme, that of the artist's responsibility towards "die Dinge." Their destiny may be only to become his "Bilder," but the need is mutual, for the various elements of his personal identity are scattered among them. Thus in seeking out and formulating the essence of "die Dinge" the poet will also be reconstructing his own identity. To complete the circle, he will thereby rescue the absolute from the neglect to which human intellectual categories have condemned it. The idea of art as "Aufgabe" is present here but only in the context of art's supreme importance. All the artist really has to do is "die Dinge lieben." Mere understanding of his cosmic role will enable him to fulfill it.

The same universality of purpose is the theme also of "Am Rande der Nacht" (January 1900), but new emphases are evident. First, the artist gives himself a more concrete location in time and space, eliminating the abstract, oracular quality which so often renders *Das Buch vom mönchischen Leben* diffuse. Second, although "die Dinge" are still in the undifferentiated plural, they are given concrete imagery ("Geigenleiber") to which the poet remains faithful throughout the poem. He is actually "realizing" the essence of "die Dinge" instead of merely claiming to do so. As a corollary to this the absolute is very much in the background. The violin image binds the absolute, the artist, and "die Dinge" together in a highly functional relationship, which has no need of rhetoric. To contrast the persona of the monk with the metaphor of the violin string may seem forced, but it does underline the point that the artist now has no "outside commitments." He is no more and no less than the articulator of the violin's depths. There is a subtle shift from the metaphor of "Aufgabe" to that of "Arbeit." This gives "die Dinge" their enhanced status in this poem. In content their nature is no different from what it has been since "Wenn die Uhren so nah" (1898)—a repository for human emotion. Formally they have become the central point of focus for the poet, the core from which his imagery emanates.

All five of these poems present "die Dinge" in terms of human subjectivity. In "Der Schauende" (January 1901) the crucial change occurs which leads to the genuine independence of "die Dinge." The change derives from the artist's loss of faith in the importance of his role. The storm both excludes him from the interaction between "die Dinge" and the absolute and makes him look at "die Dinge" themselves in a new light. They are self-sufficient as objects. Just as the absolute has no need of the artist to transmit its power, so "die Dinge" have no need of mankind's emotions in order to live in harmony with the absolute. The image of the angel in the second half of the poem offers the poet a way not of becoming indispensable again but of regaining some kind of function. In a sense the functionality of "Am Rande der Nacht" has prepared the way for this. As a violin string the artist has already "fallen" from more exalted images of himself, and now he must make "falling" the central element in his life style. For "falling," bending before the wind, is the secret of "die Dinge," their way of maintaining themselves amid the violent and contradictory forces of the world.

In "Pont du Carrousel" (1902–03) the blind man is an image of the new aesthetic. Both the emotive terms in which he is presented and the cosmic imagery surrounding him suggest that he is in part an embodiment of the artist's destiny. In the basic perspective of the poem he is a "Ding," a human being who has become inwardly and outwardly motionless not by resisting life's forces but by passively letting them flow around him. This new centrality of "die Dinge" is less a negation of the earlier subjectivity than a radical development of it. The blind man, after all, implicitly retains both his human faculties and his social status as a living criticism of society. Rilke has not lost interest in these things (as *Malte* makes clear) but is concerned to integrate them with the concrete, knowable world. His "objective" approach is no revival of realism. It does not involve the random selection of subject matter or the requirement that subjectivity be excluded. Rilke's "Dinge" always have relevance to the human world. A random glance through the *Neue Gedichte* reveals such titles as "Abschied," "Todes-Erfahrung," and "Auferstehung." Rilke seeks to bring such ultimate matters to life in everyday images, just as the significance of the blind man in "Pont du Carrousel" becomes evident only within the disorderly framework of the bridge on which he stands.

5   A Circle of Images

The three motifs I have discussed are all related to the act of creation. All three derive their peculiar resonance from a tension between the simplicity of their explicit meaning and the complexity which Rilke invests in them. This tension is especially evident in Rilke's use of the child image, an image with two wholly dissimilar sources. Rilke embraced the romantic ideal of childlike spontaneity, but remained aware that the ideal bore no relationship to the childhood he had personally experienced. The image of a child thus provoked contradictory reactions in him: pessimism at the spectacle of the early loss of immediacy in modern children, and a sense that the total darkness of his own childhood meant that a child's potentialities lay undeveloped within him. The paradoxical idea of a "future childhood" underlines Rilke's identification of the artist's mode of perception with that of the child.[1] The goal of artistic maturity and the goal of achieving his own childhood become the same for him. Hence his paradoxical insistence, in the early Paris years, on work as an end in itself. Rilke has no need to seek inspiration, because all the inspiration he could ever need lies within him in the shape of an unrealized childhood that can be drawn to the surface only through ceaseless self-discipline. The construction of a poem involves concentration and hard work. Once it is completed and a valid new "Kunstding" has entered the world the absolute rewards Rilke with that sensation of immediacy which his poetry can convey to others. Childhood is a state of mind which the poet cannot

1. In 1903, when discussing his early years in a letter to Ellen Key, Rilke evoked this paradox succinctly: "Ich lebe nicht in Träumen, aber im Anschauen einer Wirklichkeit, die vielleicht die Zukunft ist" (April 3, 1903; *Briefe aus den Jahren 1892–1904* [Leipzig, 1939], p. 336).

achieve on his own, but which he can *earn* by striving in his poetry
for the paradox of conscious spontaneity.

I have used the term "absolute" to describe that force which
rewards Rilke in his pursuit of paradoxical goals and never allows him to relax and consolidate past achievement. Life becomes
a constant confrontation with this force, and the hand image
frequently expresses the mode of that confrontation. The idea of
human striving is embodied in the image of the artist grasping
the outstretched hand of the absolute; and the acceptance of human limitations, the self-effacing affirmation of natural rhythms,
is expressed by the "falling" of the poem "Herbst" (1902), the
universal falling towards the cupped hand of the absolute. The
hand stands for relationship in all its forms, especially the relationship of the artist with his material. The hand is thus often
the only reality of which Rilke feels certain. In the act of creating,
the functional movement of the hand is at the center of a continuum between subject and object that has no firm boundaries.
In a barren period, the hand seems to acquire a life of its own,
restlessly seeking new functions and trying to pull the poet's inert
subjectivity in its wake.

"Die Dinge" are the elements of the external world to which
the artist must dedicate his work. Because objects combine inherent spatial stability with the capacity to absorb time serenely, they
represent a permanent challenge to Rilke. In their self-contained
perfection they express without effort the underlying harmony of
the world. They are models of what the hand of the absolute can
accomplish and as such a constant reproach to the poet, whose uncertain identity can achieve only momentary reality in works of
art. Rilke's criterion for a "Kunstding" is the extent to which it attains the stable simplicity of ordinary natural and domestic objects, but "die Dinge" do lack a dimension which the work of art
possesses. Like the child, they are unaware of their own significance. This limitation gives the poet his opportunity and also his
burden: to achieve a new childhood means to perceive objects

again with the immediacy of a child—but also to recapture in an enduring form what the child cannot articulate and cannot retain. In such an attempt Rilke is both adding a new dimension to "die Dinge" beyond the perfection already achieved by the absolute and turning the curse of consciousness into a blessing.

One could virtually construct the ideal image of the artist out of these essential elements. Rilke does in fact attempt to do so, in a poem of November 1902 about Rodin of which two versions exist. Later that month Rilke began his first essay about Rodin, a work which is both flagrantly hagiographical and full of instinctive insights. Rodin has been called a "man for all seasons," in his combination of vitalism and pessimism, of naturalism and formalism. This enigmatic breadth inspired Rilke to build a mythology of art around his works. In his *Geburt der Tragödie* (1872) Nietzsche made comparable use of Wagner as the central figure in his philosophy of drama. The interpretation of Wagner's music is brilliant but extrinsic—it leads away from the felt texture towards a theoretical framework. So it is with Rilke and Rodin. Rilke's discussions of individual sculptures tend always to lead into formulations of theories in terms that are essentially Rilkean. Of course, no clear line can be drawn. Rilke was already thinking sculpturally under his wife's influence, and the impact of Rodin's work profoundly affected both his ideas and his methods. Much in the essay is new and reflective of a genuine confrontation with the master's art: terms like "Oberfläche," "Raum," "Gebärde" begin only now to acquire their full significance. At the same time the picture of a total artist that emerges from the essay, the god-like figure who combines instinct with industry, love of detail with grandeur of conception, the material with the immaterial—this is a myth built by the poet from the inner needs and thematic preoccupations of his own past.

Rodin (First Version)
Er hat nicht Kindheit, nicht Alter.

Einsam steht der Gestalter
unter Gestalteten.
Seine entfalteten Hände
tragen als Flügel die Dinge.   5
Er ist allein mit seinen schweren
kreisenden Händen,
die Steine gebären.
Und er ist mit den Steinen allein
wie ein noch nicht gestorbener Stein.   10
[November 10, 1902; *Werke 3, 763*]

This poem is sculpturally constructed, in the sense Rilke attributes to Rodin: each section is a self-contained image independent of all the other images. The sections are bound very closely
by the actual words which lead associatively from one image to
another. The poem is thus a continuous whole and at the same
time a configuration of independent surfaces. Furthermore, like
the lovers in Rodin's "Kiss," two central themes mingle with each
other from varying perspectives throughout the three sections:
the theme of the artist's loneliness and that of his creativity.
Except for the first line, which is a kind of motto, the poem has
three sections, of four, three, and two lines. Each is initiated by
the theme of loneliness, and each then qualifies that theme by
placing the artist in the context of creation. The three sections
correspond to the different perspectives from which a sculpture
may be viewed. In the first the work as a whole claims its place
in the "Raum," the setting created by other "Dinge." In the
second a new "Ding" is formed by the merging, the interaction
of two formerly disparate "Dinge," which is described in the essay on Rodin (*Werke 5, 165*). In this poem it is the actual involvement of the artist with his material that gives rise to the
new reality. In the last of the three sections the emphasis is on
the texture of a sculpture, a solidity paralleled by the artist's inner
hardness and certainty.

The path from this poem to "Pont du Carrousel" (1902–03)

is clear. The problem of translating artist directly into "Kunst-ding" is too complicated by the subjectivity and ambivalence of the actual words that must be used to achieve the clear outline Rilke sought. The blind man, at one remove from the artist, can be more readily placed among "Dinge" that are not simply other works of art wrapping the "Kunstding" in reflections of itself.

The agelessness of the blind man in "Pont du Carrousel" is evoked by the opening line of the present poem, a line that at once establishes the poet's myth-making intentions. In reality Rodin has of course had a childhood and is now old, but the temporal dimension of life is subsumed in the suprapersonal single-mindedness of a creator's existence. Again the essay on Rodin reveals the full resonance of this superficially negative reference to childhood:

> [Sein Leben] wird eine Kindheit gehabt haben, irgendeine, eine Kindheit in Armut, dunkel, suchend und ungewiss. Und es hat diese Kindheit vielleicht noch, denn—, sagt der heilige Augustinus einmal, wohin sollte sie gegangen sein? Es hat vielleicht alle seine vergangenen Stunden, die Stunden der Erwartung und der Verlassenheit, die Stunden des Zweifels und die langen Stunden der Not, es ist ein Leben, das nichts verloren und vergessen hat, ein Leben, das sich versam-melte, da es verging. Vielleicht, wir wissen nichts davon.
>
> [*Werke 5*, 142]

Rilke maintains the Jacobsenesque theme of the "preserved past" at the very moment when he is focusing on new problems. There are no sharp breaks in Rilke's development; his own thinking enacts "ein Leben, das sich versammelte, da es verging."

The emphases of the individual sentences point to the under-lying direction of the poet's thought. Rodin "probably" had a childhood, he "perhaps" has it still. This "perhaps" grows into the apparent certainty of "es ist ein Leben, das nichts verloren," but a bald statement of ignorance supervenes. What is important is not

what is "probable" about Rodin but what is "certain," what can be
deduced from his work and his character as an artist. In this way
the theme of childhood can be detached from the mere subjective
experience of childhood. The phrase "Kunst ist Kindheit" is not
negated but clarified by the line "Er hat nicht Kindheit, nicht
Alter." The negative applied to childhood is inseparable from that
applied to age. Together they simply negate the notion of "werden," of a human being developing in time. Rodin "almost certainly" had a full childhood, but "wir wissen nichts davon." By
aligning himself with "die Dinge" the artist necessarily negates his
humanness, or rather that part of his humanness which remains
tied to subjectivity, to emotions that fall prey to time. "Kindheit"
and "Dinge" are indissolubly linked, but true childhood is something apart from any specific child (a very Rilkean thought—
compare the phrase "Niemandes Schlaf" from his "Grabspruch").

The artist, in other words, lives the childhood of the human
race, and his own childhood is incidental to this task. The subjective theme, broached in "Wenn die Uhren so nah" (1898), of
the individual's identity merging with that of his ancestors has
become the basis of a rigorous objectivity rooted in the artist's
mythic potentiality. In the introduction to his subsequent lecture
on Rodin (1907), Rilke expresses this very clearly:

> Mir ist zu Mute wie einem, der Sie an Ihre Kindheit erin-
> nern soll. Nein, nicht nur an Ihre: an alles, was je Kindheit
> war. Denn es gilt, Erinnerungen in Ihnen aufzuwecken, die
> nicht die Ihren sind, die älter sind als Sie; Beziehungen sind
> wiederherzustellen und Zusammenhänge zu erneuern, die
> weit vor Ihnen liegen.
>
> [*Werke* 5, 207–08]

Another poem called to mind by the phrase "nicht Kindheit,
nicht Alter": is "Der Schauende" (1901), in which the landscape
under the storm's impact is "wie ohne Alter." In that poem the
storm itself is invoked as "ein Umgestalter," and here Rodin is

"der Gestalter." He fulfills the synthesis, so desperately sought in "Der Schauende," between the need for passivity and the need to create. He can shape "die Dinge" so easily because, like them, he is "ohne Alter." The poem's first five lines situate the artist at the point of spatio-temporal intersection, the productive moment when the unformed "Dinge" are about to pass out of time into the timelessness of the artist's past creations ("Gestalteten"). I have discussed earlier the significance of folded hands, and Rodin is the very antithesis of the withdrawing nun in "Zwei Nonnenhände" (1897). He is the artist open to the world, his hands wholly involved with the second hand. The wing metaphor embodies many characteristic connections: the artist's hands now are as closely bound up with "die Dinge" as wings to a bird's body. At the same time they are not statically attached, but, again like wings, carry "die Dinge" upward towards the absolute, the power that makes possible the transformation of "die Dinge" into "Kunstdinge" outside time. The two poems of January 12, 1900, which enact the creative process, echo in this image. In "Ein einziges Gedicht" the exuberant child artist flung his "Töne" against heaven's gate, and here the sculptor moves in the same direction with the deliberate maturity of "die Arbeit." In "Am Rande der Nacht" "die Dinge" strove for the redemption of the violin string's silvery tune, and here the artist, masterful but no longer absolute, himself seeks out and transforms the passive "Dinge."

The second stanza, as if by association, concentrates on the hands themselves, the actual point of fusion between subject and object, between the pure form of the absolute and the as yet unformed "Dinge." This unifying role is stressed by the accompanying adjectives: the hands are "schwer" because imbued with the essence of "die Dinge," with the ability to fall beneath the weight of the absolute; at the same time they belong to the formed world of the absolute itself, the realm of perfect circles and universal order of which the blind man in "Pont du Carrousel" is also a part. The verb "gebären," however, suggests why the blind man is a more suitable subject of a "Kunstding" than the artist himself. This verb belongs to an essentially foreign sphere, the sphere of undifferentiated reproduction; whereas Rilke's artist is, as we have seen, not part of the world of becoming. His creative act negates mere temporality. It is anti-vitalistic insofar as it transforms something already living into something timeless. With so emotive a term as "gebären," Rilke chose a vivid image that goes against the grain of the poem as a whole. In *Das Buch vom mönchischen Leben,* Rilke used so many different images for the absolute that no clear frame of reference was ever established. In the same way the very range of imagery available to evoke the artist ultimately vitiates the present poem's coherence. It becomes clear why "die Dinge" are so important to Rilke: they anchor the governing drama of his life, the relationship between artist and absolute, a drama to be summed up in the opening lines of the First Elegy. In his earlier years Rilke lacks the poetic equipment for such cosmic tensions, and "die Dinge" act as intermediaries. They contain the constancy of the absolute outside time, and they yield to the absolute's force as the poet himself must learn to do.

The image of "Steine" dominates the last three lines, reiterated as if to draw a circle around the artist, uniting the potential with the already realized. The term seems used as a synonym for "Kunstding" in a sculptural context. But Rilke here incorporates the resonance of "Stein" as a substance as well as an isolated object. Because Rodin is a sculptor, his art yields a potent image for art as a whole—the production of that which is inert, i.e., timeless. In the last couplet the paradox is turned around and applied to the artist himself: he is like his own statues, except that he must bear the imperfection of living. The "gestorbene Steine," to crown the paradox, are truly living, in the sense of being outside time. The artist is an unfinished sculpture, continually fashioning the "Stein" of his own being.

Rilke found a striking image for the artist's situation in Rodin's "Karyatide," a figure symbolically loaded down with its own unformed substance, condemned to bear the sisyphean burden of incompleteness:

> ... ein weiblicher Akt, knieend, gebeugt, in sich hineingedrückt und ganz geformt von der Hand der Last, deren Schwere wie ein fortwährender Fall in alle Glieder sinkt. Auf jedem kleinsten Teile dieses Leibes liegt der ganze Stein wie ein Wille, der grösser war, älter und mächtiger, und doch hat seines Tragens Schicksal nicht aufgehört. Er trägt, wie man im Traum das Unmögliche trägt, und findet keinen Ausweg.
>
> [*Werke 5,* 175]

The stone on the artist's shoulder is the absolute, evoked yet again in terms of the second hand ("ganz geformt von der Hand der Last"). But the image of the caryatid implies stone underneath as well as above. The artist is sustained as well as driven on by the absolute, constantly aware of both his beginning and his end: the phrase "noch nicht gestorben" returns the reader to the dimension of the opening line "nicht Kindheit, nicht Alter." The first line isolates the artist by removing him from his subjective life. The last line returns him to that life, but in a sense that ensures the persistence of timelessness. Having observed the artist intensively in his creative context, the poet feels he can venture the words "noch nicht gestorben" as the essence of the sculptor's subjective life. Knowing his caryatid-like status between the impersonality of unformed life and the impersonal burden of the absolute, the sculptor accepts his purely temporary status as the forever incomplete prototype of his own "Kunstdinge."

Rodin (Second Version)
Er hat nicht Kindheit, nicht Alter.
Seine Kindheit war die Jugend der Steine

und sein Alter ist nicht das seine.
Einsam steht der Gestalter
unter Gestalteten;   5
in seinen entfalteten Händen
liegen die Länder.
Seine Dinge kreisen um ihn wie Sterne,
und stehn wie Sternbilder um ihn her.
Seine Nähe erbaute er,   10
und dann warf er sich eine Ferne.

[November 10, 1902; *Werke 3,* 764]

This is not so much a new version as a new poem that happens to include some of its predecessor's lines. The two poems are
related in much the same way as the two written on January
12, 1900, "Am Rande der Nacht" and "Ein einziges Gedicht."
The first presents the artist in the act of creation, the second
evokes the universal harmony that dawns as creation is completed.
There are strong indications that this change of perspective has
occurred in the second version of "Rodin." The phrase "liegen die
Länder" stands in striking contrast to the corresponding phrase in
the first version, "tragen die Dinge." In the latter image the artist's hands are recognizably his own, engaged in the presentation
of "die Dinge" to the absolute with a view to rendering them
timeless. In the second version Rilke's myth-making seems to have
led him to portray the artist as not merely emulating but actually
becoming the absolute. The passive stability of the cupped hands
recalls the image of the second hand in the nearly contemporary
poem "Herbst" (September 1902):

Und doch ist Einer, welcher dieses Fallen
unendlich sanft in seinen Händen hält.

Rodin has clearly achieved this cosmic status by the act of creation. The suggestion that the creative act is now completed is
strengthened by the description of it at the end in the past tense.

The emphasis on the harmony resulting from creation gives the poem many more points of contact with "Pont du Carrousel" than the first version has. Whereas the first version reiterates the theme of loneliness, here it is stated only once, to be virtually displaced by images of the circling cosmos. Rodin's isolation in this poem is not the subjective prerequisite of creation but the objective centrality of the blind man in a universal scheme. This universality of context is underlined by following the word "Sterne" with "Sternbilder" in the next line. A similar thematic repetition occurs in "Pont du Carrousel," in the sequence "Sternenstunde . . . Gestirne."

This poem is also more clearly oriented than the first version around the circle of images "Kind"-"Hand"-"Ding." The amplification of the first line both emphasizes the impersonality of the childhood theme and adds to the vividness of the caryatid images. The artist has unformed stone both below and above him. Below it is a support, above it is a burden. Below it is the childhood spontaneity out of which the self-formed artist grows, above it is the unattainable solidity of the absolute, against which the aging artist thrusts his head. Youth and age, raw material and absolute, artist and world—all are bound together in the unifying substance of "Stein." The initially temporal concept of childhood has led to a wholly spatial imagery. Both youth and age are negated in the first line because, as the second and third lines show, they coexist for the artist from the beginning. Indeed it is the opening words "Er hat" that are in fact negated: since the artist has no existence outside his vocation, the notion of possessing time has no meaning. Like the blind man who is the "Markstein namenloser Reiche," Rodin stands among his own creations, a timeless symbol of two simultaneous perspectives, the formlessness from which his art has been fashioned ("Jugend der Steine") and the unseen perfection which he can never quite attain ("nicht das seine"). Rilke has moved far from the lines in "Wenn die Uhren so nah" (1898): "Meine ganze Kindheit steht / immer um mich her." There the theme of childhood implied inner detachment from the visible world, here it inaugurates a celebration of total continuity between the world of objects and whatever can be known of the "inner life." Rodin, like the blind man, is interesting only for what he is *seen* to be, but "only" is inaccurate when the sensitive observer can see such a comprehensive image of harmony.

The structure of the first version, beginning with the basic scene "Einsam steht der Gestalter / unter Gestalteten," leads ineluctably to the functional moment of creation, when the thrice-repeated word "Stein" evokes both the physical contact and the spiritual oneness of the artist with his material. The second version begins with the same scene but leads away from the "Gestalter" instead of towards him. As before, the hand image is at the poem's center. Whereas in the first version the hands dynamically enclose "die Dinge" as if between wings, here, although still "entfaltet" and open, they are essentially passive. In the poem "Wenn ich gewachsen wäre irgendwo" (September 1899) Rilke portrays the absolute as a young bird in the monk's cupped hand. Now, through the mythology of the artist, he can emancipate himself from such self-conscious images. Like the blind man in "Pont du Carrousel," Rodin is at the center of the universe. Unlike him, he is there not because of his extrinsic position in a crowd but because of his intrinsic achievement, which is concentrated in "die Hände." In this objective imagery the hands are the link not so much between creator and created as between unformed "Dinge" and finished "Kunstdinge." At first glance the phrase "liegen die Länder" seems a vague way of saying this, but the phrase conveys literally the way in which the lines on hands can be seen as valleys, hills, rivers. It is as if the world outside Rodin has left its permanent imprint on his hands, which have in turn impressed that image on his "Kunstdinge," reflections of the natural world at once living and stylized.

As the hand image is used to contrasting effect in the two

poems, so also "die Dinge" carry different connotations in the two
contexts. In the first version they are the unformed "Dinge" to
which the artist is endeavoring to give shape. Here they are
"seine Dinge," the "Kunstdinge" that embody his timelessness.
The imagery, which began with "Steine" and broadened through
"Länder," now reaches the cosmic level of "Sterne."[2] As in "Pont
du Carrousel" these images are used to evoke a simultaneity of
motion and motionlessness ("kreisen . . . stehn"), a synthesis of
space and time. At the beginning of the poem the superficially
temporal notion of "Kindheit" leads into the spatial realm. Now
the superficially spatial "Dinge" restore at least the implication
of temporality as embodied in the circling stars. Thus the abstract
fulfillment of lines eight and nine is not disrupted by the past
tense of the last two lines. While maintaining the abstract level
("Nähe . . . Ferne") Rilke restores the artist's functionality ("erbaute . . . warf").

The scene he has evoked is not "eternal" like that of the blind
man on the bridge. It is constantly recreated by the artist, a sisyphean moment of harmony which, on this mythologized level, is
a harmony arising inevitably from the effort that leads to it.
The dialectic of "Nähe" and "Ferne," of detailing and overall
conception, was perhaps what fascinated Rilke most about Rodin's
sculpture:

> Hatten seine Dinge früher im Raume gestanden, so
> war es jetzt, als risse er sie zu sich her . . . Und in der Tat,
> wenn Rodin die Oberfläche seiner Werke in Höhepunkten

2. "Stern" has the dominant role in the poem's concluding lines that
"Stein" had in the first version. One of the attractions of the caryatid image
for Rilke the craftsman must have been the similar sound of the two words.
The last two lines of "Abend" (*Werke 1*, 405), probably written in 1904,
contain a caryatid-like evocation of an individual life under the impact of the
evening:

> So dass es, bald begrenzt und bald begreifend,
> abwechselnd Stein in dir wird und Gestirn.

zusammenfasste, wenn er Erhabenes erhöhte und einer
Höhlung grössere Tiefe gab, verfuhr er ähnlich mit seinem
Werke, wie die Atmosphäre mit jenen Dingen verfahren
war, die ihr preisgegeben waren seit Jahrhunderten . . . Mit
solchen Mitteln konnte er weithinsichtbare Dinge schaffen,
Dinge, die nicht nur von der allernächsten Luft umgeben
waren, sondern von dem ganzen Himmel. Er konnte mit
einer lebendigen Fläche, wie mit einem Spiegel, die Fernen
fangen und bewegen, und er konnte eine Gebärde, die ihm
gross schien, formen und den Raum zwingen, daran teilzu-
nehmen.

[*Werke* 5, 194]

These sentences read like a commentary to the second Rodin
poem. The essential components of the hand image are here. At
the beginning the dynamism is attributed to the "Raum," and
the verb "risse" clearly implies the action of the "second hand."
At the end it is the artist who compels the "Raum" to participate
in the creative act. The two images are, again, complementary.
Moreover the synthesis of the temporal and the spatial is embodied in the comparison of the artist with "die Atmosphäre":
Rodin's achievement combines the simplicity of the cathedral
sculptors with the sophistication which their creations have attained through the passing of time. The time dimension is concentrated in a single moment of spatial creation, because the
sculptor's perspective on time, like that of the absolute itself, is
circular rather than linear. He can concentrate the rhythm of centuries in his "Kunstdinge" because the natural world in which
that rhythm is revealed passes as a totality through his hands. The
concept of time arose originally from spatial observation. In Rodin's work it returns to its origins, transformed into the "Ferne,"
the "Sternbild" which fulfills the detailed "Nähe."

The myth Rilke builds around Rodin reflects the sculptor's

literal fulfillment of the dialectic outlined in "Der Schauende": himself indistinguishable from "die Dinge," he undertakes the physical subjugation of inchoate raw material in order to confront the absolute with his "Kunstdinge." It is important that the perfect Rilkean artist projected in the two Rodin poems in no way coincides with Rilke's conception of himself. Such an idealization was necessary to Rilke precisely because the personal disorientation expressed in "Der Schauende" has grown worse rather than better in the autumn of 1902. As usual, Rilke was well aware of the meaning of Rodin for his own life. In another poem from the same period, also entitled "Rodin," he makes clear how little the understanding of art has to do with its creation, how obstinately the "ich" refuses to fulfill the objective role assigned to it:

> Des Meisters Leben geht von uns so fern
> als wär es schon in Mythen umgewandelt;
> wir fühlen nur die Dinge, die er handelt
> —und nicht ihn selbst: wir haben keinen Herrn.
>
> [November 21, 1902; *Werke 3,* 765]

The typically Rilkean paradox is that at the very moment when he is elevating the ideal of objective mastery before himself and the world he is writing letters and poems about his own utter lack of mastery and total alienation from the objective world. In the following lines the hand image vividly illustrates how far removed the poet feels from the mythologized sculptor:

> Ein Verleugneter der eignen Hände,
> und vergessen wie ein totes Tier,—
> und die vielen fremden Widerstände,
> und der Aufstand gegen mich in mir.
>
> [November 17, 1902; *Werke 3,* 764]

The autumn of 1902 was a unique period in Rilke's life. His image of the artist was not always so far removed from his opinion

of himself, but that at this moment the images of "Kind,"
"Hand," and "Ding" should coalesce to produce such potent impressions of a fulfilled artist tells us something important about
Rilke and the significance these words held for him. Their
origins, as we have seen, are various: "Kind" derives its resonance from the romantic literary tradition, "Hand" from an apparently traumatic childhood experience, "Ding" from its very
blandness as an "Alltagswort." What renders them significant is
Rilke's determination to make them his own and fill them with
his own meaning. Such emphasis on individual words reflects the
unusual nature of his art. Certain words are used like leitmotifs
to denote certain aspects of the creative act. The term "leitmotif"
is not quite appropriate because the words accrue associations and
alter in emphasis as Rilke's view of the artist solidifies and becomes detached from subjective considerations. In 1896 he is
largely dependent on the poetic models of the past; in 1902 he
feels as far away as ever from an independent poetic achievement.
In the years between he has developed a full picture of what such
independence would involve, and the result is the paradoxical
situation of November 1902.

At the moment when, in the figure of Rodin, Rilke brings together all the elements of the creative ideal, he feels how unattainable such an ideal is. But the very act of articulating the
unattainable is an essential step forward in Rilke's mastery and
suggests how close he is in fact coming to the "idea" of the artist.
As his key words become integral components of his poetic style,
they acquire a resonance born of constant use, a significance that
no longer needs to be stated. Thus much more is conveyed by the
line "Er hat nicht Kindheit, nicht Alter" than its explicit meaning. The very statement that the sculptor does not possess his
childhood implies the possibility of such possession. The phraseology at once conveys to the reader not that Rodin has in any way
failed with regard to his childhood but that he has in some sense

advanced beyond the possession of childhood. The importance
of childhood is assumed by Rilke. His constant use of the child-
motif enables him to imbue a seemingly negative reference with
that assumption, to concentrate his whole poetic ethos into ever
fewer and simpler words.

I have noted the parallels between images used to describe
Rodin and those Rilke commonly applies to the absolute: the
cupped hand containing the world, the destiny summed up in the
word "Gestalter." From the vantage point of 1902 it is evident
that the absolute and the ideal image of the artist are one and the
same to Rilke. His relationship with the absolute is essentially a
relationship with himself, or rather with the perfected image of
himself. This is the sense in which Rilke is narcissistic, and in
1899 his narcissism leads to self-indulgence. At this period he be-
lieves that unlimited expansion of personal consciousness is the
foundation of art, and the wider he spreads the net of his imagery
the more certainly will be contained in it every aspect of the absolute, with which he will in effect become identical.

Almost at once Rilke shifts away from this viewpoint. Between 1900 and 1902 he employs images he has already made
his own, like "Kind," "Hand," and "Ding," in a new endeavor—
the structuring of an absolute remote from subjectivity—that will
stand before him as a perpetual "Aufgabe," a mirror that mocks
his weaknesses. In 1902 the absolute becomes, for a while, incarnate in Rodin. Much of Rilke's metaphysics, from the early aestheticism to the *Duino Elegies,* should be understood in terms of
this need for a creative model. Essentially, Rilke rejects nothing;
the truth he seeks is given to him all the time, as the ever-present
intersection between past experience and present spatial reality.
His central metaphical problem is identical with his problem as
an artist: how to express in words what is at once inexpressible
and perfectly expressed, a moment that is constantly receding, a
landscape that needs nothing added to it. When the achieve-

ment of the creative moment becomes the sole criterion of personal validity for the creator, one cannot assign the meaning of such an art to a purely aesthetic sphere. Rilke's art is not opposed to life or to human society, it is rather a dimension needed by both, a song of the earth and the city for which the artist is merely a vehicle.

6 A Later Transition: 1914

At the threshold of the Paris years we have been able to define the transition from early to middle-period Rilke in terms of a growing instrumentality. Instead of feeling the world and absorbing it as a totality, the artist must, in Rilke's view, isolate its components and reconstruct them verbally according to their own inner laws. The late Rilke, as is well known, emerged from a painfully long struggle with his own poetics lasting from 1909 (the conclusion of *Malte*) at least until 1914 (the poem "Wendung"), perhaps even until 1922. With his intensely dialectical self-awareness, Rilke tended to view this change as a negation of the Paris aesthetic, a kind of repersonalization ("Werk des Gesichts ist getan, / tue nun Herz-Werk"—"Wendung"; *Werke 2,* 83); but, as Beda Allemann in his admirable book demonstrates, the change is an "Erweiterung" rather than an "Überwindung," an opening of something closed. Anticipations of the late aesthetic can be found in the earliest Paris years. Indeed, a line from the poem on Rodin just studied—"Seine Dinge kreisen um ihn wie Sterne"—illustrates the context implicit in even the most objective of the "Dinggedichte."

That context, once established, remains constant in Rilke's life. It is his median position between "die Dinge" and an image of perfection before which he must justify himself by illuminating the existent fulfillment of the world and with which he can perhaps enter into rivalry as a re-creator. Rilke assumed in the Paris years that this functionality, once clearly understood and technically manageable, was self-fulfilling. He omitted from the equation temporality, the fact that man's life, unlike the circular cosmos, moves in a straight line from cradle to grave. Rilke does indeed fulfill his poetic mission in Paris, but for man even fulfillment takes place in time and modifies his personality to the point where repetition of a given poetic gesture becomes impossible. Then it leaves him, ironically "fulfilled," in a world in which time continues to pass, remorselessly underlining both the poet's superfluousness and the persistence of "die Dinge."

In his "Requiem" for the suicide Wolf Graf von Kalckreuth, written in November 1908 as his own troubled period was about to begin, Rilke offers the following idea as a key to the artist's self-preservation:

> Dies war die Rettung. Hättest du nur *ein* Mal
> gesehn, wie Schicksal in die Verse eingeht
> und nicht zurückkommt, wie es drinnen Bild wird
> und nichts als Bild, nicht anders als ein Ahnherr,
> der dir in Rahmen, wenn du manchmal aufsiehst,
> zu gleichen scheint und wieder nicht zu gleichen—:
> du hättest ausgeharrt.
>
> [*Werke 1*, 663]

Painfully but doggedly, Rilke takes his own advice, embracing the negative realities of his life embodied in terms like "Schicksal" and "Zeit" and making them the central themes of his poetry. As Allemann shows, the essential novelty in Rilke's late work is the notion of the conquest of time by means of time itself, the use of human memory to distill the dimension of genuine experience from that of merely being alive:

> Dabei gilt es zu beachten, dass die Wiederholung derselben Erfahrung nicht lediglich etwa Bestätigung und Verdeutlichung in sich schliesst. Vielmehr is das zunächst vereinzelt genommene Erlebnis überhaupt erst möglich auf Grund der immer schon gemachten Erfahrung, die in ihm erinnert wird. Die Dinge können nur in den Weltinnenraum treten, weil und insofern sich die Erinnerung an ihnen entzündet.[1]

The complementary spatial concept expressing this internal transformation of "die Dinge" is identified as "Figur" by Allemann,

1. Beda Allemann, *Zeit und Figur beim späten Rilke* (Pfullingen, 1961), p. 22.

who traces the origins of the term as two fold—on the one hand the plastic, self-contained entity celebrated in the *Neue Gedichte,* on the other a cosmic notion like "das Sternbild," a spatial patterning evocative of the harmoniousness of the absolute, like that of the poem "Pont du Carrousel."

The fusion of these two aspects in Rilke's mature poetics can be regarded as the culmination of his use of the motif. We have seen how, very early, he endows certain words, by repeated usage, with the exclusive associations of his personal world. In the later poetry this method becomes itself the experiential center of Rilke's writing, and the result is an extension of his language in two opposite directions. His motifs, as they become "Figuren" filled with the dimension of time, sever all but the most tenuous connections with the objects to which they nominally refer: in seeking to understand Rilke's mature usage of terms like "Ball" and "Spiegel," one is ill advised to attempt to visualize a concrete ball or mirror. Rilke's "Figuren" are his most refined weapons in a lifelong confrontation with the absolute, the means whereby a world rendered imperfect by man's conceptuality can be compelled to yield a perfection equal to the perfection that can be imagined.

The other pole of this creative process, however, enabling Rilke to escape the prison of art for art's sake, is a renewed simplicity, a conscious emptying of his motifs of the associations with creativity built up during the years before 1902. The formal perfection of the *Neue Gedichte* depends on an interlocking system of imagistic links among the creator, the world of objects, and the poem that unites them. After 1908 Rilke takes apart this system, separating his motifs from a generalized and by definition positive image of the artist and attempting to infuse them with the realities of his individual experience. These realities are obviously inseparable from the business of being a poet but they are often extremely negative. It is arguable that a fusion of these two endeavors is not achieved until after February 1922: the *Elegies* use language analytically, returning repeatedly to the same problem and the same motif in shifting contexts, while the *Sonnets* aim at synthesis, the achievement through linguistic refinement of a perfect world. Throughout Rilke's later writings one can see an attempt to blend increasingly abstract terminology with an intensity of experience that *includes* suffering without bypassing it in favor of the temptingly self-contained world of objects.

The three motifs on which the present study has concentrated are all equally important in the world of the late Rilke, with decisive changes of emphasis. The child motif retains its associations of fullness and spontaneity. From a model for the artist, a mode of being he must attempt to relive, it becomes a stage in the artist's life from which he is irrevocably separated. It lives on in him as an essence, a complete and completed life, which occasionally reveals its secrets to the adult through the faculty of memory. Already in the *Neue Gedichte,* in a poem of July 1906 entitled "Kindheit," the term "Figur" concludes a very simple and direct evocation of childhood, suggesting that even the most abstract features of a poet's craft have been lived by the child. The adult invents nothing; everything of value is remembered:

> nie wieder war das Leben von Begegnen,
> von Wiedersehn und Weitergehn so voll
> wie damals, da uns nichts geschah als nur
> was einem Ding geschieht und einem Tiere:
> da lebten wir, wie Menschliches, das Ihre
> und wurden bis zum Rande voll Figur.
>
> [*Werke 1,* 511]

Time is further stressed in the "Requiem" for Paula Becker (1908) when Rilke coins the term "ein Kindgewesensein," and it is dominant when the child motif moves to the very center of Rilke's concerns in the unfinished "Elegy" of December 1920:

> Lass dir, dass Kindheit war, diese namenlose
> Treue der Himmlischen, nicht widerrufen vom Schicksal,

selbst den Gefangenen noch, der finster im Kerker verdirbt,
hat sie heimlich versorgt bis ans Ende. Denn zeitlos
hält sie das Herz.

[*Werke 2*, 130]

Allemann points out that "zeitlos," as used by Rilke here and
elsewhere, does not mean "outside time" in any mystical sense,
but rather on the level of "vollzählige Zeit" when "Schicksal" is
momentarily reborn as "Figur." Childhood itself stays permanently within, but the experience of it is by definition fleeting,
savored and transformed in the interstices of adult time. The
interaction of the permanent and the ephemeral is the necessary
condition of human fulfillment. One cannot be celebrated without
the other, as Rilke emphasized in a terse paradox from the years
1913–14: "nur was vergehen darf, kann dir gehören" (*Werke 2*,
402). The child understands this because in him adult categories
are reversed; he is open to the past, closed to the future. Thus
the child becomes a twofold "Figur" for the later Rilke: on the
one hand the unfinished being of the Third Elegy, embracing the
wildness and confusion of the past that is achieving new life
within him, on the other the perfection of "der junge Tote,"
spared the necessity of a future.

The hand motif undergoes a more extensive change in the later
poetry, because the very notion of relationship changes for Rilke.
The bond with the second hand that underlies the harmonious
cosmos of the early and middle periods no longer functions in
the later works. The idea of an absolute is more important than
ever, but, as the first line of the First Elegy announces, it is an
inaccessible absolute. Instead of drawing sustenance from it, Rilke
is in rivalry with it. The hand is still the instrument of creativity,
but it constructs its world from inner resources only. Thus the
closing lines of the Seventh Elegy can be read as an exultant overcoming of the vivid experience delineated in "Ich weiss, als Kind:

Mein Spielzeng fiel" (1896), when the absolute first invaded the child's world:

> Wie ein gestreckter
> Arm ist mein Rufen. Und seine zum Greifen
> oben offene Hand bleibt vor dir
> offen, wie Abwehr und Warnung,
> Unfasslicher, weitauf.
>
> [*Werke 1*, 713]

The aspect of the hand motif that is increasingly prominent in the late poetry is the one already suggested by the poem about Rodin: "in seinen entfalteten Händen / liegen die Länder." The hand is seen less as an instrument, more as an object with its own expressivity, its own inner world. As Rilke's experience becomes infused with time, bonds between human beings are viewed less directly, more as symbolic reenactments of a timeless "Figur." The lovers in the Second Elegy, for example, touch each other in order that the gesture itself may become eternal. Going one step further into the world of "Figur," Rilke then celebrates the fulfillment of hands already fulfilled by belonging to the sphere of art, the hands of figures on a Greek vase: "Gedenkt euch der Hände, / wie sie drucklos beruhen. . . ." And in the poem "Handinneres" (1924) the meeting of two hands is like a meeting of two worlds, the recreation of a "Figur" imbued with the spatial ("Landschaft") and the temporal ("Ankunft"):

> Die auftritt in anderen Händen,
> die ihresgleichen
> zur Landschaft macht:
> wandert und ankommt in ihnen,
> sie anfüllt mit Ankunft.
>
> [*Werke 2*, 178]

With the loss of the feeling of oneness with "die Dinge" characteristic of the Paris years, Rilke entered a long period of alienation from the world of objects, as many agonized letters from the years 1910–12 testify. If it is an illusion to think he can model himself on "die Dinge," what kind of relationship can he have with them? Are they by definition other? At times he comes close to a rejection of his involvement, seeking instead a more generalized terminology reminiscent of the "Melodie" of his earliest years, as in the following lines from sketches for the "Requiem auf den Tod eines Knaben" (1915):

> Wehen, nicht Worte nur Wehen
> keine Spur nehr von Dingen.
> Nur ein Durchdringen. Nur ein Geschehen
> Ein Gelingen von Sternen
> und ich Knabe mitten darin.
>
> [*Werke 2,* 439]

With the growing centrality of time, however, Rilke gradually evolves the solution of the late *Elegies,* a solution that involves a partial dethronement of "die Dinge." The poet creates not just an equivalent of "die Dinge" but something greater than they are that rescues from them qualities destined in the real world for eventual oblivion. It has often been pointed out that the increasing devaluation of things by modern technology played a part in Rilke's conception of his mission, adding a historical dimension to the urgency of poetic memory:

> Was in der gerichteten Zeit unweigerlich ins Vergehen verhängt ist, wird in der Erinnerung aus diesem negativen Aspekt gerettet. Das sagt mit aller Deutlichkeit die siebente Elegie. Die Dinge selber sind, wo sie für sich bleiben, nicht im Offenen. Denn gerade das dinghafte In-der-Welt-Sein ist ja das Gegenständliche, das Entgegenstehen, welches die Welt abschliesst. Das Nurgegenständliche ist chaotisch und geschlossen. Das Haus erhält erst mit dem Brauchen durch den Menschen die Gestalt, die als dauernd erkannt wird. Und

wenn der Mensch es auch wieder zerstört, um an seine Stelle
erdachtes Gebild zu setzen, so ist es doch wieder der Mensch
allein, der das im Äussern Vergehende retten kann, indem er
es erinnert in der noch erkannten gültigen Gestalt.[2]

Rilke was slow to develop the emotional equipment for so self-
confident a stance. To conclude this study, I have chosen a poem
which is, in the fullest sense of the word, transitional. It reveals, in
both theme and structure, the persistence of the poetic world of
Rilke's youth into his maturity. By the way in which hitherto
valuable and comforting motifs are ruthlessly analyzed and inverted, it illuminates once again a point repeatedly stressed in this
study, that Rilke was no magical manipulator of words, but a man
who never ceased reexperiencing and reexamining his own values.
We need not accept those values, but we cannot deny the eloquent
honesty with which they were forged.

Vor Weihnachten 1914

I

Da kommst du nun, du altes zahmes Fest,
und willst, an mein einstiges Herz gespresst,
getröstet sein. Ich soll dir sagen: du
bist immer noch die Seligkeit von einst
und ich bin wieder dunkles Kind und tu   5
die stillen Augen auf, in die du scheinst.
Gewiss, gewiss. Doch damals, da ichs war,
und du mich schön erschrecktest, wenn die Türen
aufsprangen—und dein wunderbar
nicht länger zu verhaltendes Verführen   10
sich stürzte über mich wie die Gefahr
reissender Freuden: damals selbst, empfand
ich damals *dich?* Um jeden Gegenstand
nach dem ich griff, war Schein von deinem Scheine,

---

2. Jacob Steiner, *Rilkes Duineser Elegien* (Bern, 1962), p. 189.

doch plötzlich ward aus ihm und meiner Hand   15
ein neues Ding, das bange, fast gemeine
Ding, das besitzen heisst. Und ich erschrak.
O wie doch alles, eh ich es berührte,
so rein und leicht in meinem Anschaun lag.
Und wenn es auch zum Eigentum verführte,   20
noch war es keins. Noch haftete ihm nicht
mein Handeln an; mein Missverstehn; mein Wollen
es solle etwas sein, was es nicht *war*.
Noch war es klar
und klärte mein Gesicht.   25
Noch fiel es nicht, noch kam es nicht ins Rollen,
noch war es nicht das Ding, das widerspricht.
Da stand ich zögernd vor dem wundervollen
Un-Eigentum . . . . .

2

(. . . . . Oh, dass ich nun vor dir   30
so stünde, Welt, so stünde, ohne Ende
anschauender. Und heb ich je die Hände
so lege nichts hinein; denn ich verlier.

Doch lass durch mich wie durch die Luft den Flug
der Vögel gehen. Lass mich, wie aus Schatten   35
und Wind gemischt, dem schwebenden Bezug
kühl fühlbar sein. Die Dinge, die wir hatten,

(Oh sieh sie an, wie sie uns nachschaun) nie
erholen sie sich ganz. Nie nimmt sie wieder
der reine Raum. Die Schwere unsrer Glieder,   40
was an uns Abschied ist, kommt über sie.)

3

Auch dieses Fest lass los, mein Herz. Wo sind
Beweise, dass es dir gehört? Wie Wind

aufsteht und etwas biegt und etwas drängt,
so fängt in dir ein Fühlen an und geht   45
wohin? drängt was? biegt was? Und drüber übersteht,
unfühlbar, Welt. Was willst du feiern, wenn
die Festlichkeit der Engel dir entweicht?
Was willst du fühlen? Ach, dein Fühlen reicht
vom Weinenden zum Nicht-mehr-Weinenden.   50
Doch drüber sind, unfühlbar, Himmel leicht
von zahllos Engeln. Dir unfühlbar. Du
kennst nur den Nicht-Schmerz. Die Sekunde Ruh
zwischen zwei Schmerzen. Kennst den kleinen Schlaf
im Lager der ermüdeten Geschicke.   55
Oh wie dich, Herz, vom ersten Augenblicke
das Übermass des Daseins übertraf.
Du fühltest auf. Da türmte sich vor dir
zu Fühlendes: ein Ding, zwei Dinge, vier
bereite Dinge. Schönes Lächeln stand   60
in einem Antlitz. Wie erkannt
sah eine Blume zu dir auf. Da flog
ein Vogel durch dich hin wie durch die Luft.
Und war dein Blick zu voll, so kam ein Duft,
und war es Dufts genug, so bot ein Ton   65
sich dir ans Ohr . . . Schon
wähltest du und winktest: dieses nicht.
Und dein Besitz ward sichtbar am Verzicht.
Bang wie ein Sohn ging manches von dir fort
und sah sich lange um, und sieht von dort,   70
wo du nicht fühlst, noch immer her. O dass
du immer wieder wehren musst: genug,
statt: *mehr!* zu rufen, statt Bezug
in dich zu reissen, wie der Abgrund Bäche?
Schwächliches Herz. Was sol ein Herz aus Schwäche?   75
Heisst Herz-sein nicht Bewältigung?
Das aus dem Tier-Kreis mir mit einem Sprung

der Steinbock auf mein Herzgebirge spränge.
Geht nicht durch mich der Sterne Schwung?
Umfass ich nicht das weltische Gedränge?   80
Was bin ich hier? Was war ich jung?

[*Werke 2, 95*]

This work was written shortly after three extremely famous
poems, "Es winkt zu Fühlung fast aus allen Dingen" (with the
unique occurrence of the word "Weltinnenraum"), "An Hölderlin," and "Ausgesetzt auf den Bergen des Herzens." In length and
analytic style it stands in relation to them as an Elegy stands to an
Orpheus sonnet. In another respect the relationship is the reverse:
whereas the *Sonnets* were ecstatic by-products of the fulfilled *Elegies,* the present poem is an agonized examination of why the
values so painstakingly given shape in the three achieved poems
simply do not work for their creator. In his language and ideas
Rilke has advanced beyond his own emotional development. He
finds that the basic problem of perception is as enigmatic as ever.
"Die Dinge" are still totally other. True to his own precepts,
Rilke pours his situation into verse, hoping perhaps that "Schicksal" will after all become "Figur," that the poem itself will show
the way forward. In this he fails. The desolation of the ending is
hard to match anywhere in his work, but in the course of the work
many of Rilke's central motifs are reorchestrated in the new, more
abstract language he has evolved and is struggling to absorb.

The poem is built on the theme of time, the dimension Rilke
senses is crucial to his emotional future. Together with the tripartite structure, time is also rooted in Rilke's earliest poetic
practice. Of the poems we have studied, "Aus Nächten" (1898),
"Wenn die Uhren so nah" (1898), and "Am Rande der Nacht"
(1900) are all constructed in this way: a period of preparation is
followed by a brief moment of transition and then fulfillment. Of
course the emotional sequence is by no means so harmonious
here. But the structural analogy goes deeper still. The rhyme

scheme of the poem's first section is as follows: *a a b c b c, d e d e d, f f g f g, h i h i, j k l l j k j k m*. These five groupings correspond directly to movements in the text itself. Indeed, in lines seven, twelve, seventeen, and twenty-one caesuras clearly mark the transition. Thus Rilke's early practice of using irregular but recognizably distinct four-, five-, or six-line groupings as the emotional segments of a longer poem is given new life. The temporal movement is in reverse, as the poet restlessly examines the past for answers to the present, but each of the five sections represents a distinct moment in time. In the first the poet almost sarcastically greets the Christmas of the present; in the second he evokes the moment of anticipation before the child is granted access to the Christmas tree; in the third the toys are infested with the plague of possession; in the fourth he looks back at the state of the toys before he touched them; and in the negatively lyrical final section that state lives again in words as a paradise lost.

The theme of Christmas is appropriate to Rilke's purpose on many levels. In its recurrence and its festiveness it supposedly embodies the dimension he is seeking to create in his "Figuren." Because it is given, externally imposed, it tends to produce the opposite extreme from "Figur," the dutiful, meaningless mask. In its connection with the acts of giving and receiving and with the entry of new "Dinge" into individual lives, Christmas concentrates Rilke's thoughts on his relationship with objects. In its time-honored role as the fulfillment of childhood, the feast provokes Rilke to an analysis of the reality of that childhood, to a stripping away of "der behübschende Irrtum." The gulf between present and past hardly needs stressing. With the repeated "einst" Rilke dismisses the charade of adults' mimicking the joys of children, and with the peremptory "Gewiss gewiss" he turns to the deeper question, *was* there ever an "einst"? What is secure about adults' memories of childhood experience? The word "doch" in line seven overshadows the vivid depiction of anticipation that follows. The

anticipation was undoubtedly real and pure, devoid of calcula-
tion, but the term "verführen" recalls the warning "doch" of
three lines earlier and draws the child's experience into proximity
with that paradigm of human aspiration, adult love. Something
about human desires precludes their fulfillment. Whereas the
possessiveness of a child is normally casual and unselfconscious
(toys, picked up only to be discarded), the intensification of the
giving process at Christmas time, the organization of feelings in a
conscious pattern reveals to the child the central human defect—
insistent possessiveness that destroys its object.

The suddenness of the object's transformation recalls the sudden revelation produced by children tugging at imagined ropes in
"Ein einziges Gedicht, das mir gelingt" (1900). In each case the
instrument involved is the hand, which now appears in all its
ambivalence. As it can create, so it can destroy; it stands for both
relationship and the negation thereof. The wording of lines fifteen–seventeen recalls vividly the diary entry of November 20,
1900, quoted earlier: "Ein Ding mehr plötzlich und ein Ding, das
immer schwerer zu werden scheint, gleichsam alle Trauer auftrin-
kend." As the wreath Clara Westhoff created acquired a life of its
own, a terrifyingly independent life, so the "neues Ding" of the
present poem mocks its progenitor. The difference is that the
present object is an abstraction, "das besitzen heisst." Clearly the
child's experience (like Clara's in its earlier context) has become
an analogy for the artist's relation to his material. These lines
have an equally striking similarity with a contemporary poem
about the act of creation, the "Spanische Trilogie" of January
1913:

> aus mir und alledem ein einzig Ding
> zu machen, Herr: aus mir und dem Gefühl,
> mit dem die Herde, eingekehrt im Pferch,
> das grosse dunkle Nichtmehrsein der Welt

ausatmend hinnimmt—, mir und jedem Licht   5
im Finstersein der vielen Häuser, Herr:
ein Ding zu machen. . . .

[*Werke 2, 44*]

Creation and destruction are aspects of the same process; there is
no avoiding the endless repetition of the child's feeling by the
Christmas tree. As Rilke broadens the implications of the scene,
it seems that he hopes, by dwelling on this negative childhood
experience, to regain, through a new "Umschlag," the positive
features, the spontaneous creativity of the child, which until recently had seemed so securely a part of him. The word "Anschaun" makes this unmistakable. Rilke had used the term repeatedly to describe the process underlying the *Neue Gedichte,* a
process to which, in the poem "Wendung" (June 1914), he has
just officially bid farewell: "Denn des Anschauns, siehe, ist eine
Grenze" (*Werke 2,* 83). As a poet he has appropriated, possessed, too much of the external world and now he can only see
"die Dinge" at one remove, through the medium of his own
language. Possibly the phrase "das Ding, das widerspricht" echoes
Mephistopheles' self-description as "der Geist, der stets verneint."
Certainly there is an analogy between Faust's desire for rejuvena-
tion and Rilke's yearning to recover a lost stage in his artistic life.
As with Faust, Rilke's way forward lies through the very instrument of negation, the flexible, increasingly abstract language at
his command.

In the middle section, placed like an aside in parentheses, the
poet translates the child's experience into the terminology with
which he is experimenting. The hand motif returns, again as an
inversion of a very early usage. The poem "Wenn ich manchmal
in meinem Sinn" (1897), in which the second hand is embodied
in a woman concludes:

. . . in meiner Hände hingehaltne Schale
legst du sie leichtgelenk,
wie ein Geschenk.

Here Rilke attempts to emancipate himself from the imagery of
the second hand because his imagery no longer answers his needs.
By force of habit he still seeks the gift of "Die Dinge," but he
can do nothing with it. Significantly, "ich verlier" has no object,
because the verb evokes his whole condition: his very identity is
slipping from him, his hands functioning as their own negation,
destroying instead of creating, giving away instead of fruitfully
meeting in personal relationships:

> Meine Hände gingen ein
> in der andern schicksalvolle Schliessung;
> alle, alle *mehrte* die Ergiessung:
> und ich konnte nur vergossen sein.
>
> [February 1914; *Werke 2,* 216]

Rilke's answer to the problem typically demands radicalization of
what is happening anyway, total elimination of personal identity.
Now he attempts to do what he is often wrongly thought to have
done in the Paris years, remove himself from the artistic equation.
In a poem for Lulu Albert-Lazard written on October 7, 1914,
just two months before the present one, Rilke presents simply the
image of a "leere Mitte." An important image in his later conception of "die Dinge," here its negativity leads Rilke to offer it
as a substitute for personal identity, free from tangibility and
hence from possessiveness:

> Sieh, ich bin nicht, aber wenn ich wäre,
> wäre ich die Mitte im Gedicht;
> das Genaue, dem das ungefähre
> ungefühlte Leben widerspricht.
>
> [*Werke 2,* 224]

Lines thirty-four to thirty-seven of the Christmas poem seek to
give form to "das Genaue" to evoke a new kind of art. Their im-
perative form stresses how far Rilke feels from his goal. The
term "Bezug," central to his later poetry, is best defined negatively,

as the opposite of possession. Rilke puts it thus in a letter of 1923: "Das Fassliche entgeht, verwandelt sich, statt des Besitzes erlernt man den Bezug."[3] The image used here to evoke "Bezug," the flight of birds through the poet's inner being, is also the prime illustration of "Weltinnenraum" (in "Es winkt zu Fühlung," August / September 1914), a word which is virtually a synonym for "Bezug" in 1914:

> Durch alle Wesen reicht der *eine* Raum:
> Weltinnenraum. Die Vögel fliegen still
> durch uns hindurch.

[Werke 2, 93]

Allemann points out the contradictions of "Weltinnenraum," contradictions which underly the spiritual crisis in the present poem:

> Wir haben im Zusammenhang mit dem Weltinnenraum darauf hingewiesen, dass sein Wesenzug die Aufhebung der Schranke zwischen Innen und Aussen ist. In ihrer radikalsten und erst eigentlich angemessenen Form würde diese Aufhebung auch den Verzicht auf die Termini Innen und Aussen verlangen. Die Begriffsbildung "Weltinnenraum" selbst ist ein Versuch, mit Hilfe eines Oxymorons die Aufhebung zu vollziehen, aber indem in ihm die Begriffe von Aussen (Welt) und Innen doch erhalten sind, bleibt er zwiespältig.[4]

The difficulty is twofold: on the one hand, if the poet is indiscriminately open to the outside world, voiding himself of all existence in time, then the inner dimension will quickly seem unnecessary and the poet's superfluousness the more apparent; on the other hand, the poet's past existence is irrevocably there—the world of objects is imbued with the evidence of past possession—and hence the discriminations of memory are forced upon him. The problem can be summed up in a single word: responsibility.

---

3. An Ilse Jahr, February 22, 1923, *Ausgewählte Briefe 2*, 395.
4. Allemann, p. 279.

From his earliest work Rilke has felt entrusted with a mission towards "die Dinge." in lines thirty-seven to forty-one of the present poem he views the mission as foundered, but cannot simply walk away from the wreckage. The limits of his emancipation from the past are revealed in the use of another key word: "Abschied." Here the connotations hark back to the child by the Christmas tree, guiltily abandoning a toy he has just clutched to him. "Abschied" is the ultimate expression of possession, the confession of human enslavement to whim and temporality. Like "Schicksal" and "Zeit," the term "Abschied" is capable of inversion, and indeed becomes a central "positive" concept in Rilke's later poetry. Allemann describes it as "die intensivste Form der Begegnung" and goes so far as to say:

> Die grundlegende Weise, in der sich für den späten Rilke der Übergang aus den blossen Abläufen in jene senkrecht stehende Zeit vollzieht, ist der Abschied.[5]

To achieve this insight, Rilke must learn what in this poem he cannot bring himself to accept: the impossibility of direct perception, the inescapability of being "gegenüber."

The poem's final section is the most agonized of all. The form is similar to that of the first, with irregular groupings of lines reflecting an emotional movement, but there is no progression. Each section takes up the same contrast between man's inadequacy and the world's completeness and batters at it with varying imagery. Rilke, caught in the present moment, tries by repeated assaults to extract a meaning from his predicament. The section's opening line is reminiscent of the precept that introduces "An Hölderlin" (September 1914): "Verweilung, auch am Vertrautesten nicht, / ist uns gegeben." Indeed, in that the title "Vor Weihnachten" suggests Christmas has not yet arrived, the line anticipates the injunction of the famous Sonnet to Orpheus II,

5. Ibid., p. 169.

13: "Sei allem Abschied voran." But at once the line's real meaning here is established: Rilke releases the feast not because he will
not possess it but because he cannot. Obsessed with time, he cannot
yet see its real significance for him. It is not yet the state in which
"die Dinge" acquire their true resonance. Instead it is treated as if
it were *itself* a "Ding," a man-made entity, a preordained starting point for human feelings. Because man is doomed if he lives
merely inside time, Rilke tries to stand outside time, to encompass
it in verse.

This posture, a redirection of "das Anschaun," is no more satisfactory. His feelings simply will not attach themselves to an object, however metaphorical. Another early image recurs, that of
the storm in "Der Schauende" (1901) which bends "die
Dinge" before it. At that time Rilke sought to combine the attributes of both storm and "Dinge"—now his feelings are like the
wind, wandering restlessly but capriciously in search of an object.
That he still seeks a restoration of the lost synthesis is shown by
his attribution of the term "Überstehen" to the external world.
The word expresses the most inward of human aspirations (cf. the
last line of the "Requiem" for Kalckreuth: "Wer spricht von Sie-
gen? Überstehn ist alles."), and the alignment of such a notion
with "Welt" underlines the hopelessness of the idea of self-dissolution. If Rilke divests himself of specifically human qualities,
these qualities will not simply disappear but will pass over into
the world of objects. This would be all right if subjective identity
really could be eliminated, but it cannot: "ein Fühlen" remains,
stripped of purpose and dignity.

Awareness of the poet's fundamental median position also remains. Lines forty-three to forty-seven stress the poet's isolation
from "Welt," and lines forty-seven to fifty-two distance him even
more radically from the absolute (here clothed in the late
imagery of the angel), both sections culminating in the despairing
"unfühlbar." As he castigates the inadequacy of human feeling,
the time dimension is insistently present, in the participle con-

struction of line fifty and the emphasis on the brevity of "der Nicht-Schmerz." Time is still wholly negative, contributing to the loss of that intensity of feeling which is still Rilke's goal. Self-dissolution must be seen as the ultimate formulation of that goal, going beyond the humanness of feeling to a realm of pure intensity.

Lines fifty-eight to seventy-one, built of rhyming couplets, really form a single section, evoking the event of the poem's third part. This event exactly parallels that of the first part (lines 13–17) in which the gold of the Christmas toy turns to the dross of possession. Together the two events summarize symbolically the utter perversity and incapacity of human nature. For the original fall of man lies in his rejection of the fullness that is offered him. The vice of possessiveness follows inexorably from this —what is not rejected is possessed, and thus the whole of human experience is devalued. Rilke often implies that the child's wholeness is destroyed by adults. The truth, which he is increasingly prepared to face, is that the child himself abandons this wholeness, as self-awareness leads to self-assertion. The child image is by no means reduced in importance as a result of this insight; rather, the notion of achieving childhood becomes more urgent than ever as "achieving" loses all connotations of "recovering." Childhood exists, but by definition a child cannot consciously experience it. Ultimately, Rilke's acceptance of the loss of wholeness gives him a certain security, a protection against self-pity, as the following lines from an elegy fragment of February 1922 suggest. They echo the imagery of the 1914 poem, even the omnipresent bird flight, now subtly transmuted into a "Figur," a component of subjectivity rather than a replacement for it:

> . . . oder des Vogels reichlicher Flug
>   schenke uns Herzraum, mache uns Zukunft entbehrlich.
> Alles ist Überfluss. Denn genug
>   war es schon damals, als uns die Kindheit bestürzte

mit unendlichem Dasein. Damals schon   5
war es zuviel. Wie könnten wir jemals Verkürzte
oder Betrogene sein: wir mit jeglichem Lohn
längst Überlohnten . . .

[*Werke 2*, 140]

In 1914 Rilke can find no consolation. The child's experience reaches a climax in the synaesthesia of lines sixty-four to sixty-six, followed by the bleakly rational exclusion from paradise (line 68). Lines sixty-nine to seventy-one postulate the neglected universe which obsesses Rilke at this period. On the one hand he cannot concentrate his feelings even on what is closest to him, on the other he is more than ever aware (especially after his extensive travels in the years before 1914) of endless harmonies and monuments to the past in the physical world that insistently demand rebirth and recreation. Desperately, the poet seeks metaphorical equivalents for the act of creative union which are not tarred by the deadness of possession. The first metaphor is physical (lines 73-74) and "der Abgrund" recalls the closing lines of "Das Lied vom Kehrreim" (1899): "so tief bin ich im dunklen Reich / des Grunds." There the traditional conception of God as "der Grund" was combined with the physical image of a "Teich" and the emphasis was on the poet's absolute stillness. Here the poet seeks the same posture of being both underneath and inside reality, but because he has experienced loss the metaphor is assertively dynamic, as if by violently heightening the gesture of possession ("reissen") he can negate it and achieve the paradoxical openness for which he yearns.

The second metaphor (lines 75–76) is intellectual, an attempt to develop an answer according to the precept of the poem "Wendung" (June 1914): "tue nun Herz-Werk." The difficulty is that Rilke is unfamiliar with the term "Herz," which never becomes acclimatized in his poetry. In trying to legitimate the dangerously possessive word "Bewältigung" by identitfying it with

"Herz-sein" he is not advancing the situation, just conceptualizing it once again. The most successful development of "Herz" as an image occurs in "Ausgesetzt auf den Bergen des Herzens" (September 1914). That poem is directly echoed here in the third, wholly spiritual metaphor (lines 77–78):

> Da geht wohl, heilen Bewusstseins,
> manches umher, manches gesicherte Bergtier. . . .
>
> [*Werke 2,* 95]

The openness of animals is a persistent Rilkean theme, and the arrival of a "Steinbock" on his inner landscape would symbolize the new access of perceptual immediacy which the poet craves.

Lines seventy-nine and eighty restate the poet's anguish once again, the interrogative form underlining the impossibility of his aspiration. At one extreme he wills self-dissolution, merging with the ordered "Figuren" of the objective world most vividly manifest in the stars' motion. At the other he yearns to stand *outside* the universe, concentrating both order and chaos into a single consciousness. The paradox is heightened by the contrasting metaphors: if the stars are the reality most remote from man Rilke will claim them as his brother; if the world's turmoil is the immediate and overwhelming reality, Rilke will embrace and order it. He has pressed his self-questioning to its extreme point, to "der Gipfel reine Verweigerung" (of the poem "Ausgesetzt auf den Bergen des Herzens"). The last line falls back into a comprehensive cry of despair. Its spontaneity is not lessened by the fact that both questions have already been asked during 1914. The first occurs in similar wording and a similarly cosmic context, although its anguish is there much lessened by Rilke's hope, in the next stanza, for consolation from a meeting with Benvenuta:

> ach, die Nacht verlangte nichts von mir,
> doch wenn ich mich zu den Sternen kehrte,

der Versehrte an das Unversehrte:
Worauf stand ich? War ich hier?

[*Werke* 2, 216]

The second, also in a poem of dedication (December 2, 1914), refers to the night in 1899 when Rilke wrote the *Cornet*. It is phrased not as a question but in a tone of wistful wonderment, the meaning of "was" being closer to "wie" than to "warum":

Noch weiss ich sie, die wunderliche Nacht,
da ich dies schrieb: was war ich jung.

[*Werke* 2, 226]

The juxtaposition of the two questions, however, places them in a new light. The repetition of "ich" concludes a series of urgent references to the first person. Since Rilke cannot formulate his questions without these references, now he focuses on the very nature of this "ich," this unavoidable pronoun. By asking simultaneously about his meaningless present and the enigmatic but undeniable existence of his past, Rilke is on the verge of his ultimate way forward, the fusion of the spatial and temporal dimensions.

Rilke did in fact attempt an answer at the time, in sketches for the poem's continuation. The answer is an almost schematic avoidance of the problem of possession, a projection of fulfillment in terms of "Herz-Werk":

Nicht dass ich etwas in mir unterbringe—
dass ich ihm sage: sei geliebt:
das ist mein Herzblut. Sei geliebt du Blatt,
das einmal fiel von irgend einem Baume,
von irgendwem in irgendeinem Traume   5
geträumte Stadt
und du, im Zwischenraume zwischen zwein
geflüsterten, gefühlten Worten, rein
entstandne Stille: sei geliebt.

[*Werke* 2, 430]

One cannot avoid a feeling of attenuated texture, of artificial lyricism in these lines. The loving atmosphere has induced a return to the dreams and whisperings of the early years. The mature verbal magic is there, but the content is sentimental. Evidently Rilke himself became aware that the dimension of love cannot simply be summoned in this way. When it is used as an instrument to overcome the problem of the neglected universe, it is felt merely as a rhetorical trick. Rilke's elaborate determination to evoke "Dinge" he has *not* himself experienced is also uncharacteristic. The way forward can only lie in his own life, not in the lives of others. Otherwise he is condemned to "das Ungefähre" ("einmal . . . irgendwem . . . irgendeinem"), the word that epitomizes for Rilke all that is alien to poetry. So the questions at the end of the final version remain. Indeed they cannot be finally answered; for poetic identity changes not only with each new day but with the effect each new day has on the totality of the past.

To conclude, I would like to consider anew the implications of my title. In a sense, it is obvious tautology: when is a man not in transition? With Rilke it is unusually appropriate because of the uncanny way in which, without ever joining a movement, his life became a part of the history of his times, entered immediately into the public domain. The mystical Russophilia of *Das Stundenbuch,* the cubism of *Neue Gedichte,* the fractured modernity of *Malte,* and finally the cosmic range of the *Duineser Elegien,* confidently surpassing the millennial gesturing fashionable at that time: these very different formal achievements are instantly recognizable as the products of a single consciousness. Since his writing adapted to, and indeed preceded, such contradictory movements, the continuity of his life and work is remarkable. His life did not lack major events, but always he seemed inwardly ready for them. Thus Rilke's correspondence during the first half of 1902 testifies to great uncertainty as to the future; but from the moment of his arrival in Paris and meeting with Rodin, the appropriateness of the event is obvious: destruction of any remaining unworldliness on the one hand, encouragement of the

sculptural tendencies in his poetry on the other. Less obvious, but
no less significant, is Rilke's relationship to the world war. For
five years he had been suffering under his alienation from "die
Dinge," searching, with intermittent successes like the beginning
of the *Elegies,* for a way to reconstruct his personal world. Then,
with the advent of war, his confusion suddenly became universal.
From the general destruction two personal goals emerged: rescu-
ing the reality of the prewar world and enduring the present. With
the future preempted, a burden was lifted. Rilke was well aware
of his complex relationship with the surrounding social changes:

> Mehr ist auch jetzt nicht zu leisten, als dass die Seele über-
> steht, und die Not und das Unheil sind vielleicht gar nicht
> vorhandener als vorher, nur greifbarer, tätiger, sichtlicher.
> Denn die Not, in der die Menschheit täglich lebt seit Anbe-
> ginn, ist ja eigentlich durch keine Umstände zu steigern.
> Wohl aber sind Steigerungen der Einsicht da in des Mensch-
> seins unsägliche Not und vielleicht führt das alles dazu; so-
> viel Untergang—als suchten neue Aufgänge—Abstand und
> Raum für den Ablauf.[6]

If there is an explanation for Rilke's strange symbiosis with
his own times, it lies, I think, in what is perhaps the cardinal
paradox of his life. Without obvious talent at the outset, Rilke was
compelled to be extremely open to outside influences, and as
his distinctive personality developed, he still did not feel compelled to reject anything. Rather, with an autodidact's eagerness,
he absorbed more and more. His own style emerges from an accre-
tion, not a selection, of influences. With this artistic openness
goes a total absorption in a single, entirely private goal: the quest
for his own childhood. Nothing deflected him from this aim. Rilke
survived the strains of the period after 1909 in part because sur-
vival was essential to the preservation of his childhood. Signifi-

6. An Karl und Elisabeth von der Heydt, November 6, 1914, *Ausgewählte Briefe 2,* 15.

cantly, Rilke regarded letter-writing as an aspect of his creativity. The easy transition from the private to the public realm was at the heart of his self-sustaining transitions in time. Thus when his doctor, Count Stauffenberg, attempted a form of psychoanalysis, Rilke formulated in a letter his reasons for resisting, then incorporated parts of the letter in an unfinished essay, "Erinnerung" (September 1914):

> Mit Schrecken empfand ich manchmal eine Art von geistigem Brechreiz, den er hervorzurufen bemüht war; es wäre furchtbar, die Kindheit so in Brocken von sich zu geben, furchtbar für einen, der nicht darauf angewiesen ist, ihr Unbewältigtes in sich aufzulösen, sondern ganz eigentlich dazu da, es in Erfundenem und Gefühltem verwandelt aufzubrauchen, in Dingen, Tieren—, worin nicht?—wenn es sein muss in Ungeheuern.[7]

This fusion of the intensely private and the deliberately public is fundamental to Rilke's use of motifs. By filling simple words from the public realm with his personal associations, he established a deep continuity in his work long before the theme of temporal recurrence became so important to his later poetry. Each new development in his writing is an intensification rather than a transformation of the previous one. As the motifs become filled with ever more personal meanings, so the surrounding language is ever more carefully selected, the singleness of vision more insistently focused. The ultimate purification, inaccessible even to the poet, is the unsullied perception of the young child, for whom there is no cleavage between private and public worlds, no barrier between past and present.

7. An Lou Andreas-Salomé, September 9, 1914, *Ausgewählte Briefe 2,* 10.

Selected Bibliography

For a complete listing of critical materials on Rilke I refer the reader to Walter Ritzer, *Rainer Maria Rilke: Bibliographie* (Vienna, 1951). I have included here only books and articles related to my topic by methodology or subject matter, together with certain basic works on Rilke.

SOURCES

Rilke, *Ausgewählte Briefe, 1897–1926,* 2 vols. ed. Karl Altheim, Wiesbaden, 1950.

———, *Briefe 1902–06, 1906–07,* ed. Ruth Sieber-Rilke and Carl Sieber, Leipzig, 1930.

———, *Briefe aus den Jahren 1892–1904,* ed. Ruth Sieber-Rilke and Carl Sieber, Leipzig, 1939.

———, *Briefe und Tagebücher aus der Frühzeit, 1899–1902,* ed. Ruth Sieber-Rilke and Carl Sieber, Leipzig, 1931.

———, "Kindheit, Bild der Kunst," Brief an Charlotte Scholtz, April 7, 1899, in *Die Erzählung 1* (1947), no. 3, 11–13.

———, *Sämtliche Werke,* ed. Ernst Zinn, Wiesbaden, vol. *1,* 1955; vol. *2,* 1956; vol. *3,* 1959; vol. *4,* 1961; vol. *5,* 1965; vol. *6,* 1966.

———, *Tagebücher aus der Frühzeit,* ed. Ruth Sieber-Rilke and Carl Sieber, Leipzig, 1942.

——— and Lou Andreas-Salomé, *Briefwechsel, 1897–1926,* ed. Ernst Pfeiffer, Wiesbaden, 1952.

SECONDARY MATERIALS

Allemann, Beda, *Zeit und Figur beim späten Rilke,* Pfullingen, 1961.

Angelloz, J.-F., *Rainer Maria Rilke: L'évolution spirituelle du poète,* Paris, 1936.

Baer, Lydia, "Rilke and Jens Peter Jacobsen," *PMLA 54* (1939), 100–32, 1133–80.

Belmore, H. W., *Rilke's Craftsmanship,* Oxford, 1954.

Berger, Kurt, *Rainer Maria Rilkes Frühe Lyrik,* Marburg, 1931.

Blume, Bernhard, "Das Motiv des Fallens bei Rainer Maria Rilke," *MLN* 60 (1945), 295–302.

———, "Ding und Ich in Rilkes Neuen Gedichten," *MLN* 67 (1952), 217–24.

———, "Die Stadt als seelische Landschaft im Werk Rainer Maria Rilkes," *MDU 43* (1951), 65–82, 133–49.

Bohning, Elizabeth E., "Childhood in the works of Rainer Maria Rilke," *Canadian MLR 18* (June 1962), 13–22.

Bollnow, O. F., *Rilke,* Stuttgart, 1951.

Butler, E. M., *Rainer Maria Rilke,* Cambridge, 1941.

Corcoran, Mary B., "Zur Bedeutung wichtiger Wörter in den frühen Schriften von Rilke," Ph.D. diss. Bryn Mawr College, 1958.

Demetz, Peter, *Rene Rilkes Prager Jahre,* Düsseldorf, 1953.

Emde, Ursula, *Rilke und Rodin,* Marburg, 1949.

Feise, Ernest, "Rilkes Weg zu den Dingen," *MDU 28* (1936), 151–56.

Gray, Ronald, *The German Tradition in Literature,* Cambridge, 1965.

Greifenstein, Karl, "Der Engel und die Dimension des Unsäglichen bei Rainer Maria Rilke, Ph.D. diss. University of Heidelberg, 1950.

Guardini, Romano, *Zu Rainer Maria Rilkes Deutung des Daseins,* Bern, 1946.

———, "Kindheit: Interpretation eines Elegienfragments von Rainer Maria Rilke," *Literaturwissenschaftliches Jahrbuch 1* (1960), 185–210.

Hagen, H.-W., *Rilkes Umarbeitungen,* Form und Geist, ed. Lutz Mackensen, 24 Leipzig, 1931.

Hamburger, Käte, *Philosophie der Dichter,* Stuttgart, 1966.

Heerikhuizen, F. W. van *Rainer Maria Rilke,* trans. F. Renier and A. Cliff, New York, 1952.

Heidegger, Martin, "Wozu Dichter?," in *Holzwege,* Frankfurt, 1950, pp. 248–95.

Holthusen, Hans Egon, *Rainer Maria Rilke: A Study of his Later Poetry,* trans. J. P. Stern, New Haven, 1952.

Jaszi, A. O., "Names and Objects in Rilke's Poetry," *New Mexico Quarterly 25* (1955), 73–81.

Kippenberg, Katharina, "Rainer Maria Rilke und die Dinge," *Das Inselschiff* 17 (1935), 18–23.

Kohlschmidt, Werner, *Rainer Maria Rilke*, Lübeck, 1948.

——, *Rilke-Interpretationen*, Lahr, 1948.

Kretschmar, Eberhard, *Die Weisheit Rainer Maria Rilkes* Weimar, 1936.

Kunisch, Hermann, *Rilke und die Dinge*, Cologne, 1946.

Mágr, Clára, *Rilke und die Musik*, Vienna, 1960.

Mason, Eudo C., *Lebenshaltung und Symbolik bei Rainer Maria Rilke*, Weimar, 1939.

——, *Rainer Maria Rilke: Sein Leben und sein Werk*, Göttingen. 1964.

Mendels, Judy, and Spuler, Linus, "Zur Herkunft der Symbole für Gott und Seele in Rilkes Stundenbuch," *Literaturwissenschaftliches Jahrbuch* 4 (1963), 217–31.

Meyer, Herman, "Rilkes Cézanne-Erlebnis," *Jahrbuch für Asthetik und allgemeine Kunstwissenschaft* 2 (1952–54), 69–102.

——, "Die Verwandlung des Sichtbaren. Die Bedeutung der modernen bildenden Kunst für Rilkes späte Dichtung," *DVLG 31* (1957), 465–505.

Mövius, Ruth, *Rainer Maria Rilkes Stundenbuch*, Leipzig, 1937.

Musil, Robert, *Rede zur Rilke-Feier in Berlin am 16. Januar 1927*, Berlin, 1927.

Parry, Idris, "Malte's Hand," *GLL 11* (1957), 1–12.

Peters, H. F., *Rainer Maria Rilke: Masks and the Man*, Seattle, 1960.

——, "Rilke's Love-poetry to Lou Andreas-Salomé," *MLQ 21* (1960), 158–64.

Salomé, Lou Andreas-, *Rainer Maria Rilke*, Leipzig, 1929.

Sieber, Carl, *René Rilke: Die Jugend Rainer Maria Rilkes*, Leipzig, 1932.

Simenauer, Erich, *Rainer Maria Rilke, Legende und Mythos*, Frankfurt, 1953.

——, "Rilkes Darstellung der Dinge im Lichte der 'Metapsychologie' Freuds," *Schweizer Zeitung für Psychologie und ihre Anwendungen* 8 (1949), 277–94.

Spoerri, Theophil, *Präludium zur Poesie*, Berlin, 1929.

Steiner, Jacob, *Rilkes Duineser Elegien*, Berlin, 1962.

———, "Das Motiv der Puppe bei Rilke," in *Kleists Aufsatz über das Marionettentheater,* ed. Helmut Sembdner, pp. 132–70, Berlin, 1967.

Tubach, Frederick C., "The Image of the Hand in Rilke's Poetry," *PMLA* 77 (1961), 240–46.

Wood, Frank H., *Rainer Maria Rilke: The Ring of Forms,* Minneapolis, 1958.

———, "Rilke and the Time-factor," *GR 14* (1939), 183–91.

Index of Titles and First Lines

All poems are listed both by titles (if any) and first lines, including those whose first lines are not directly cited in the text.

Index of Proper Names